HEALERS OR DEALERS?

Richard P. Allison

Foundations Book Publishing
Brandon, MS 39047
www.FoundationsBooks.net

Healers or Dealers?
By Richard P. Allison

Cover by Dawné Dominique Copyright © 2021
Edited and Formatted by Steve Soderquist

ISBN: 978-1-64583-064-1

Published in the United States of America
Worldwide Electronic & Digital Rights
Worldwide English Language Print Rights

This is a work of nonfiction. Only the names and identifying details of the individuals involved have been changed. Those who are innocent of any wrongdoing described in each story must be protected.

For Brad, our son. Always continue to grow and learn...

and

In memory — J. Larry Burris 1949-2021
A good man and a sad loss

Table of Contents

"First, do no harm," or "primum non nocere."
- Hippocrates, Of the Epidemics

We as professionals have caused an epidemic that is bigger than the HIV epidemic. We have more deaths from drug overdoses than occurred at the peak of the HIV/AIDS epidemic in 1995. That's how big this is. It is more deaths than motor vehicle accidents. The cause in the opioid epidemic starts with getting prescriptions of opioids from physicians. — Atul Gawande, MD. Surgeon, writer, and researcher. Boston, Massachusetts.

PREFACE

You've got the biology of dependence or addiction to opioids driving it. You also have financial incentives for people to stay sick through Social Security insurance compensation. You've got doctors who are incredibility incentivized in many ways to continue to prescribe. I really feel like the opioid epidemic is the canary in the coal mine with regards to our health care system. We have some serious infrastructure issues that we need to reform. — Anna Lembke, MD. Author, Drug Dealer, MD.

The good news is that most physicians are well trained, perform as expected, and genuinely want to help their patients to be free of suffering from disease or injury using appropriate care and management. Thank goodness for all of us! The not-so-good news is the subject of this book. According to various sources,[1] 10-17% (some say the figures are too high, others say they are too low) of physicians nationwide do not always do the right things. They may be impaired by drugs, alcohol, mental illness, or just do not conform to acceptable medical standards. These are so-called "bad actors." Only approximately 67% of doctors who knew of an impaired doctor reported the doctor.[2] That left the remaining impaired doctors to be uncovered or reported by patients, families of the doctors, employees, medical board staff, or other means. My personal experience leads me to believe the figures quoted above about impaired doctors are much lower than reality. Add to

[1] Including the American Medical Association and the *Journal of Medical Ethics* (December 2003). See also Harbin, Tom, MD, MBA, "Doctors and Addiction," (May 2017) and Tagliareni, Sonia, "Physicians with substance abuse disorders" (May 2018).

[2] Survey, *Journal of the American Medical Association* (2010).

the impaired doctors those who have nefarious motivations of various kinds and non-conformist doctors, and figures go up, thus exposing large numbers of patients to risky, substandard care. There are more bad actors in some states than others, and a correlation exists, depending on the actions and reputation of the state medical boards. Those states known for fewer efforts are a destination for those physicians seeking the "Mobile Cure." The bad actors know which states they are. In the 1980s, the Mississippi State Board of Medical Licensure (MBML), even with a perception of Mississippi being a rural and regressive state, built a strong reputation by being one of the most proactive boards in the country.

From 1982 until the turn of the century, the Mississippi medical board, which is made up of nine doctors nominated by the State Medical Association and appointed by the governor, oversaw the practice of proper medicine and the protection of the public seriously as parallel goals. During the majority of this period, the board's executive officer was former surgeon Frank J. Morgan Jr., MD, who expected his colleagues to maintain the highest standards of practice in medicine. After Dr. Morgan retired, Doyle Bradshaw and Tom Stevens, MD served respectively as executive officers. They shared the same high expectations concerning practice standards as their predecessor. Also significant in helping the Mississippi medical board be so very successful was the board's attorney, Stan Ingram, a former medical board investigator who composed most of the laws and regulations under which the board operates to date. Stan graduated third overall in his law school class – quite an accomplishment!

He is probably the most knowledgeable and experienced attorney in the state concerning the Mississippi Medical Practice Act and board regulations. Stan and I hunted deer and fished together for many years (and we could write another entire book about some of those stories!). Many times, while sitting on a deer stand, Stan was working on case preparation while I hunted or was asleep. No one could out-work Stan Ingram in preparation for a hearing.

Shortly after the death of Tom Stevens and just before the turn of the century, medical politics in Mississippi precipitated the Mississippi medical board losings its way. The board shifted priorities from the protection of the public to the protection of the physician, mirroring a nationwide trend. Some doctors were salvageable, but many were recidivist offenders undeserving of a license.

Trying to reduce a doctor shortage by keeping bad actors in practice is not a safe or viable solution to protect the public. Shortly before I retired in 1998, one board member told me after a board meeting, "We [i.e., the state medical association and a few other board members] are tired of being number one in disciplinary actions in the country. This is a physician's board for physicians." I took his comment as a sign of ominous things to come, as they did! One way to measure the result is by the depth and extent of the current opioid epidemic. More recently, the news has been better. It appears the actions and thinking of the boards, in general, are once again making a priority of taking serious action to protect the public. And, I dare say, the boards are better at keeping the public informed through somewhat improved transparency. However, much, much more proactive efforts and transparency are still needed. Every Mississippi citizen who must see a physician should become familiar with the Mississippi State Board of Medical Licensure's website (https://msbml.ms.gov) and demand any and all details pertaining to their doctor's licensure or disciplinary history. Information from every state that includes *specific* details of the violations should be in the public domain.

It would be foolish to think that all of the bad actors, of the types described herein, just disappear or cease practicing the healing arts or, at a minimum, see the error of their former ways. Some doctors do make remarkable turnarounds, but not all! Many play the same games but employ tactics to make themselves harder to catch. They play the same games using different names, and sometimes even the same names or techniques to game the regulatory system. Many times, I would personally hear so-called knowledgeable members of the legislature say, "I would rather have my drunk doctor than any other (sober) doctor." Not a logical thought process, especially when you consider several of these legislators have had their own public incidents involving alcohol.

In 1981, early in my tenure as chief investigator with the Mississippi medical board, a prominent physician in state government commented to me and Frank Morgan, concerning doctors in difficulty with drugs or alcohol, "A physician can heal themselves better than any medical board."

Dr. Morgan leaned over to me and quietly commented to me after that doctor had left the meeting, "Now you see just a little of what we are up against in getting anything done to address impaired doctors."

Shortly after this exchange, fate would intervene to help us. Mississippi experienced a series of six to eight physician suicides and fatal overdoses involving controlled substances and/or alcohol over an eight to ten-month period. The doctor who had commented that doctors could heal themselves had a forced change of heart. In response from the medical community, a doctor husband and wife team, along with others, were highly instrumental in early impaired doctor intervention efforts. Thus, the disabled doctor program (as it was known then) began to gain traction in Mississippi for the identification, intervention, and treatment of physicians in difficulty.

Every investigation, whether by a federal, state, or local agency takes on a unique opportunity and/or challenge. Whether it is solving a mystery, following an evidence trail wherever it leads or being able to touch the "untouchables." That is the attraction that binds the investigator. That is part of the magnetism of being an investigator and is why many cannot do anything else for a career. Considering the motivations and before presenting particular cases, a description of qualifications and training of medical board investigators is warranted.

The practice of medicine is referred to as a practice because it is as much an art as science. While there is a vast amount of science in medicine, the application of that science by the physician is truly an art form. Investigations are similar in many ways. There is a massive amount of science and knowledge involved to become a qualified investigator. Like physicians, investigators can specialize in an investigative category. These include controlled substances, robbery, homicide, rape, fraud, embezzlement, and many others. How an investigator applies that training and knowledge is just as much an art form. Just how do physicians gain their knowledge and confidence to practice medicine? The answer is years of intense training and supervision. That knowledge and acquired skill is the primary source of their confidence.

With the same purpose and objective in mind, I developed a two-year training program for all incoming medical board investigators. The first step was the most important. The MBML applicant had to pass a thorough background investigation. No stone was left unturned. The applicant had to have impeccable credentials and integrity, along with a college degree and three years of investigative experience. All of this was required to even be considered for an MBML investigator slot. There was no substitution allowed for the requirement of a college degree. My philosophy was simple. Investigators must be able to present at a physician's clinic in a professional and diplomatic manner. Discussions with a physician, matters of law, and regulations governing the practice of medicine demands incorporation of proper training. To gain the knowledge and confidence to confront the physician, trainees had to be very diligent in their preparation.

If they could not, or would not, put in the time and effort to learn, the physician would hand them their head! Many criticized the training program for being too long, but I stood my ground. Earlier in my career, I had seen more than one trainee who could not perform due to the fear of confronting a doctor about anything. One trainee had such fear of talking to a doctor that he literally could not utter a sound during an interview. On more than one occasion, I had to step in and take over the presentation. The board did everything it could to help him, including speech therapy. However, he could not overcome what was diagnosed as a "cultural deficit." One trainee would not travel in his assigned area for fear of finding something about which he would have to confront a doctor. He broke out in cold sweats. Both individuals went on to have successful law enforcement careers that did not involve doctors.

These lessons taught me that to overcome these obstacles, the training had to be comprehensive, intense, and include role-playing. The investigator had to be knowledgeable and conversant in the following: controlled substances, chemical names, generic names, drug forms (injectables, pills, capsules, tablets), controlled substance schedules (federal and state), indications, contraindications, dosages, prescription language, reading and comprehending patient files, medical terminology, diseases, handling body fluids, diagnoses, evidence handling, chain of custody, probable cause, warrants, affidavits, testifying, federal law and regulations, state law, and board regulations governing the practice of medicine.

The most important part of the training is drilled into the new investigator on the very first day. No investigator will have any adversarial contact with a licensee without first obtaining executive approval. The executive officer is the investigator's lifeline, and he must know the details of the purpose of the visit before giving approval. In other words, there is a tremendous amount of knowledge and communication that provides the confidence to confront a physician who may have a proprietary advantage. Most investigators were able to grasp all training components with success. As with any systematic protocol of training, some trainees were not successful and either left the position or were terminated.

Problem physicians fall into one of five categories known as the "Five Ds: Dated, Duped, Dishonest, Disabled, and Disruptive". This book will detail <u>actual</u> cases from each of the categories. The reader should note that these are actual cases, not fiction! I will not divulge the names, dates, or locations of violators or their victims because personal information serves no positive purpose. My intention is solely to heighten the public interest in board action and/or inaction. No fair hiding behind executive sessions to give the benefit of the doubt to the licensee. The public has a right to be informed and protected from bad actors. The public has a vested interest to know if and/or when the medical board gives a license to a doctor that is patently unqualified or even dangerous based on well-documented problems or disciplinary history. This information allows the patient to make an informed decision about care for themselves and/or their family. The primary goal of any medical board should be the protection of the public.

The following were actual participants: MBML Investigators Charlie Moses, Neil Breeland, Mickey Robbins, and your author, Chief Investigator Richard Allison; Stan Ingram, MBML attorney and prosecutor; Steve Campbell, Mississippi Bureau of Narcotics (MBN), retired; Randy Corban, MBN, retired; MBML executive officers Frank J. Morgan Jr., MD, retired; Doyle Bradshaw, deceased; and Thomas Stevens, MD, deceased. Other participants include: Jerry Nickels, chief deputy of a sheriff's department, retired; Sammy Webb, investigator for a district attorney, retired; Gordon Kennedy, state investigator, retired; Jim French, assistant chief of police, retired; Sam Aldridge, MBI/DEA task force, retired;

Oscar Mackey, assistant attorney general, deceased; Lee Spencer, chief toxicologist at University of Mississippi Medical Center (UMMC); Arthur Hume, PhD, deceased. All these individuals were either investigators or employees of the medical board, investigative staff of other agencies, forensic toxicologists, or professors at the time these cases were investigated by the medical board or criminally prosecuted. All other names have been changed to protect the identities of the accused and their victims. The names of doctors who were investigated have been changed so no one can identify their victims. Key facts are unchanged, but minor details have been embellished or omitted where necessary to protect victims and sources. Although the reader may be appalled by the facts and circumstances reported herein, they are real and true and represent a snapshot in time of the history of our medical profession. *If, perchance, you recognize a victim, please respect their privacy. They have been through enough.*

If anyone who reads this suspects a problem with their doctor in their own case management or that of a friend or family member, contact the appropriate medical board. As you will soon learn, these cases are not as rare as you might think.

Many newly appointed doctors to the medical board, after sitting in judgment for their first few hearings, made comments to me afterward such as, "I thought the board appointment was more of an honor, I had no idea a physician would act in such an irresponsible manner," or "It's hard to hear what some of these doctors have been doing." Their eyes were opened! It is also important to open the eyes of the public as well. On one occasion, I had forwarded a complaint to Tom Stevens, seeking his approval to assign for investigation. Early the following morning, he appeared in the doorway of my office with the complaint in hand. He told me that now I was requesting to investigate the very last friend he had in medicine. He said, "You have already investigated all of my other friends!" I told him, "Well, boss, maybe now you will pick better friends." True to his character, he approved the complaint for investigation.

Who has any interest in writing such a book? Not many! My only previous experience in writing was doing mainly ROIs (reports of investigation). My spouse, friends, and other family members who helped with early editing were reminded of my investigative/law enforcement writing style. I have attempted to learn a softer, more flowing style. Occasionally, as a chief investigator, I was requested to write an article for a publication concerning medical board cases, regulations, or drug diversion trends. Those efforts were nothing approaching serious manuscript writing. I am not now, nor will I ever be, a Charles Krauthammer or Tom Clancy. I have tried to make this book accurate, interesting, informative, sincere, and honest, avoiding highly technical jargon in favor of relatively simple words.

My education consists of a BS in business management with a minor in criminal justice from Delta State University in Cleveland, Mississippi. My senior year (1972), I was recruited and hired by what was then known as the "Bureau of Drug Enforcement," a division of the State Department of Health. This division later became the Mississippi Bureau of Narcotics (MBN), where I worked for seven years. Later the MBN became a division of the Mississippi Department of Public Safety.

My investigative experience also included time as a special agent with the Illinois Central Railroad and the Performance Evaluation and Expenditure Review Committee (PEER) of the Mississippi Legislature. The controlled substance training and investigative experience at MBN opened the door to the chief investigator position at the physician licensure division of the Mississippi State Board of Health, and I was hired in 1981. One year later, the Mississippi legislature, at the wishes of the Mississippi State Board of Health, and one doctor in particular who chose to wash his hands of dealing with bad actors, created the Mississippi

State Board of Medical Licensure. (See "Controlled Substances and Strippers Galore" for more details.) My career in state government ended with retirement in 1998. After retirement, I served briefly as manager of the fraud unit at Blue Cross and Blue Shield of Mississippi and finally fourteen years as a Loss Prevention investigator with a nationwide retail distributor.

The cases described in this publication are derived from my experiences at the Mississippi State Board of Medical Licensure. All of these cases and investigations are ones that I either personally investigated, supervised as chief investigator, or worked in coordination with law enforcement agencies and regulatory agencies such as sheriff's departments, police departments, the Mississippi Bureau of Narcotics, Mississippi Bureau of Investigation, United States Attorney's offices, the Drug Enforcement Administration, Board of Pharmacy, the Board of Nursing, and the Board of Dental Examiners.

One person or agency cannot be successful in such a complex and detailed investigative endeavor without assistance. Fortunately, at the medical board, I had, for the most part, highly motivated and effective investigators and support staff, tremendous outside agency assistance, along with an accomplished and experienced attorney/prosecutor. Most importantly, we had a medical board, starting with the nine doctor appointees of Governor William Winter, when the Mississippi State Board of Medical Licensure was first created, that made it clear to the Executive Officer and myself that they would act accordingly when necessary to effectively deal with bad actors. One new board member appointee, whom I knew personally, and who had stitched me up several times growing up, told me directly at his first meeting, "Richard, if you bring us the case examples of real problems and put them on the table, we will deal with them." From the beginning, the boards I served were committed to informing and protecting the public. Just prior to my retirement, medical politics began to turn the board in a very different direction away from strong, reliable, consistent action and leadership. I hope to see a turn again, back to the laudable goal of putting the public first.

To all involved, in helping to develop this project, I will always be eternally grateful!

THE PILL DOCTOR
SPECIAL PREFACE

In many cases, the doctors involved were outright malicious – establishing "pill mills" in which they gave away opioids with little scrutiny, often for hard cash. — German Lopez, VOX journalist.

Just by way of an explanation, I selected this case to be the first presented in this publication not because it was the first diversion case that I investigated or was involved in, because it was not. "Controlled Substances and Strippers Galore" was my first significant diversion case. I selected this case to be first because it most clearly exemplifies how just one single, small-town "country" doctor (not a manufacturer), by prescribing dangerous controlled substances without legitimate medical need, causes not only untold widespread community and family destruction but also creates his own statewide opioid epidemic.

CHAPTER 1

THE PILL DOCTOR

While every case of my career was significant in its own way, some were "larger" than others, "a large case" being defined in different ways. The case involving "the Pill Doctor" (I will refer to him as PD from now on) was the largest in terms of diversion of Schedule II and IIN drug amounts that I investigated in my entire career. By the term "diversion" I am referring to controlled substances that are diverted, mainly by prescribers, from legitimate medical channels for illegal use and/or abuse. Diversion is one of the primary sources of drugs feeding the opioid epidemic. PD practiced in a relatively small town with close proximity to a large city and became well-known for prescribing basically whatever the patient requested and not what was necessarily needed. That is an important distinction: who was practicing medicine, the patient or the doctor?

The Mississippi State Board of Medical Licensure (MBML) had recently been created by the Mississippi legislature, and the staff had barely moved into the new offices when the complaints began to come in. Before I forget, my name is Richard Allison, and I was the Chief Investigator for MBML from approximately January 1981 until April 1998. For much of that time, it was easy being identified as the Chief Investigator because, for most of the early years, I was the only investigator. Initially, there was a second investigator who was well trained, knowledgeable in diversion investigations, and wiser. By "wiser," I mean that once he had finished training me, he chose to leave state employment and enter the private arena in corporate loss prevention. As the years went by and successful cases were prosecuted, the workload increased resulting in other investigators being added. There is nothing like good PR and strong, consistent action to boost the public's faith in a regulatory/investigative agency.

Even before the completion of board action on Dr. Ludes from the "Controlled Substances and Strippers Galore" caper (see next chapter), the phone was ringing with complaints about PD. The complaints came slowly at first, but as time passed, many more began to pour in. The calls were from private practice pharmacists, Board of Pharmacy Inspectors, doctors, law enforcement, ministers, family members of drug addicts, recovering drug addicts, treatment centers (not many existed at the time), nurses, concerned citizens, and even politicians including a United States Senator.

Two facts about the sources of complaints are noteworthy: First, the fact that so many came from doctors was revealing and underscores an important lesson from my career; if a doctor is complaining about another doctor, one best pay-attention. Second, not a single complaint came from a pharmacist who I will call "Big Al" and about whom I will tell you more later.

Steve Campbell, a very close friend of mine and a Special Agent with the Mississippi Bureau of Narcotics, described PD as the worst problem in the state when it came to the over-prescribing of controlled substances. He said many of the Bureau's informants were talking about him as a main source of street pharmaceuticals. Clearly, PD was a problem! When Steve spoke, people listened. He was likeable, knowledgeable, and confident with natural leadership qualities fine-tuned from a background in Marine aviation, flying as the RIO (i.e., Radio Intercept Officer) in the back seat in F4s in Vietnam strafing Viet Cong or NVR (North Vietnamese Regulars) on the ground and later chasing Russian Migs and Bear Foxtrot bombers off the coast of Northern Japan that occasionally harassed U.S. Navy reconnaissance aircraft.

With all the complaints coming into the new MBML, Frank J. Morgan, Jr., MD, the executive officer, directed me to drop everything and work on PD as a top priority. This was a daunting task for just one investigator. I decided to focus all my pharmacy profiling efforts on just Schedule II and IIN prescriptions to better manage the vast number of pharmacies to be profiled. The plan was fairly simple in concept, but the scope was far-reaching. I just needed to identify *every* patient receiving suspicious amounts of Schedule II and IIN prescriptions from PD.

One pharmacist, Big Al, was of particular interest. Big Al's pharmacy was in the same town and close to PD's clinic. However, he was about the only pharmacist who was *not* complaining about the number, size, type, and frequency of controlled substance prescriptions coming out of PD's clinic. Wonder why? Could it be that Big Al was making so much money he was not about to complain? You better believe it!

But first things first. I suggested to the executive officer that before we tip our hand and go overtly into the pharmacies, which would alert PD that we were looking at him, maybe we should seek assistance from the MBN to do an undercover operation first. This was the first time I had proposed an undercover operation on a doctor since I began work at the medical board and, surprisingly, Dr. Morgan agreed. A few days later I was able to meet with MBN Agent Steve Campbell, commonly known by his peers as "Rambo," to propose the possibility of a joint investigation starting with an undercover (UC) operation on PD.

Agent Campbell got the nickname "Rambo" from the board's executive officer, Frank J. Morgan Jr., MD, and the name stuck! Steve was good at what he did, which was catching drug dealers and dealing with errant doctors by convincing them that a brighter future in medicine was contingent upon them being compliant with controlled substance laws. His intimidating manner with the doctors led to the long-standing nickname. I don't know if he boxed or not but my money would be that he could hold his own with just about anybody.

I would follow up the UC operation with a wide area profile of all pharmacies to identify any suspicious patterns of prescribing. Steve agreed it was worth a shot and stated he had two agents in mind for the operation who were good at UC and experienced. He said he would talk to the Chief of Operations and seek approval for the joint operation. A few days later, he called me back and told me the UC operation on PD had been approved. It would be an MBN special op supervised by Rambo in cooperation with the medical board.

Since we already knew PD was prescribing to known addicts and abusers, we planned to have the two MBN operatives make three undercover visits each using the direct approach, by presenting as abusers or addicts seeking more drugs for themselves. Since we already knew PD was doing this, it would remove the entrapment defense. All visits would be recorded for evidence and surveilled for back up, if necessary.

Over the next two months, the two agents, using undercover names, made their three visits each and obtained controlled substance prescriptions on each visit. During all of the UC visits, the agents carried wireless transmitters (commonly referred to as code 10 units) allowing all of the conversations to be recorded and monitored by backup agents. All of the recordings were maintained and transcribed for the prosecution. One of the agents, on her first visit, told PD she was a college student and needed Preludin (a Schedule II diet pill containing Phenmetrazine, no longer on the market) to help her study. PD wrote her a prescription for thirty Preludin and charged her $30 for the visit which she paid directly to him in the examining room, not at the front desk. No exam of any kind was performed. The prescription was for a thirty-day supply, however, in just two weeks, the agent returned and received another prescription for the same drug and amount. After another two weeks, she again returned to PD's clinic and received yet another prescription for thirty Preludin along with a barbiturate for sleep. Again, no examination of any kind took place on any of the visits. Preludin was not indicated to be used for "academic" purposes. On all three visits, PD wrote the requested prescriptions charging $30 per prescription paid in cash directly to him.

A similar circumstance took place with the other UC agent. She complained of having a difficult time getting Percodan (a Schedule IIN pain pill containing Oxycodone) and Dilaudid (a Schedule IIN pain medication containing hydromorphone) for her drug problems and not being able to lose weight. She said she did not have money for drug treatment. She obtained the requested prescriptions, including a Schedule II barbiturate for sleep and a Schedule IV diet pill, although anyone could see the female UC was not a weight loss candidate. Again, no medical exam of any kind was performed and each prescription cost $30. Most legitimate doctors are suspicious of any patient when they request specific drugs, especially when they admit to drug abuse. Also, prescribing any controlled substance to a patient just because the patient cannot get the drug for their addiction problem is not a legitimate or indicated use. The direct approach strategy that Agent Campbell suggested had worked well. Each prescription was filled at Big Al's pharmacy, which was the closest pharmacy to PD's clinic and which therefore filled many of PD's prescriptions but somehow produced none of the complaints about his prescribing.

Now the fun part began for me: pharmacy profiling, which took the better part of six months in late 1982 and early 1983. I profiled over 100 pharmacies in a multi-county area around PD's clinic by documenting every Schedule II and IIN prescription issued by PD over the past several years to some patients, and just the past year for some others. The profile identified over a hundred patients receiving suspicious amounts of Schedule II and IIN narcotics for a year or more. Several of the patient profiles went back for five or more years!

I will call one patient, a forty-three-year-old female, "Alice" in the spirit of *Alice in Wonderland* or, perhaps, the term "Go Ask Alice" referenced in the song *White Rabbit* by Jefferson Airplane. During the previous two years, Alice had received a total of 4,000 Dilaudid 4 mg tablets and 6,000 Numorphan 5 mg suppositories (known as rectal rockets on the street). Numorphan is a highly addictive Schedule IIN drug primarily used for cancer pain with the chemical name Oxymorphone. The suppository form is in Schedule IIIN due to being, theoretically, less abused in that form and like the suppository form of most drugs is used when the patient has trouble swallowing or keeping anything down orally. Dilaudid is a highly addictive, highly abused Schedule IIN drug. Four thousand Dilaudid 4 mg tablets over approximately 730 days averages over five tablets per day, every day! The Numorphan average was over eight per day. Both drugs are usually directed to be taken in four-hour increments and not in combination. It should be noted that Dilaudid 4 mg tablets were selling on the street for as high as $150 per 4 mg tablet at the time. That comes to a grand total of only

$600,000 cash, tax-free! Numorphan went for only about $10 per suppository. No human being could function or even live taking half that amount. Not to get ahead of myself, but just for the record, her medical file in PD's clinic when seized had one entry for "headaches," not cancer, with no follow-up or evaluations, and few of the prescriptions were documented in the file.

Just out of curiosity, based on the large quantities prescribed to Alice, I conducted brief surveillance to try and determine what she might be doing with all of the pharmaceuticals that she was being prescribed. The surveillance documented that she went to work every day for a local business with no signs or apparent symptoms of being an abuser and that she had no problems swallowing or keeping food down during and after meals. She rarely went out after work and when she did it was grocery shopping or to PD's clinic. It appeared she was in it for something other than a legitimate medical need and PD was her source. Most of her prescriptions were filled by Big Al, mentioned earlier, who did not complain about PD's prescribing, not one single time. I considered that a clue, especially when numerous other pharmacies, filling a mere fraction of PD's prescriptions, had complained or expressed concern with PD's prescribing. When I was finally in Big Al's store, I asked him if he ever became concerned about the huge amounts of drugs to Alice and several other patients. His only comment was, "I just fill 'em, I don't ask any questions." I deliberately went to Big Al's pharmacy last, because I knew that when I went in, the next call he made would be to PD to let him know the medical board was asking questions, but it would be too late then. I did a follow-up at Big Al's approximately a month after my original visit just to see if PD had cut back, he had not. Some doctors feel they are untouchable, then and now.

A second patient from the pharmacy profile garnered a lot of attention in this case due to his reputation for criminal activity and the amounts of controlled substances prescribed to him by PD. I will call this patient "Buddy" (not his real name). Buddy and I had crossed paths many times, long before this investigation. Many years earlier, Buddy shot and wounded one of his fellow drug abusers in a bar, then followed him outside into the parking lot. Two MBN agents, who responded to the scene, pulled out their weapons and ordered Buddy to put down his weapon. When he refused and appeared poised to administer the coup-de-grace to his wounded "friend," they opened fire, shooting him four times. Although Buddy was shot in the chest, neck, shoulder, and arm, miraculously, he lived thanks to the very fine care he got immediately in the ER and on a long-term basis at what was known then as Hinds General Hospital in Jackson, MS. At the time of the shooting, I worked at the MBN and was assigned as a part of the shoot team. Most of what a shoot team did in that era was document what the primary shooter had done. This helped in preparation for the defense of an excessive force lawsuit that may be filed by the perpetrator. Such a lawsuit was filed by Buddy but later thrown out by the court. However, the wounds suffered by Buddy followed him for the rest of his life as a totally chemically dependent patient on Dilaudid and other controlled drugs. He would appear in and out of my career at MBML as a professional patient hitting up doctors all over the state until he found PD. During the profiling, I found prescriptions to Buddy, mostly at Big Al's pharmacy and a few at other pharmacies, for Dilaudid, Percodan, and Ritalin. His amounts were in the "off the chart range," with multiple prescriptions monthly for all three drugs.

One of our expert witnesses on the case, and one of my longtime best confidential sources, was the Director at a major treatment center. I'll call him "Dr. White" (not his real name). Dr. White frequently called me to report doctors throughout Mississippi, and occasionally other states, who were over-prescribing to patients he was trying to rehabilitate. Dr. White never identified the patients, just the over-prescribers. He did not care for doctors who profited by selling prescriptions to chemically dependent patients. Dr. White had encountered and treated several of PD's so-called patients, including Buddy. Dr. White admitted he and other treatment staff were fond of Buddy because of his almost mythical but violent life, and his personality that communicated his experiences much like that of an old western outlaw. The last time Dr. White said he saw Buddy, he had discharged him clean and sober from the treatment center, but in less than a week, Buddy was dead. Dr. White would literally tear up whenever he discussed Buddy. During my profiling, I found three prescriptions from PD to Buddy for Dilaudid, Percodan, and Ritalin (a Schedule II drug containing methylphenidate, a stimulant) issued shortly after his discharge and just one day before he was found by his mother in bed deceased. The theory was that Buddy had taken the same high doses he was accustomed to taking before treatment. The large amounts simply overdosed and killed him. We attempted to have his body exhumed for an autopsy to test for the drugs. If the drugs were found to be the cause of death, a manslaughter charge could be added to the case against PD. Everyone in Buddy's family encouraged the exhumation except, unfortunately, his mother. The manslaughter case stopped there, but not the prescribing case.

A third patient identified in the profile and used in the prosecution was a male patient we dubbed "Percodan Man." He received Percodan in quantities of an average as high as 100 doses per day. All of his prescriptions were from PD and also mostly filled at Big Al's pharmacy. No one can take 100 Percodan daily and survive. The number of aspirin alone (325 mg per pill), would destroy the stomach, liver, or kidneys, not to mention the massive amount of oxycodone that would probably stop pulmonary function at half that daily amount. Percodan Man was totally dependent on oxycodone, the primary drug in Percodan, and was said to be a significant supplier of the drug on the street.

Yet another patient identified from the profiles was a middle-aged female who was receiving massive quantities of Percodan, Dilaudid, and other Schedule IIN controlled substances from PD. She was described by family members as bedridden and completely non-ambulatory, unable to function in any way.

After completing the time-consuming task of the pharmacy profiling, the next monumental task involved breaking out the prescriptions by individual patient name, date, and drug. While this manual process was very slow – remember, there were no Excel spreadsheets! – it was revealing because it identified which patients were receiving the larger amounts of controlled substances over the longer periods. From our analysis of the data, we identified the key patients, including the four patients described above, for the next step in the investigation.

Steve Campbell, Stan Ingram (our board attorney) and I then began to put together the administrative warrant and affidavit to seize patient files from PD for analysis. We compiled an affidavit of facts and circumstances that ended up being four legal pages long, not including the separate inspection and search warrant. The affidavit followed to the letter the format spelled out in state law for MBML to seize the patient files of a doctor under investigation. Since we knew PD to be well connected in state and local politics, Stan took extreme care to cross every "t" and dot every "i." I do not recall ever having a more well-prepared legal document to serve. However, I had to get it past the Senior Circuit Judge first and, as it turned out, that was easier said than done.

The Senior Circuit Judge in the district covering PD's clinic, at the time, was a highly respected jurist and recommended to review the application for the search warrant on PD.

I telephoned his office and was told he was in court, but I could probably catch him during a break to present my warrant and affidavit. The very nice receptionist did not ask, and I did not volunteer, who the warrant was for. I traveled to the courthouse where he was presiding and waited for a break. This hurry up and wait was not at all uncommon for obtaining signed warrants, so I took a seat in the courtroom and waited my turn.

At the first break, I approached the bench and asked to present a warrant and affidavit. The judge took care of some other items in front of me, then directed that I approach and state my business. I identified myself to him and presented my credentials. I handed him the warrant and affidavit for him to read while at the same time identifying the doctor on whom the warrant was written. After a long reading session, he put the affidavit down and, in a somewhat surprised and incredulous voice, asked me why I needed to seize almost 100 patient files for examination. I referred him to the affidavit that explained the huge amounts of controlled substances prescribed by PD to the patients, all of whom were listed. We needed the files to verify the legitimate medical need. All of this was detailed in the four-page affidavit.

The judge requested to see my identification again. While he was looking at my ID, I handed the judge copies of statutes establishing the authority of MBML under state law to obtain the files by warrant. He did not look at the copies. He immediately requested his court reporter to come back into the courtroom. He told me he was going to make a record of the proceedings for future reference. He then swore me in, which put me under oath. I had never previously had a judge ask a court reporter to record a presentation for a search warrant, either criminal or administrative. A judge will always place the agent/investigator under oath to swear to the veracity of the contents of the affidavit prior to signing the warrant, but never to cross-examine him during the review of the affidavit *before* the warrant being signed.

Worst of all, having the court reporter present significantly increased the possibility of a leak, which could have adversely affected the investigation or endangered the integrity of the evidence or the safety of the investigators. He identified the date, all parties present, being the judge, court reporter, and myself. He then began asking me a variety of questions about the investigation, including how and when it was initiated, what was involved, identification of all parties or agencies, if PD knew, any possible consequences, when I planned to serve the warrant, and if the sheriff or local police would be present. Being cognizant of the court reporter present, I answered the questions as completely as I could, trying not to reveal too much information.

The judge sat back in his chair and took a long time reading the affidavit and warrant. Perhaps he was stalling, wondering what to do. After the long pause, he indicated he could not sign the warrant authorizing the service because the affidavit was deficient on its face. I asked the judge if he could be more specific on the deficiencies for me to advise my board attorney for corrections. The judge then handed the entire warrant and affidavit back to me. The judge said, "The entire document is flawed, from the codes to the inadequate probable cause. I can't allow you to serve a warrant on my good friend – especially one as weak as this."

I told the judge I would convey his message as said directly to our board attorney. Suddenly, he changed course, demanding the warrant and adding, "I will sign your warrant and you go ahead on and serve it."

I began to be suspicious of his change of strategy. Having a eureka moment, I suddenly realized what he was planning to do. He was going to sign the warrant but throw out the evidence later in a motion to suppress the hearing. A blind man could see it, and the court reporter is recording all of this which could possibly be used against me since he had already said on the record that the warrant was deficient. I said, "Your honor I am not serving a warrant signed by you after you have told me on the record that it is deficient. That is not going to happen." I pointed over to the court reporter.

He told me again, in a calmer tone, "Give me the warrant. I will sign the warrant so you can serve it."

I gave him the warrant and affidavit. He swore me in again. After I testified to the affidavit being true and correct, he then signed the warrant and handed it back to me.

I again said, "I am not going to serve the warrant. We will do something else. I would like to have a certified copy of the court reporter's transcript for the investigative file."

The Judge responded, saying, "You could request it, but you would not get a copy." He then hit his gavel and said, "Dismissed."

When I told Stan Ingram, the board attorney, of my meeting with the judge, the explosion was nuclear and read at least a seven on the Richter scale. It took Stan quite a while to cool down and begin to explore various options. He thought about another judge, but that would not work because we could still face the same judge who issued the warrant in a suppression hearing. Stan considered subpoenaing the files to a hearing, but that allowed almost no time for analysis of the files since the files do not have to be produced until the day of the hearing. The Mississippi medical board statutes do not allow investigative subpoena power, only subpoena power to a hearing. The options were few and far between. The only realistic choice was the federal route. Maybe we could somehow interest the DEA or the United States Attorney (USA) to pursue the case criminally. There was a very large number of controlled substances diverted in this case and with the patient files in hand, I was confident I could prove it.

Stan and I presented the option to the executive officer who agreed there was not much choice. I contacted Agent Steve Campbell who, while surprised at the judge's response, also felt we had no other option. In all fairness, the judge enjoyed a reputation for being fair-minded and very hard on the criminal element. That is why Agent Campbell recommended we take the affidavit and warrant to him. The judge's reaction and comments caught everyone who knew him by total surprise.

Agent Campbell set up a meeting with an assistant United States attorney (AUSA), DEA, MBN, and MBML for a briefing on the case at the AUSA's office. Since Agent Campbell had worked with the AUSA on other cases and knew all the participants at the meeting, I was more than happy to let him take the lead on the briefing. At the meeting, he explained all of the processes in the development of the case to date. He started with the stack of documented complaints, the pharmacy profiling results, several specific patient examples of the amounts, types, and frequency of the controlled substances prescribed. He advised the AUSA of the UC visits and the results and identified several patients of PD's that were sufficiently in recovery to testify and of at least two expert physicians who would be available to testify.

I then explained the MBML attempt to get an administrative search warrant for the badly needed patient files before the circuit judge as well as his response and, thus, our reason for presenting the case for consideration by the AUSA. The AUSA could not believe the unusual conduct by the judge. I suggested that PD probably had a reasonable idea that he was under investigation by now. Either his "good friend," the judge, the court reporter, or a pharmacist had probably spread the word. However, follow-up profiles on a few selected patients had not changed: PD's prescribing was still out of control.

The AUSA developed an immediate interest. He agreed that a search warrant for the patient files should be developed and served as soon as possible. George Phillips, the USA appointed for the Southern District of Mississippi personally approved the joint operation but emphasized one major point. There would not be any leaks to the media. If this case goes to trial, it will be tried in the courtroom, not the media. We all clearly understood.

It only took a short time for the AUSA working with Agent Campbell to develop the federal search warrant. After I had a chance to read the warrant, prior to it being served, I observed that most of the wording was very similar to the language used by Stan Ingram in the MBML affidavit and warrant that the state circuit judge described as deficient. John Countiss, the local federal magistrate, was presented the application for the search warrant and after a careful review issued a signed warrant authorizing the seizure of the patient files. The magistrate was long considered one of the most thorough and capable magistrates to serve the federal court system in Mississippi. He was universally recognized as a man of judicial integrity.

The warrant was served on PD the following day by agents from DEA, and MBN. It was suggested by the AUSA that since the warrant was a federal criminal warrant it might be best if only DEA and MBN be in on the service of the warrant. During the service, few of the patient files were found. The building where PD "practiced" was multi-story and quite large. An extensive search had to be conducted and PD was not cooperative. Agents had to be certain that most of the files that were not found did not exist, or at least that they did not exist in the clinic.

During the search of the clinic, and unrelated to the investigation, some shocking things were found. The top floor of the clinic consisted of several rooms where stacks of pornographic movies, tapes, and magazines were found. Several television sets connected to VCRs were found loaded with porno tapes. The first thing we thought was PD was making tapes of himself having sex with patients in return for prescriptions. After viewing a sample of the tapes, it appeared they were professionally prepared, and none contained PD himself. PD refused to talk with investigators or answer any questions per his attorney.

Once they were convinced that they had found as many of the files that existed, a receipt for seized files was prepared and provided to PD. Agents departed the clinic and made the return of the warrant to the federal court.

The detailed analysis that followed revealed exactly what was expected. PD was basically selling prescriptions, not practicing medicine. Of the very few files that could be found, most were of the patient "Alice" type, with little to no entries, medical evaluations, or referrals. Most of what did exist in the files was payment information. Those files mostly reflected the money that was owed for prescriptions previously issued. PD seemed more interested in tracking the money, not the medical issues. No files on either of the undercover agents were found. It appeared the accounting was simple. If the patient paid, no file was made. If they did not pay, a file was made to track and/or collect the money. Not exactly the way it was taught in medical school.

After the warrant was served, the file analysis allowed investigators to narrow the focus to the top eighteen "regular" patients to be used in seeking indictments against PD, in addition to the two undercover agents who had already participated in the investigation.

The total patient pharmacy profiles contained almost 10,000 prescriptions. I was able to go through the multicounty pharmacies picking up almost 3,500 prescriptions on the patients of primary interest. That number was later reduced to approximately 1,500 prescriptions to be used in the indictment and possible prosecution including the UC prescriptions. I provided a receipt for every prescription to the pharmacy where the prescription was obtained. This is necessary for the pharmacist to have a record of the prescription in the event of an audit by the pharmacy board. Most were very cooperative and glad to see these patients go away, except for one. Guess who got upset about PD being investigated and prescriptions being taken out of his pharmacy? You guessed correctly! Big Al balked when I attempted to pick up the prescriptions in his store, and initially refused, demanding a warrant or subpoena to release them. I told him I would go to the USA and get a grand jury subpoena requiring him to personally deliver the prescriptions to the federal grand jury handling the case. He then could present them in person and hang around to answer a few questions. He could justify to the grand jury how he filled some Dilaudid, Percodan, and other prescriptions for some patients at the rate, at times, of up to 100 doses a day. I told him I really would like to hear him explain why he filled prescriptions for patient Alice that averaged at times, five to ten Dilaudid 4 mg per day. If he wanted to go that route, we would. I informed him that I planned to leave an investigator in his store to make sure the evidence was secure until the subpoena arrived. If it took overnight, we would have someone watching the store just to be certain lightning did not strike the store and burn up all the evidence. (That actually happened once but was not going to happen again. As it turned out, it was not lightning that burned the store as the pharmacist claimed, but the pharmacist himself. Imagine that!) Big Al decided it was in his best interest to let the prescriptions go. At this point, I was convinced I could talk the AUSAs handling the case into indicting Big Al as a co-conspirator along with PD.

At this stage in the investigation, we had the complaints, the pharmacy profiles, the original prescriptions, the patient files that we knew existed, undercover agent visits, cooperating former patients, family members of patients who did not survive, two expert witnesses, and the law on our side, with a grand jury waiting. Most importantly, we had two of the most experienced and successful AUSAs in the business in our corner to prosecute the case. I almost felt sorry for PD and his entourage of lawyers. Well, almost!

The case was presented by the AUSAs to the federal grand jury with Steve Campbell, me, and an expert witness called to testify. It was a real pleasure to watch consummate professionals do their job. They were organized, precise, and knowledgeable. The organization and legal research on the case law and evidence were conducted by an intern at the USA office at that time. He went by the nickname RICO. RICO is an acronym for Racketeer Influenced and Corrupt Organizations Act, a federal statute used primarily by federal law enforcement against organized crime families. It required tremendous legal research and investigation to apply. RICO did that level and quality of work for the USA on this and many other cases. The nickname was meant as a well-earned compliment, as he was very effective at legal research, preparation, and presentation.

The grand jury returned a twenty-one-count indictment charging PD with twenty counts of illegal distribution by prescribing controlled narcotics and non-narcotic drugs without any legitimate medical indications and one count of conspiracy with the patients. Unfortunately, I was not able to convince the AUSAs to indict Big Al. I have regretted my inability to convince them of that my entire life. To this day, every time I see him, it digs at me because I know that Big Al needed to go to jail.

After the indictment, PD was arraigned before a federal magistrate to determine if enough evidence existed to bind PD over for trial. At the arraignment, the magistrate heard all the evidence and the challenges from the defense. He ruled sufficient probable cause existed for trial and, at the request of the AUSAs, required PD to surrender his DEA certificate pending trial. That immediately shut down his controlled substance prescribing operation for the foreseeable future.

After several months of pre-trial motions, the trial, with Judge Tom Lee presiding, began. Due to a shortage of federal courtrooms, the trial started in the old Mississippi Supreme Court, a courtroom within the Mississippi state capitol building. I have to admit to a certain amount of awe when I thought about the history of Mississippi that passed through that old courtroom. Here we were making history, in a very small way, by having one of the most significant cases in medical board history, before or since, taking place in that old courtroom. Nobody saw that coming.

The trial followed the standard script in format and presentation with one or two surprises. The witnesses testifying for the prosecution included MBN agent Steve Campbell, Dr. White, one other expert physician, the MBN UC agents, DEA agents serving the warrant, several recovering addicts, family members of deceased patients, and myself. Through these witnesses the AUSAs were able to have entered into evidence the following: the complaints concerning PD's practice, all of the original prescriptions used for the indictments based on the pharmacy profiles, the patient medical files (such as they were and if they were found), expert testimony concerning the lack of any medical indications or justification for the prescriptions found, and testimony from patients of PD who were in recovery, describing how easy it was to obtain their drugs of choice. Even with fresh track marks clearly visible, PD would prescribe whatever they said they needed. Finally, the undercover agents spoke about the details of their visits to PD.

The defense objected to the introduction of all of the evidence on every occasion, as was expected. The defense team even entered an objection to one of the judge's courtroom bailiffs! We never could figure out what or why that happened. The defense consisted of four attorneys, all from the general area of PD's practice. They were overruled on every single objection. Of particular interest or surprise was one of the defense objections to some underlining of text in an original report from one of the expert witnesses expressing his opinion on the inappropriateness of the prescribing by PD. It turned out that any tampering, such as the underlining on original documents is possible grounds to have the piece of evidence excluded. The defense had every member of the prosecution team cross-examined concerning that evidence being underlined but no one on the prosecution team knew anything about it. The defense team was not put on the stand for questioning on the matter. We on the prosecution team were certain it was done by one of the members on the defense team, for whatever reason. Judge Lee was satisfied after the prosecution team testified, there was no legal taint to the document and allowed it to be admitted into evidence. The trial moved on.

By this time, we were in our third courtroom. The moves were necessary due to constant repair work taking place throughout the old federal courtroom building.

The next surprise happened when one of the prosecution's expert witnesses was testifying concerning the large amounts of narcotics inappropriately prescribed by PD. The lead defense attorney made a rather boisterous, loud comment to one of the other attorneys, sitting at the defense table, describing the testimony as inappropriate and stating that he would be, "G--damned if he was going to let it stand."

The defense table was situated directly in front of the jury in very close proximity. I heard the comment all the way into the seating area of the large courtroom a long way from the jury. Judge Lee's reaction, by the way he looked at the defense team indicated he also heard the vulgar comment. The jury consisted of seven women and five men. In the front row of the jury, were five women and one man. From their reaction, they clearly heard the inappropriate comment as well. The one male member of the jury sitting on the front row near the defense table, after the comment, sat straight-up, rolled his eyes, and vigorously shook his head. I hate to say this because you never really know, but I think the trial was over when the jury heard that comment. They were upset and the defense team lost all credibility.

The trial continued with the defense portion. The defense moved for a directed verdict of acquittal based on insufficient evidence to justify a conviction, a standard move and in this case almost laughable. The judge overruled the motion thus requiring the defense to put on a case. Their first witness was PD. He began to testify as to the legitimate need of every single prescription, one by one, admitted into evidence on each patient. If this were continued it would add another two or three weeks to the trial. PD would be testifying about approximately 1,500 prescriptions, one at a time! After one full day of this testimony, prosecutors stipulated that each prescription issued by PD was issued "in PD's opinion" for a justified medical condition. It was the prosecution's opinion that they were not and that it was a judgment for the jury to make, based on the evidence. The judge accepted the stipulation with defense concurrence and the trial moved on.

PD testified that each patient needed what he prescribed and they really were in pain. When asked on cross-examination why he did not refer patients with long-term pain for consults or evaluations to determine the cause of the pain, PD said in his experience, they rarely offered anything useful.

When asked how he justified the grossly excessive amounts prescribed to patients like Alice, Percodan Man, and others, he said they said they needed the drugs and he really believed they were hurting. His standard response, but with no documentation dictated by the proper practice of medicine to back it up. When asked why he had so few files available on the patients, PD said he knew his patients well. When asked why so little amount of information was contained in the files that had data, again he said he knew his patients. PD was asked how he justified prescribing to a patient 100 Dilaudid 4 mg to take one every four hours or six per day, assuming they woke up every four hours at night and then prescribing another 100 Dilaudid the next week, ad infinitum. PD's answer defined the case: he said the patients said they really needed it! The gist of the prosecution's case was now established. The jury would have to ask themselves: Who was practicing medicine here – the patient or the doctor?

I attempted to have an AUSA, question PD to explain the "love palace" on the second floor. They said there was not a basis, no law against that, and the judge would probably sustain the defense objection to the question as just trying to inflame the jury. Still, in my opinion, PD did not help himself on the stand.

Next to testify was my favorite, Big Al. Big Al was supposed to be a character reference witness and he was, but cross-examination can be revealing. Big Al extolled the virtues of PD on and on. He talked about all the good he had done with patients and the community. He talked about how PD was always available to patients and wanted to be certain he took good care of them and their pain. When asked, on cross-examination, about patient Alice and the number of prescriptions he filled for her, he gave the standard answer, "I just fill 'em." The same answer applied to Percodan Man and many others. He was asked how he justified filling new Dilaudid, Percodan, or Demerol prescriptions for patients when previous prescriptions, based on directions, should have had over half the prescription remaining. Big AL said he does not question the doctor or the patient, my job is to fill the prescriptions. When asked why he charges over twice the amount for some of the prescriptions written by PD for certain patients, he said pricing is a business decision. When asked if he overcharged due to the patient being addicted, Big Al said that it was just a business decision. The AUSA said, "You knew the patient would pay whatever price you charged. Isn't that correct?" Big Al gave the same old answer: "Pricing is a business decision." The USA replied, "You were just milking the patients, right?" Big Al responded, "I was just filling the prescriptions." Big Al was asked if he ever thought about acting in the best interest of the patient. Big Al said he did, by filling the prescriptions. "Somebody had to fill them, why not me?" He was asked to explain why there were complaints from numerous other pharmacists filling far fewer prescriptions than he did, but no concerns or complaints from him. The defense objected strongly to that question but was overruled. Big Al's response was that he had nothing to complain about. About this time, Big Al began to emotionally breakdown. Fighting back heavy tears, he said in a loud, crying voice, "The prescriptions were all issued by PD and I just fill 'em!" It should be noted that during the cross-examination the defense entered a "continuous objection" to all the questioning by prosecutors. After the cross-examination was completed on Big Al, the AUSA doing the questioning of Big AL, walked to the prosecutor's table and sat down. He then turned toward me sitting in the courtroom and mouthed silently, "We should have indicted Big Al, too!" At least I was not the only person who thought he should have gone to jail. Sadly, he did not.

Defense attorneys put on an expert witness to rebut the prosecution's experts concerning the inappropriateness of the prescriptions. He testified that PD should be able to write prescriptions for his patients based on his treatment plan for the patient with an appropriate diagnosis. The "expert" tried to give PD wide latitude to justify the outrageous amounts that had been prescribed to the patients but had to admit on cross-examination there should be a medical file on each and every patient, and every prescription should be documented in the patient's file. When asked what if there was not a file, a diagnosis, or anything on a patient, the expert had to admit that the prescriptions should not have been issued. The admission was a big "uh-oh" for the defense – not what they wanted to hear. Finally, a plethora of politicians, city and county officials, sung the praises of PD before the defense rested. I was surprised the State circuit judge who initially denied the MBML warrant did not testify on PD's behalf.

Closing arguments began after over four weeks of trial. The AUSAs mentioned the over 10,000 prescriptions profiled in the investigation involving thousands upon thousands of controlled substances diverted by PD. They described how he indiscriminately and without any medical indications or justification provided the patients the drugs they said they needed. The patient files or lack of patient files clearly established PD's criminal intent. PD did not bother to maintain medical files correctly because he did not use them for legitimate care. This established PD was selling pills at $30 per prescription, not practicing medicine. The AUSAs described PD's clinic as a meeting place for addicts. It was described as a virtual shopping center for pharmaceutical drugs. PD was described by prosecutors as nothing more than a high-level drug dealer.

The defense team, in closing, described PD as a caring and compassionate doctor who did not want his patients to hurt. PD was described as an old, trusting doctor. They accused the UC MBN agents of being outright liars about what happened between them and PD. The MBN agents just lied to PD about being sick or needing medication. The defense said PD would take patients that no other doctor would try to help. He was just too kind and soft-hearted. The defense said that whenever a patient told PD they hurt, he believed them and tried to help their pain. It is amazing how just the MBN agents were liars, but all of the seriously addicted patients were truthful. Don't think the jury didn't see through that.

After a five-week trial, it took the jury *less* than an hour to reach the verdict of guilty on all twenty-one counts. At the sentencing hearing, held several weeks later, PD was sentenced to four years in prison and fined $100,000. He was released on $50,000 bail pending notice of appeal. He could still practice medicine until the MBML had time to call him to a hearing based on the conviction. However, he could not prescribe controlled drugs. Remember, PD had been required to surrender his DEA certificate at the preliminary hearing before trial. While waiting for the appeal to be completed, ironically, fate was to intervene!

While driving his vehicle in his hometown, PD was hit in a high-speed car wreck that seriously injured him, resulting in his death two weeks later. I was told by law enforcement that the driver of the other car had run a red light. He was said to be one of PD's former "patients," who was "drunk on drugs" at the time of the accident. Justice can be served up very cold at times!

An interesting side-note to the case. Since PD was convicted of one conspiracy count and all substantive counts involving the unlawful dispensing and distribution of controlled substances, 21 U.S.C. Secs.846 and 841(a)(1), the sentence included a period of confinement, probation, and a fine of $100,000. Prior to PD's death, his attorneys had appealed the conviction. Acting according to a motion under Rule 38(a)(3) of the Federal Rules of Criminal Procedure, the District Court entered an order directing PD to deposit with the Clerk of the District Court, as assurance for the payment of the fine if the conviction were affirmed, the sum of $100,000 "to be held by the Clerk in an interest-bearing account pending final resolution of the matter." PD complied with the order and made the deposit. Also, the 5th Circuit long had a firm rule that prescribed that an entire criminal proceeding be abated, meaning the indictment and conviction be dismissed, should the defendant die before the appeal is concluded. That means PD's estate got the $100,000 plus interest back! I am not a student of the law sufficient to understand the logic or theory of that legal thinking, I was just disappointed PD would get anything, dead or alive. PD had caused tremendous long-term harm to families and communities alike. I just could not feel sorry for him or his family. I had seen too much of the human destruction caused by his unscrupulous prescribing up close and personal. The Fifth Circuit Court of Appeals completed the full review of the appeal filed by PD's attorneys in 1984 and affirmed the conviction. Not a single item in the appeal was considered to have merit.

Steve Campbell retired from the MBN many years later after a long and successful career. Before he retired from MBN, I had the privilege of working several other cases with him. After retirement, he began a second career in law enforcement with a large county sheriff department and subsequently with one of the larger police departments in the state. He finished his career working in the private sector and still resides in south Mississippi. To this day, I consider him one of my most trusted friends.

The lead AUSA on the case retired from the United States Department of Justice after a very distinguished career. He went to work for a well-known and prestigious law firm.

The second AUSA on the case was appointed in 1985 to be a federal district judge. He continues to serve today.

RICO has a very successful law practice in the State of Mississippi. As hard as he worked on this case, no one doubted he would be successful and respected in his career.

Big Al continued to "just fill 'em." I was never welcome in his pharmacy. I would not have it any other way. There are some people that you just do not care if they do not like you. In fact, you prefer it that way!

The State circuit judge who denied the MBML warrant continued to serve on the State bench until appointed as a federal magistrate many years later. To say the least, I was disappointed. However, I was not given a survey form on that. I have often wondered if the judge ever realized that he and he alone was the sole reason that his "good friend" PD was federally prosecuted. All he had to do was his job of signing a completely valid and legal administrative search warrant without all his drama or just recuse himself from the process involving the search warrant. The case could have had a very different outcome. PD may even still be alive. Very few people knew about the judge's role in all of this, until now.

Dr. White left his local treatment center after a few years to run a much larger treatment center in another state. Unfortunately, he eventually lost his medical license due to a relapse in chemical dependency which could not be successfully treated. Not long after that, he passed away. A truly sad loss.

As far as Alice, Percodan Man, and the bedridden female patient referred to in the narrative, I only received follow-up information on the bedridden female. She was said by family members to have made a remarkable recovery after PD could no longer prescribe her any more controlled substance prescriptions. Amazing!

CHAPTER 2

CONTROLLED SUBSTANCES and STRIPPERS GALORE

Over-prescribing is the major contributor to the opioid crisis. — British Medical Journal, 2017: 359: j 4792.

One thing I learned early in my career as an investigator while working with and around physicians is that money is all-important. And why not mine the gold while the mining is good? The insurance companies are not doing badly either, kind of the same approach. There is nothing amiss about that thinking as long as the patient receives proper care. The case I am about to describe revealed to this investigator just how important the mining of that gold really is in medicine. It even resulted in the legislature creating an entirely new state agency. This case was one of the first cases that involved a long, drawn-out, legally contentious hearing. Prior to 1982, the physician licensing and regulation functions were still a division of the Mississippi State Board of Health. The actual board that made up the State Board of Health consisted of nine physicians appointed by the Governor from across the state. The physicians on the state board frequently commented how they did not want to spend a great deal of time away from their clinics. Sitting in the board's conference room making decisions about state health issues and not seeing patients cost them dollars. Then why accept the appointment? Previously, cases brought to the attention of the full Board of Health by the Physician Licensure division involved minor actions such as uncontested surrenders of DEA certificates or licensure decisions. Without a DEA certificate, physicians cannot legally prescribe controlled substances. Most cases were primarily informational only and took up a small amount of time at the Board of Health meeting. This case was the straw that broke that camel's back, resulting in the separation of the Physician Licensing division from the State Board of Health. As a result, the Mississippi State Board of Medical licensure was created. Time is money.

Before getting too deep into the cases in this publication, it is necessary to explain some of the operational processes and controlled substances scheduling. Early in the business of investigating physicians, investigators had four primary tools for gathering information. One was the telephone to receive complaints, of which there were very few because the public did not know we existed. If the board is not doing its job or is not believed to be doing its job, the public will not call. The second tool was a program called Area Development Profiling (AD). This program preceded computers and was extremely effective in identifying suspicious controlled substance prescribing patterns by physicians. The last two tools were pen and paper (profile sheets). The profile sheets were used to document the controlled substance prescriptions in pharmacies and were developed by one of the earlier board investigators. They were used by the medical board for over three decades. The process was slow but very effective. Using AD, investigators scanned prescriptions and used the pharmacy profile sheets to manually record recurring patient prescriptions. The date, drug, amounts, patient, and prescriber would be documented and analyzed. Schedule II and IIN (explained below) were the drugs of greatest interest and abuse.

At the time of this and subsequent cases described in this book, controlled substances were classified by a schedule based on actual or potential abuse or addiction. The federal and state-controlled substance schedules were very similar in structure. They were: Schedule I, II, IIN, III, IIIN, IV, and V. The letter "N" by II and III simply denote "narcotics." There exist some Schedule II and III drugs that are not narcotics. An example would be the controlled substance Ritalin, which is a Schedule II drug but not a Schedule IIN drug. More recently, DEA certificate schedule numbers for providers have been changed to Arabic rather than Roman numerals.

Schedule I includes those drugs with no accepted medical use in the United States. It includes heroin, LSD, and marijuana, etc. (Although some jurisdictions have since reclassified marijuana, Mississippi has not yet done so). Schedule II and IIN include those drugs that have proven medical value but also a high potential for abuse or addiction. This schedule includes Oxycontin, Oxycodone, Dilaudid, Hydrocodone (formerly in Schedule IIIN), morphine, Demerol, Fentanyl, and Ritalin, etc. Schedule III and IIIN include drugs that have accepted medical value but *less* potential for abuse or addiction and includes Tylenol #3, #4, and certain cough products containing Codeine. Schedule IV drugs have accepted medical value but (supposedly) even less potential for abuse or addiction and include Valium, Xanax and other benzodiazepines, and Ambien, a non-benzodiazepine. Schedule V drugs have the lowest potential for abuse or addiction and include low dose opium cough medicines and or low dose codeine cough syrups.

At the time of these investigations, Schedule II and IIN prescriptions were required by state pharmacy regulations and federal regulations to be maintained separate and apart from all other prescriptions. In addition, the major pharmaceutical drugs being abused were primarily in Schedule II and IIN. These included most forms of narcotics, amphetamine or amphetamine-like substances, and barbiturates. This also included Preludin (Phenmetrazine, a highly abused Schedule II amphetamine-like diet pill) and Quaalude (Methaqualone, a highly abused Schedule II sedative-hypnotic). Neither of these two drugs is currently on the market. Thank goodness!

While profiling a rural part of the state, I began to identify a suspicious pattern of prescriptions for Preludin in combination with Quaalude. The recipients were all young females, described as strippers by several reliable sources, including pharmacists and law enforcement officers. All the prescriptions were written by the same physician, who I will call "Dr. Ludes."

By regulation, Schedule II and IIN prescriptions cannot be called into a pharmacy unless it is an extreme emergency. They are required to be written/issued by a physician. Each prescription was for thirty dosage units with instructions to take the Preludin once daily and the Quaalude once nightly with no refills. Schedule II and IIN prescriptions cannot be refilled; they must be rewritten. Based on the prescribed dosage, each prescription should last at least thirty days. However, these "ladies" were getting new prescriptions sometimes weekly from the doctor. Mathematically, ethically, and legally, that is a big "oops" for the physician. When a patient is returning for additional prescriptions way too early, that is a red flag indicating potential abuse and the physician should no longer reissue such prescriptions without investigating addiction, abuse, or diversion problems. The medical record on the patient, if properly maintained in good faith, should readily identify such potential abuse patterns for the doctor to address.

While continuing to build the profile, I visited one pharmacy in particular. Although I did not know it at the time, Doctor Ludes had two primary practice locations. One clinic happened to be in the back room of the pharmacy I was currently visiting. As I began to go through the Schedule II prescriptions, I noticed the stack was very thin. I asked if there were any more Schedule II prescriptions to review. The pharmacist pointed to a stack of prescriptions at least six feet high that was impaled on a long heavy metal wire hanging in a back corner of the pharmacy. The pharmacist told me that the doctor comes to a backroom area attached to, but behind, the pharmacy area that serves as a clinic two days a week where he sees patients. The pharmacist said he "files" the scripts by putting them on the metal wire after he fills them. The prescriptions on the wire were all for the same drugs, Preludin and Quaalude. Most of the patient's names were female and, according to the pharmacist, just happened to be young females who worked as strippers in night clubs located in Biloxi, MS. They were all getting weekly prescriptions for thirty dosage units each. Preludin, being a strong stimulant, amphetamine-like drug, allowed the girls to "work" all night long. The Quaalude taken in the morning after "work" would allow the girls to sleep all day and start the cycle over the next night. What a healthy lifestyle!

There were suggestions that the doctor was being paid in more than one way by the strippers. A not-so-subtle hint of drugs-for-sex operation. The prescribing of these drugs was clearly outside the course of a legitimate professional practice based solely on the time period and amounts alone. The use of these drugs as determined by the manufacturer in the Physician's Desk Reference (PDR) was intended for short periods (thirty to sixty days maximum) and contraindicated for concomitant prescribing. The prescriptions had been issued to most of the girls for periods in excess of eight to twelve months with little to no interruption. Obviously, the pattern indicated a serious potential problem. The only way to determine what, if any, justification exists for such prescribing patterns is a detailed analysis of their patient files.

All the investigative material collected, along with the analysis of the prescribing patterns, were presented to the executive officer and board attorney for their directions. The girls averaged taking at least four tablets a day of each drug, assuming they took all the drugs and did not divert any. At those amounts, it is not likely to be considered legitimate medical care. Clearly, Doctor Ludes was not managing patients, just supplying prescriptions for whatever reasons. Regardless of the facts of a case, any responsible investigator wants to hear the other side of the story. Frankly, I was very curious how Doctor Ludes could justify the level of prescribing.

An inspection search warrant and affidavit were drawn up and approved by the board's attorney. Mississippi state law allows the medical board to gain access to patient files, via an inspection and search warrant, based on probable cause. These warrants, once reviewed and signed by no less than a circuit judge, allow medical board investigators to enter the clinic of a licensee at the address listed, during operational hours, and inspect designated patient files. Those patient files to be used in the prosecution of a case can be seized and the permission of the patient is not required.

I was able to track down the district's senior circuit judge at a dinner party at the Broadwater Beach Hotel in Biloxi, MS. He was dressed in a tuxedo when he met with me in a private room off the ballroom dance floor. He was not a real happy camper about the interruption but said he knew what the job was when he took it. He reviewed the affidavit and warrant carefully and asked a lot of questions. He admitted he was not very familiar with the authority of the medical board. I had, at our board attorney's suggestion, made copies of specific statutes for reference, since we knew most judges were unfamiliar with our authority. I continued this practice in the future and it served me well several times. The judge finally signed the warrant and affidavit authorizing it to be served.

I traveled to Doctor Ludes' pharmacy clinic location the next day. I was greeted by an employee who indicated the clinic was open, but the doctor would not be in. I explained to the employee the reason for the visit, showed her the warrant and recommended she contact Doctor Ludes. The doctor does not have to be present or give permission for the warrant to be served, however, we prefer them to be in the clinic, if at all possible. She contacted the doctor and was told that he would not come to the clinic, but to cooperate with the investigator and provide what I wanted. I provided her with a list of names of patient files to be reviewed. After a search by myself and the employee, only a few files were located. I asked the employee if it was possible that some of the patient files needed were at the other clinic location. The employee explained that if the prescriptions were filled at the in-house pharmacy, of which the vast majority were, the patient file would be at this location. An inspection of several of the files found virtually no data documenting a proper examination or justification for the treatment of the patients with the drugs prescribed. Only a few of the medical files contained a recorded weight even though the primary reason for prescribing Preludin is a diagnosis of obesity. I did not see a weight scale anywhere in the clinic. There were almost no entries for the prescriptions entered into the patient files. All the listed patient files that could be located were seized. I left a detailed inventory of the patient files taken with the clinic employee.

The data from the profiles along with the analysis of the few medical files found and seized were reviewed by the executive officer and board attorney. Based on the long-term prescribing pattern and the woefully inadequate medical justification found in the patient files, a decision was made to contact Doctor Ludes and seek a voluntary surrender of his DEA certificate.

Upon graduation from medical school, and after passing the Licensing exam known then as the Federation Licensing Exam (FLEX), a doctor is issued a license to practice medicine. Today, that exam is known as the United States Medical Licensing Exam (USMLE). Once licensed, the doctor can then apply for a United States Drug Enforcement Administration (DEA) certificate. The certificate is assigned a unique number and lettering combination that applies only to that practitioner and allows that practitioner to administer, dispense, and prescribe controlled substances, but only for well documented legitimate medical reasons supported by documentation. When I contacted Dr. Ludes, he refused to surrender his DEA certificate.

When a doctor refuses to cooperate with the board voluntarily, no other option is available except to summon the physician to a hearing before the full board. The action is accomplished by issuing a summons and an affidavit. These documents specify the date and time of appearance as well as the charges. The summons and affidavit were prepared by the board's attorney and served by me on Dr. Ludes.

A full-board licensure hearing had rarely been undertaken by the State Board of Health. Numerous other physicians had appeared before the full board to plead their case, but only a few had a full adversarial hearing. Effectively, it is a trial, based on the evidence, with the board serving as the jury.

At that time, whenever the State Board of Health met, an agenda was prepared and disseminated to board members before the meeting for their review. The hearing of this doctor was handled as any other routine item. Like other items, it was expected to be handled in just a short period of time. This was not the case! The attorney defending the doctor presented motions for summary judgment, continuance, and discovery. Also, there were numerous objections to admissions of evidence, a change of venue motion, and other assorted procedural arguments. Dr. Ludes was not going down without a fight. As a result, several hours passed and the case was carried over to the next scheduled meeting. This scenario repeated itself for several more months. After a very lengthy period of combined hearing days, the board was finally able to revoke Doctor Ludes' DEA certificate. Almost immediately, Doctor Ludes appealed the board's action and petitioned the board for the return of his DEA certificate pending appeal. Understand, all of this was new to the Board of Health. None of this legal bantering had ever taken place before, to this extent, and it appeared yet another protracted hearing process was about to begin. However, it ended rather abruptly.

According to information that I received from ambulance sources and local law enforcement, Doctor Ludes was apparently having an ongoing romance with his "nurse" and was found deceased in bed at her residence. My source indicated he literally died "in the saddle" from a heart attack.

It was shortly after this case ended that the Board of Health directed staff to create legislation, separating the Physician Licensure division from the State Board of Health and creating the Mississippi State Board of Medical Licensure as a separate independent state agency. The bill passed in the next legislative session and the Mississippi State Board of Medical Licensure was born. The Board of Health had made it clear they had neither the time nor inclination to deal with such "Bad Actors." A full-time separate board was needed to handle licensing and discipline of physicians. Time is money!

CHAPTER 3

DR. BRIDGE and DR. BLUES

The epidemic began when doctors prescribed a huge number of opioids – leaving the drugs to proliferate not just among patients but also among teen (and family members) who rummage through their parent's medicine cabinets, friends and family whom they shared the drugs with, and a black market where patients sold excess pills. Over time these drug users move to other opioids, including heroin, fentanyl, and fentanyl analogs. — Anonymous.

For approximately two years, early in my career, I was the only investigator for the medical board covering the entire state of Mississippi.

So, on the rare occasion when I could work more than one case at a time, I considered the reduced travel a blessing. Proximity plays a big role in deciding to try and handle two cases at one time. As long as the investigations do not involve large numbers of witnesses, serving warrants, or conducting area profiling of numerous pharmacies, the cases can usually be handled fairly quickly. Such were the cases of Dr. Bridge and Dr. Blues (not their real names).

While these two doctors were in close proximity to each other, they were not located in the same town. Information concerning the two doctors came to the medical board at about the same time from different but reliable sources. Dr. Bridge came to the board's attention by means of the DEA ARCOS report. The ARCOS (an acronym for Automated Report and Consolidated Orders System) is a report function used to record all purchases of any controlled substances by the individual practitioner or provider DEA number. An ARCOS report is generally published every six or twelve months by the DEA and provided to the respective state agency that has a real need to know and requests the report. The information cannot be disseminated outside the agency to which the report is provided. I was immediately able to identify a suspiciously large amount of a Schedule II controlled substance ordered by Dr. Bridge. The ARCOS report became a vital source of potential investigative targets. Almost every time we received a report, we identified six to ten new suspicious situations that almost always produced either an impaired doctor or a doctor diverting controlled substances in violation of multiple regulations.

Dr. Bridge was a doctor whose practice was in a specialty whose practitioners are commonly known as "doctors' doctors." He was a pathologist and, as such, would not encounter or treat live patients. Pathologists encounter parts, samples, or pieces of patients for study to help make a diagnosis for another doctor. On those rare occasions when they do encounter an entire person, the "patient "is usually well beyond help because the pathologist is performing an autopsy.

Sometimes the pieces of the puzzle are not hard to put together. Why would a pathologist be ordering 5,000 dosage units of dextroamphetamine 10 mg (five 1,000 container bottles) when he does not treat patients that need the drug? As common-sense dictates, it does not take rocket science to identify a suspicious situation that begs follow-up. Dextroamphetamine is a Schedule II controlled substance, rarely used by most doctors, much less a pathologist. It is primarily prescribed to treat narcolepsy, attention deficit disorder, and as an appetite suppressant for "grossly obese" patients. However, it is considered somewhat of an obsolete medication even for use in its primary indicated diseases. There are simply safer, more effective medications now available. I provided the order information to the executive officer who authorized an immediate visit to Dr. Bridge. I did the cursory homework to obtain his DEA certificate information and the address for his clinic or lab.

While preparing for my visit to Dr. Bridge, information came to me by telephone concerning Dr. Blues. This information was provided to me by a health care professional. I will identify the caller only as "James" to protect his identity. James said a package had been dropped at his residence by UPS but he did not know how long it had been sitting at the house because the front door is not used very often and he had just found and opened it. He assumed the package was for something previously ordered but forgotten about. After opening it, he realized immediately that there was a big mistake! The large package contained ten thousand 10 mg Valium tablets (ten 1,000 container bottles). They were brand name Valium, not generic. Each tablet was blue with the trademark "V" hollowed out in the middle. Every health care professional recognizes that tablet immediately. The 10 mg Valium is commonly known as blue Valium or "Blues" and is chemically known as diazepam. It is a Schedule IV controlled substance, primarily used to treat anxiety, but is useful in many other diagnoses. It is also, unfortunately, highly abused.

When James checked the package delivery address, it was supposed to be delivered to Dr. Blues at another address on a different street. James had enough training and integrity to realize something was very wrong and decided to call the medical board. He said because of his personal experience with health care dependency problems, he felt that Dr. Blues was going down a bad road or was already there. James personally knew Dr. Blues and knew that his specialty, radiology, was not the type of practice that uses a lot of this type of medication. Some patients need a sedative for an MRI due to the noise and confined space of the procedure, but Valium is not the drug of choice for that. All of Dr. Blues' practice was hospital-based. Any medication for a radiology patient would be ordered in-house and not on an outpatient basis. I asked James to hold on to the package for now and advised that I would be able to pick it up in one or two days and provide a receipt for the package. I asked him not to discuss the package with anyone. If for some reason UPS realized their mistake and came to retrieve the package, he should cooperate and let them have it. I would then deal with UPS and/or the doctor if that occurred. I collected all of the appropriate contact information from James to meet and pick up the package.

Since I already had the most recent copy of the ARCOS data printout, I looked up the orders for Dr. Blues under his DEA certificate. There was no report of the Valium order during the most recent reporting period. Two things were possible: either the supplier had not reported the purchase to DEA, which would be a major faux pas, or the order simply had not been entered in time to make the latest print out.

Consistent with the Executive Officer's training directives, I advised him of this latest development and suggested that I should be able to handle both cases, assuming there were no complications. He agreed that it would be cost-effective if I could handle the cases at the same time. He, too, was curious why a radiologist would need such a large amount of Valium in his practice. We then discussed what we both were thinking about each doctor. We both felt that we were dealing with two impaired physicians who needed help. Both situations would likely require an accountability audit to account for the drugs and determine what they had been used to treat. The executive officer decided that if they could not provide legitimate justification and records, both doctors should be asked to voluntarily surrender their DEA certificates, all of the controlled substances ordered, be evaluated for chemical dependency at a board-approved facility, and follow the recommendations of the evaluation. If found to be chemically dependent, they would have to agree to a consent order with the board that includes urine and/or blood monitoring for five years or else face a full license revocation hearing. The plan was to contact each doctor and seek accountability of the drugs and the purpose for which they were ordered. If the doctors were cooperative, the cases could be handled fairly quickly. We tried to keep cases low key and avoid costly hearings if possible. Sometimes it works out, sometimes it does not.

I first traveled to meet with James since there was a hot piece of evidence waiting to be picked up. I knew he was probably anxious to be rid of the 10,000 Valium tablets that any self-respecting drug dealer would probably kill for. I met with James at his residence and inspected the bottles for container integrity. All of the seals on the bottles were intact and did not appear to have been tampered with in any way. I provided James a receipt for the Valium. He had nothing new to report and assured me complete secrecy had been maintained. In my car, I inspected the address on the package more closely. The house numbers and the street names of Dr. Blues and James were not even close to being similar. How did UPS make such a mistake? Every once in a while, you just get lucky. Why can't that happen to me with a lottery ticket?

If my luck continued to hold out, I would find Dr. Blues doing his radiology thing in the local hospital. At the hospital, I followed the floor lines to the radiology department. I talked with a receptionist and asked to speak with Dr. Blues if he was in. She said he was. My luck was holding so far. She very politely asked who I was and the nature of my visit. Usually, this means the doctor does not want to see a drug rep and has instructed staff not to let them by under penalty of death. In my most polite and diplomatic tone, I told her my name and assured her that I was not a drug rep or an attorney. I said that the nature of the visit was private and confidential and that I was certain the doctor would not want me to discuss it with anyone else. She left to inform the doctor.

The doctor returned with the receptionist and motioned with his hand to follow him. He led me to his private office just a few doors from the waiting area. Dr. Blues said he was very curious to find out the "confidential" nature of my visit. I then identified myself to him and advised him the board was aware of the 10,000 Valium 10 mg tablets he had recently ordered. I told him that the medical board wanted to know the medical justification for such a large order. I provided him my usual speech about how he was not under any obligation to talk to me. However, if he chose not to talk to me, the board would be forced to proceed on a more formal and more public course to a hearing. After a long pause, clearly weighing his options, Dr. Blues said he was treating a family member for extreme anxiety. He identified the patient as his elderly grandmother who resides in a nursing home in another state whom he had been treating for several years. He described her as in generally good physical health but suffering from various anxiety disorders primarily related to her age. The order was for her to theoretically have a ready supply for the rest of her life. I explained to Dr. Blues how the board and good medical practice discourages a physician from treating a family member with controlled substances, especially one so remote. I told Dr. Blues that I would need to see the medical file he maintained on his grandmother and any inventory ledgers or dispensation records reflecting the ordering and use of the Valium. Dr. Blues said he personally did not maintain any medical file on her or any kind of ledgers on the Valium. He said he simply sends her about a ninety-day supply every three or four months. I handed him a copy of the board's regulations on controlled substance record keeping and referred him to the specific page number. He simply put the booklet down on his desk without looking at it. I then told Dr. Blues that DEA has similar regulations and he might think about who he wants to deal with, the DEA or the medical board. I then asked Dr. Blues for the name of his grandmother and the name and address of the nursing home where she currently resides. He asked why I needed that information? I told him without any records or files, I would have to be in contact with her to verify his explanation of the use of the Valium. Dr. Blues then became very quiet. After a long pause, he then leaned over towards me and asked me to follow him to his residence. He said we could talk more freely at his home.

As he drove out of the hospital parking lot, I pulled in behind him and followed. After about a five-minute drive, we pulled up in front of a very nice older home located on top of a low bluff with steps leading up to the house from the street. He met me at the base of the steps that led up to his front porch and I followed him up the steps and into the residence. Once inside, I immediately stopped and did a 180 looking at the strangest sight. On my left was a beautiful, wooden entranceway table, topped by a large mirror. On top of the table were maybe hundreds of blue Valium tablets scattered about in plain sight. To my right was a tastefully decorated living room with a coffee table in front of a leather couch. On the coffee table I could see, again, possibly hundreds of blue Valium tabs scattered in plain sight. My mind finally caught up to what I was actually seeing. Dr. Blues did indeed have a problem and needed some help and right away! I think it was safe to say he did very little in-home entertainment. Well, on second thought, maybe he did a lot of entertainment. After all, it was Valium, one of the most abused and popular drugs of the time!

Dr. Blues observed me staring at the coffee table and the Valium. As I raised my head and looked at him somewhat stunned, he asked me to follow him. He led me back to the kitchen area where we sat down at the kitchen table. On the table were, you guessed it, more Valium tablets scattered about. I used my notebook edge to clear an area for me to put the notebook down on the table. Dr. Blues looked at me and asked, "What do you want to know?"

I said, "Based on what I have seen, I am assuming that your grandmother is not the person receiving the Valium."

At this point, his tone was much softer. He said, "That is correct, she has been deceased ten or more years. All of the Valium is for my own personal use. I knew when you were asking for her name and address that you would try to contact her and then you would know that I was not truthful. It is true that I was stocking up for the rest of someone's life, but not my grandmother's. I know I have a problem. Now, what do we do next?"

I told him that the board would appreciate his acting in such a prudent and appropriate manner. I advised him of the key details of what to expect, such as being required to enter a board-approved treatment program immediately. I gave him a copy of the board's list of approved treatment centers, with the contact person and their number. I also gave him the contact information for the doctor running the Recovering Physicians program in Mississippi. I explained that after successfully completing treatment he would return to practice under a board consent order that would contain certain restrictions on his license. The main restrictions would be the surrender of his DEA certificate and random, unannounced, and witnessed blood and urine monitoring for at least five years. I told Dr. Blues it would show good faith if he surrendered his DEA certificate now and allowed me to pick up all the Valium in his residence. The Recovering Physicians Program would help him with his recovery and possible withdrawal problems until he could enter formal treatment. I also gave him my executive officer's number in case he felt he needed to hear all of this from a physician. At this point and to his credit, Dr. Blues was fully cooperative. I suggested he might want to give the hospital administrator a heads-up call to make him aware of the situation. The administrator would need to know in order to provide a leave mechanism of some sort while he was in treatment and to make arrangements to cover his practice. I told him that the hospital would receive an official notification, but it was best if they had time to plan ahead and not be ambushed. He readily agreed.

I executed a form required for the surrender of his DEA certificate which he signed. He indicated he would have to find the actual certificate and forward it to me. I had him write out a brief form letter granting me the authority to search his residence with him and seize the Valium tablets. We then went through the entire house counting and bagging blue Valium tablets. They were found on every counter or tabletop and in every room in the house. Even the bathroom countertops were covered. The total was in the thousands. Did I find all of his "stash?" Did he reveal his entire "stash" to me? I doubt it. Most chemically dependent patients have a real fear of withdrawal and will do just about anything to postpone the withdrawal symptoms. I knew when he checked into treatment, they would do a toxicology screening for current drug use. Also, the recovery program would be helping him with any withdrawal complications. They could get a copy of my report if they wanted and go from there. I prepared a handwritten inventory of items taken from Dr. Blues' residence for his records.

While in Dr. Blues' residence, I contacted the executive officer and brought him up to date on the situation. He said he would contact the head of the Physicians Recovery Program and ask him to give Dr. Blues a call. I asked Dr. Blues if he wanted to talk to the executive officer, but he declined, so I hung up the phone. I told Dr. Blues to expect a call from the recovery program and that they would advise him how to proceed. Also, that he would need to notify the board's executive officer of the treatment center he chooses and to enter as soon as possible. While going over the inventory with me just before my leaving the residence, Dr. Blues received a call from the recovery program. While he was talking to them, I picked up all of my evidence bags and paperwork, put them in my briefcase, waved goodbye, and quietly exited the house.

Dr. Blues did as he said and immediately entered an approved treatment center and was diagnosed as chemically dependent, as he knew he would be. He successfully completed treatment and returned to his practice as a radiologist at the same hospital. He entered into a consent agreement with the board and complied with all requirements for the full five years. He never attempted to reregister for his DEA certificate, and all randomly collected and observed blood and urine samples tested clean.

The next morning, at approximately nine o'clock, I entered the pathology lab where Dr. Bridge practiced. I was surprised to find he was the only person working in the entire lab. I could see him moving about toward the rear of the very large facility. There was no secretary or any other kind of assistant in the reception area. I had to bang on a large viewing window to get Dr. Bridge's attention. When he unlocked and opened the main door, I held up my identification and asked to speak with him. He said he was very busy and wanted to know what this was regarding. I told him it was in regards to 5,000 dextroamphetamine tablets he had purchased a couple of months earlier. With just his head stuck through the door, he looked down at the floor while at the same time asking what I needed to know. I told him I needed to see the drugs and do an accountability audit to account for each dose. He asked what authority I had to request all that. I told him the request was by the authority of the board's regulations that required all physicians to maintain accountability records of all controlled substances purchased or acquired for use in their practice. I handed him a copy of the regulations and told him the page number. He then opened the door far enough to get both hands on the booklet and still be able to turn pages to find the specific regulation. While he was doing that, I took a good look at his eyes which were blood-red with the pupils widely dilated, both being primary symptoms of stimulant use. After viewing Dr. Bridge up-close, it was apparent that he was not a weight loss candidate. I thought that I knew now who was taking the drugs, but I recognized that I could be wrong. After all, there is a reason why there are investigations.

After scanning the regulation booklet, he opened the door and invited me to come in. I followed him through the lab back to his private office, where we both sat down. He asked me to explain just what the accountability audit involved. I told him I had to count every single dose remaining in the inventory as of today. I would then subtract that amount from the total amount ordered. The balance figure would be the amount that would have to be accounted for in dispensing ledgers. I emphasized that every single dose had to be accounted for, no exceptions. He asked me how I would account for any used? I told him by examining the patient files and ledgers used to document doses provided to patients. He asked, "What if there are not any files or ledgers?" I told him, "Then you have a real problem and I have a mystery to solve. We need to find out who got or took the pills." I told him I think I knew who took the pills but we can talk about that later. First, I needed to see the pills and do the physical count. Dr. Bridge then said the pills were stored at his residence, not in the lab. He then asked for a few minutes to finish a couple of procedures in progress that he did not want to interrupt. I told him that was fine, but I had to stay in his presence or at least in close proximity to him. It took him about thirty minutes to complete whatever test or tests he was doing. When he finished, he washed up and suggested I follow him in my car to his residence. He said he lives in a nearby state, not in Mississippi, and it would take approximately thirty to forty-five minutes to get to his house, depending on traffic. He locked up the lab and we departed. Traffic was light on the interstate, so I had little difficulty following him to his residence.

I can only describe his house as a beautiful mansion. I followed him inside and up a flight of stairs into a huge room containing several lounge-type couches spread out over the room. Two entire sides of the room consisted of huge floor-to-ceiling solid pane windows with a view overlooking a forest and pasture area. One side was a large bar covering the length of the entire side of the room. The bar was well stocked for entertainment and from the large “dance floor” area, it appeared he entertained quite a bit. He told me to pour whatever I wanted from the bar. I told him I was on the clock, but that I might take a rain check on that. He said he would be right back, he had to go collect the pills. I told him I needed to stay with him to be certain nothing was overlooked or left behind. He waved me to follow.

He led me to a huge walk-in closet by the master bedroom. There he retrieved three full, unopened bottles of 1,000 pills and a fourth bottle approximately one-fourth empty. I noticed he continued to look around the closet with some sense of urgency. My math skills were average at best, but I was pretty sure I knew why. While he carried the pill bottles, I followed him back to the main entertainment room and sat down on one of the bar stools. He placed the pill bottles on the bar. He said he needed to make a phone call for just a minute. I told him I would begin the count of the inventory. I spread several large paper towels on the bar on which to pour and count the pills from the opened bottle. There was no need to count the unopened bottles because the seals were intact. Once a batch was counted, I picked up the corners of the paper towel and poured them into a large clean plastic bowl. I had to avoid physically touching the pills to prevent any contamination. A large knife from the bar, which I cleaned and dried, served as a nice counting spatula. Dr. Bridge walked to the far side of the large room, sat down on one of the couches, and placed a landline phone call (remember, there were no cell phones yet!). I overheard most of the conversation. He called his wife, who was obviously with friends. He asked her where she had put a large bottle of the pills that were supposed to be in his closet. There was a long pause while he listened to his wife's response. Dr. Bridge suddenly stood up, still holding the phone. I heard him shout into the phone, "What do you mean you gave them to your g—d—— bridge club players! They did not need them for weight loss or any other reason. I have an investigator here that needs to account for the pills." Dr. Bridge was more than a little excited. He closed the phone call with, "No, I am not kidding. This is serious!" He then hung up the phone.

In the meantime, I continued my count, which took quite some time because I always do a double count just to be certain of no counting errors. While I was counting, Dr. Bridge was thinking. My final count revealed that out of 5,000 doses ordered and received, 3,650 were in what I will loosely call "remaining inventory." That left 1,350 to be accounted for. I gave Dr. Bridge the bad news. While he was thinking, I guess he thought he had best come clean since he now realized his wife had become a major known supplier of pharmaceutical controlled substances to the "city streets" via the bridge club "gang."

Dr. Bridge sat down by me at the bar and started talking. He said he had ordered the drugs for his personal use and averages taking about one pill a day but not every day in order to stay focused and energized. He said there should not be more than seventy-five to eighty pills gone. He had told his wife about the drugs but never expected her to take them or even worse, give them to all of her bridge club members and friends. He commented, "I am sure you heard what I just found out myself."

I asked him how he could explain not noticing an entire bottle missing. He said he just did not notice it was gone because he had not counted the drugs since they had been delivered. With his head shaking side to side in frustration, he added that he did not know what else to say.

I told Dr. Bridge that I appreciated his being forthright and that what he said based on what had transpired was creditable. I then explained there are a few hoops that he will have to jump through. First, he would have to enter a board-approved treatment center to be evaluated for chemical dependency. To this point, Dr. Bridge strongly resisted. He commented that asking a doctor to enter a treatment center for evaluation for chemical dependency was ensuring a diagnosis of the same, and it never ends well. I made no immediate response and just stared at Dr. Bridge. After a long pause, attempting to carefully form my words, I told Dr. Bridge that most treatment centers do not "make up" a diagnosis, especially those monitored by medical boards for physicians. Dr. Bridge again admitted he was taking the drugs but insisted he was not dependent. I told him if that was the case, the evaluation would be short and sweet and he would be back in his lab in a very short period of time. However, he would still probably face some monitoring requirements concerning his practice. I made it clear to him that this was not going to be negotiable. I explained that the board must do its due diligence to *know* that there is not a dependency problem and could not just make an assumption. If found to be chemically dependent, he would have to complete treatment in a board-approved facility and afterward there would be considerable monitoring of his blood and urine for controlled substances or alcohol. I then asked him, on behalf of the board, to show good faith by voluntarily surrendering his DEA certificate and all the remaining controlled substances in his possession to me at this time. Dr. Bridge asked if that was really necessary.

I emphatically told Dr. Bridge that failure to cooperate could result in his facing several administrative charges and his wife could face criminal charges based on the disposition of the drugs.

In response, he said he did not think they had intentionally done anything wrong. I responded that intent, at this point, did not matter because they had already committed numerous violations of federal and state laws and regulations dealing with the administering, dispensing, accounting, and storing of controlled substances. I explained that he could order all of the controlled substances he wanted. However, sooner or later he was going to be audited, like at the present time. I told him that he had stored the drugs at an unregistered location, his house, and in an unsecured manner, thus the local bridge club was riding pretty high with his wife as the dealer and him as the source. All of that activity could potentially result in not just administrative charges but big-time criminal charges. I emphasized that these acts alone were enough to revoke not only his DEA number but also his medical license. I pointed out that he had no records as to the legitimate medical use of the drugs and that he had admitted they had been diverted illegally by his wife. Finally, and probably most importantly, I told him he had been treating himself with a highly abused Schedule II controlled substance for no legitimate medical reason. I ended my efforts at persuasion by telling him that in my career I have seen very reputable people go to federal and state prison for fewer and less severe violations.

I told Dr. Bridge that he needed to be reasonable and prudent and that, based on my experience, he did not want to go before a full board hearing with the evidence against him. I said that he had the right to an attorney for a consultation. However, I thought any attorney worth their fee, once all the evidence was in full view, would tell him exactly what I was telling him now. To his credit, he finally agreed. I assured him that cooperation was the right decision and gave him a copy of the approved treatment centers and contact numbers. I stressed to him that this needed to be accomplished ASAP. Any unnecessary delay could be misinterpreted and formal charges filed. I gave him the executive officer's contact information so he could talk with another doctor if he wished and so he could let the EO know which treatment center he had chosen. We then executed the surrender of his DEA certificate and I took possession of the controlled substances. I reminded him that, as a pathologist, he did not even need a DEA number, and that a lot of pathologists did not have or want one. Some hospitals require a DEA number for staff privileges and in those cases, the pathologists and other specialties that did not really need a DEA number, just have the certificate for Schedule V. Since Dr. Bridge did not have a hospital-based practice, he did not need a DEA number, but it was his decision.

Dr. Bridge promptly entered an approved treatment center for evaluation and was found not to be chemically dependent despite his fears, but nevertheless was found to be an abuser. He did enter into a consent order with the board agreeing not to attempt to reregister for his DEA number without permission from the board and agreeing to random, unannounced, and witnessed urine testing for three years. All samples collected during the three years were clean and to the best of my knowledge, Dr. Bridge never attempted to reregister for a DEA number.

As far as I know, neither Doctor Blues nor Dr. Bridge had any more problems requiring medical board intervention. I do not know what happened to the high-flying bridge club. I would speculate that attendance dramatically fell off after the dextroamphetamine supply was interrupted!

CHAPTER 4

OVERABUNDANCE OF PROBABLE CAUSE

We certainly prescribe the medicine, and some become addicted to it. I am quite sure I am a part of the problem. Right now, I am trying to be more a solution than a part of the problem. – John Fothergill, MD Indian Stream Health Center.

Politics, it is said, is the tie that binds and at times, it can definitely be a tie that binds very tightly. Throughout my travels in the state of Mississippi, it was always a pleasure to visit the small towns. The small-town square is a feature unique to Mississippi and the South in general. In other states, most towns were planned very differently. Before Walmart or other big box stores arrived, all commerce, including most pharmacies, were all centrally located on the town square. This layout made it easy to conduct pharmacy profiles by simply walking "around" the square.

Such was the case when I found myself walking around the square in a small town in a rural county in Mississippi. I was not working in the town on an assigned case or based on any particular evidence, just profiling the Schedule II and IIN prescriptions as a continuation of the board's "Area Profiling" effort to identify any suspicious patterns of possible diversion. I knew it had been quite some time since any board effort had taken place in this area. In the first pharmacy, I found nothing of interest. The problem became apparent immediately after I began profiling the second pharmacy on the square. The very first prescription in the Schedule II file was for four vials of Demerol 30ml, 50mg/ml, followed by multiple prescriptions for the same about every three days. I immediately asked the pharmacist if he could give me any details on the justification for the prescriptions. He said the patient was a male, terminal cancer patient, approximately sixty years of age. I did not think too much about it until I was further into the profiling effort. Over the next three hours, I documented approximately two years of the prescriptions for the Demerol injectable.

A quick analysis identified several issues that I found unusual. Although I stopped profiling at two years of prescriptions, the pattern continued back much further. A terminal patient is generally short-term, maybe six months or less. Also, with increasing pain in most terminal patients, Demerol is not the drug of choice for that type and level of pain management. Dilaudid, morphine, or methadone were more effective and longer lasting, and would have been the drugs of choice at that time. Demerol has a quick tolerance build-up and would have required increasing amounts for pain management. Self-administration of this type of drug over such a long period is always highly suspicious and a source of concern. Finally, the prescriptions were from a local surgeon, not an internist or oncologist. I will call the surgeon "Dr. Springs." Surgeons just do not usually prescribe much beyond a surgical convalescence period of two to six weeks. This situation was a suspicious prescribing pattern if I ever saw one!

I contacted the executive officer and advised him of the profile, what the pharmacist had said about the patient's diagnosis, and my concerns. He agreed the prescribing pattern was of significant concern and authorized a visit to the doctor to inspect the patient file and determine exactly what was going on. This type of visit to a doctor's office was a common occurrence for medical board investigators. A quick visit with the doctor, review the documented patient diagnosis and treatment plan, offer some recommendations and we were usually out of the clinic in short order. After all, it was only one patient. Well, to my surprise, I was out of the clinic in very short order, but not for the reason I hoped or expected.

At Doctor Springs' clinic, I presented my credentials and requested to see Dr. Springs when he was available. The receptionist asked about the nature of the business. I told her it was about one of his patients. She asked the name of the patient, to which I replied, "Ivan Hopkins" (not his real name). She left to tell the doctor but came back immediately and told me the Doctor would not see me and could not discuss any patients under any circumstances. I thanked her and exited the clinic. Like I said, out in short order, with egg on my face! The failed visit taught me an important lesson early in my career that I passed on to future MBML investigators: never give the name of the patient to anyone but the doctor. It never happened again. I immediately contacted the executive officer and told him of the cold shoulder from Dr. Springs. He told me to continue the profiling effort and we would discuss it with Stan Ingram, the board attorney early the next week.

As directed by the EO, before leaving the area, I continued the profiling effort in the town and documented several more prescriptions to Ivan Hopkins at three other pharmacies. These additional prescriptions added considerably to his daily amount totals.

The following Monday at a staff meeting, we conferred with Stan Ingram by phone. The executive officer briefed him on the events of the previous week, the amounts of Demerol prescribed, and expressed the need to see the medical file to determine the validity of the suspicious prescribing. Stan agreed and suggested, since the doctor would not meet with an investigator, the only option was an administrative inspection warrant. I met with Stan the following day to draw up the warrant and affidavit.

Once they were completed, I traveled to the county seat location where the senior judge for that circuit had his office. I was told by his staff that he was currently conducting a trial in a neighboring county. They suggested that I drive to the county and just let the clerk or bailiff in the court know I needed to see the judge when there was a break in the trial.

Some of the trials I had to sit in while waiting to see a judge were quite interesting. This one involved a motorist that had been pulled over for speeding by a state trooper. The motorist got upset about being stopped and had stabbed the trooper in the hand with a hunting knife. The trooper, while wounded, somehow managed to disarm the motorist, subdue him, and place him under arrest. Quite frankly, the motorist was lucky to be alive. Most law enforcement officers would have been justified to shoot and kill the attacker. I got to sit in on the trial for approximately four hours. It was late into the evening before the judge finally called it a day.

When I approached the bench, the judge asked if I was the investigator with the medical board. I told him I was, and he said to follow him. Obviously, he had gotten a message I was coming. The judge led me to a small back room that reminded me for some reason of what Appomattox Courthouse must have looked like when Grant and Lee met to end the Civil War. It was old, dark, and stark. There was a small desk and chair where the judge sat down.

The other chair in the room, for me to sit in, looked like it came out of a saloon from an old western movie set. The only light in the room was from a single, bare, low watt light bulb hanging down from a high ceiling just above the desk. When you want to get rid of auditors or investigators, take them where it's hot and no lights. Works every time!

I introduced myself to the judge as I handed him my credentials along with the warrant and affidavit for him to review and, hopefully, sign. I also gave him copies of the Mississippi code that gave MBML the authorization for such warrants. The judge, while looking at my credentials, said he did not recall ever having a representative from the medical board in front of him before. He then handed the credentials back to me. I told him this was my first time to have a warrant to serve in his circuit. The judge then lifted the affidavit toward the dim light and began to read.

After reading for some time, he put down the warrant and began to read the copies of the codes I had provided. The judge then asked me if I was familiar with Ivan Hopkins. I told him I was not. He asked me if the FBI was involved in this warrant in any way. I told him we are an administrative investigative/regulatory agency of state government and never crossed paths or worked with the FBI. He asked again, "You are sure the FBI does not know about this?" I told him I had not had any contact with the FBI about this case. He began to read the affidavit again for several minutes. He then looked at me and said, "This is a large amount of Demerol."

I told him, "It is. That's why I'm here today. The medical board wants to know what's going on."

The judge said, "I understand."

I thought I was about to get my warrant signed when the judge threw me a serious curveball. He said, "I want to make a couple of changes to the warrant and affidavit. I will tell you what to change so your secretary could make the changes overnight."

I said, "Do you mean your secretary or my secretary to make changes?"

The judge said, "Your secretary. You do have a secretary with you?"

I said, "Your honor, I am lucky to have pen and paper – a traveling secretary is out of the question on my agency's budget."

He then told me that he was going to hold onto the warrant and affidavit until tomorrow. The judge told me to meet him in his regular office tomorrow at 9:00 a.m. to make a couple of changes to the documents.

I said, "Your honor I have never left a warrant and affidavit with a judge before. Can I keep it and just bring it to your office in the morning?"

He said, "No, I will keep it for corrections."

This had big-time never happened before!

When I got back to my motel, I called Stan Ingram and told him what had transpired with our warrant and affidavit. He, too, was surprised by the judge's decision. He said, "Well, let's just see what happens in the morning."

The following morning at 9:00 a.m. I walked into the judge's office. No one was in the outer office, so I proceeded toward a back-office area where I heard voices. I saw the judge and a young man, dressed in a business suit, talking, and looking at the warrant and affidavit. The judge waved me in and introduced the man to me as an attorney from the Prosecutors Association, who he had requested to help him review the warrant and affidavit. Now I was seriously wondering what in the hell was going on! The judge told me that, unfortunately, his secretary was going to be out of the office with a sick child. Therefore, changes to the warrant and affidavit could not be made then and there. He said that he and the attorney had carefully reviewed the warrant and affidavit, along with applicable law, and found one problem. I had a rare legal problem known as an overabundance of probable cause. He said,

"Usually an affidavit before me lacks probable cause, but not in this case. You clearly have entered an overabundance of probable cause."

Looking and feeling completely perplexed, my only utterance in response was, "Really!?"

The judge said, "Yes, I and the attorney here agree that to correct the problem we have to remove all references to the patient, Ivan Hopkins, on both documents. Then the warrant could be served. I am going to hold both documents until I can have my secretary make the corrections, but in the meantime, you can serve the warrant, just like you had it in hand."

I then asked the judge, "How can I possibly serve a warrant I do not have in hand? And how will the doctor know what patient file to give me?"

The judge told me not to worry. "The patient file will be waiting for you when you get to the doctor's clinic."

I said, "With all due respect, your honor, how could that possibly happen?"

He said, "I am going to call the doctor and tell him to have it ready for you to pick up, and to give it to you." To say the least, I was stunned and speechless.

The judge then told me to make the return for the warrant directly to him and not to the circuit clerk's office. Normally, a return for a warrant is to the circuit clerk in the county where the warrant was served so the return could be filed with the original warrant and affidavit as a public record. Clearly, the judge did not want the documents filed as a public record, but why? He said he would hold on to all of these documents himself. I watched him slide them into his desk center drawer.

I left the judge's office and made a call to the executive officer to advise him of the bizarre conversation that just took place and what the judge told me to do. He called Stan Ingram who in turn called me back at a payphone. I repeated what happened. Stan said that this was unprecedented. I asked him what to do; I was totally stumped. How could I serve a warrant when I do not have the actual warrant? Stan told me to take the judge at his word and go try to get the patient file and see what happens. I asked Stan if he should maybe call the judge personally and ask for some legal clarification. He said he did not want to question the judge's decision and take the chance of upsetting him. So off I went.

After about an hour, I arrived at the clinic of Dr. Springs. I introduced myself to the receptionist who said she had the patient file and immediately handed it to me. I did not have to tell her my reason for the visit, the patient's name, refer to a warrant, or see the doctor. I offered to allow the receptionist to make a copy of the file, but she said that had already been done. After leaving the clinic, I contacted Stan Ingram and advised him that I had the file and how it was waiting for me when I arrived at the clinic. The file at first glance was fairly thick. I wondered how much of it had been generated overnight. I made the return to the judge's office confirming I had been given the file by staff at Dr. Springs' clinic.

The analysis was surprising. While the file contained numerous documented visits to Doctor Springs over several years by the patient, there was no mention of cancer, major surgeries, serious illnesses, or injury justifying the Demerol prescriptions. In fact, there were no prescriptions for Demerol documented at all. Since I did not have an opportunity to interview the doctor, I had to assume this was the entire file. There were still several unanswered questions. Did the patient have a chemical dependency problem? Did the doctor have a chemical dependency problem? Did both of them? Finally, what was the medical justification for prescribing the Demerol?

After reviewing the patient file and the prescription profile, the executive officer decided to call Dr. Springs before the full board in a revocation hearing. There was no information in the patient file remotely justifying the prescribing of the Demerol. Since Dr.

Springs would not talk to an investigator of the board, he could talk to the full board. A summons and an affidavit for a license revocation hearing was prepared and served on Dr. Springs through his attorney.

For every board meeting, the executive officer prepared an agenda. The agenda lists all of the items to be discussed, with necessary supporting data, including hearings that were scheduled. Each member of the board was sent an agenda approximately two weeks before the actual meeting to become familiar with the meeting topics. One was also sent to the attorney general appointee, (at that time, Oscar Mackey, now deceased) and our board attorney. Since Mr. Mackey's office was close by, I would usually hand-deliver the agenda to him as a courtesy. When I dropped it off, if time permitted, he would review the agenda with me present, just to talk and become familiar with what to expect. When he got to the hearing on Dr. Springs, he became really interested. He said that he knew Dr. Springs and that he was from his hometown. He wanted more details. I told him of the profile and the name of the patient, Ivan Hopkins. He immediately repeated the name in a loud, forceful, but questioning manner, and began to read the summons and affidavit that outlined the amount of Demerol for the patient and the charges against the doctor. His first comment was, "I do not believe this, I just do not believe this!" Mackey then asked me if I knew who Ivan Hopkins was. I told him no, I did not.

He said, "You do not know who you are dealing with here."

I said, "I guess I don't."

Mackey said, "He was the most powerful politician in forty counties." Mississippi only has eighty-two counties. "Hopkins got me elected to the legislature. He and he alone made the decisions on who holds an elected office or dog catcher job in half of the state of Mississippi." By this time, he was white-faced.

I told him, "That might explain a lot of what had happened."

I then told him of my adventure with the judge and how he handled the affidavit and warrant and how I came to obtain the patient file. I also mentioned that the judge asked me twice if the FBI knew about the warrant.

Mackey said, "I have to make a few calls because Hopkins and the doctor do not want a public hearing. They needed to do what was necessary to avoid public exposure."

I said, "I guess that was why the judge wanted to hold the documents himself and keep them out of the circuit clerk's office."

Mackey said, "You're damn right that's why!"

I told him that I would just leave him to his phone calls and left the office. Oscar Mackey, the normally laidback, jokester personality type, was clearly in full serious mode.

I do not know who Oscar Mackey called that day. I have no way of knowing and did not ask if it had anything to do with what happened next. All I know is that in two days, the doctor through his attorney agreed to a consent order with the board in lieu of a hearing. This really made me wonder who had what on who and who had the "pictures" that gave them the power to compel such action. It was like the doctor was told what to do and had no say in the decision. I never solved that mystery but, Dr. Springs got an opportunity to talk with the board whether he liked it or not.

At the board meeting, Dr. Springs admitted he had not handled the patient's situation properly. He knew that the patient, who he described as his friend, had a dependency problem, and had tried several times to get him to go to treatment. He admitted he should have stopped the prescriptions, but just did not do it. During the discussion, I noticed the name of the patient was never mentioned. I also noticed this was a rare board meeting where no members of the press were present. Why had the press not attended? They were usually the first to arrive for a hearing. In the consent order, Dr. Springs agreed to surrender his DEA certificate, undergo an evaluation for chemical dependency, and attend courses on prescribing controlled substances and record-keeping with documentation of successful completion sent to the board. As a surgeon, Dr. Springs was allowed to use the hospital DEA number for inpatient surgery and care, but nothing on an outpatient basis. Documentation from his evaluation indicated he was not chemically dependent. He successfully completed the training on proper prescribing, handling, and documentation of controlled substances. It took almost five years, but he was gradually able to obtain full DEA privileges.

Oscar Mackey later told me that Ivan Hopkins entered treatment for chemical dependency the day after I met with the judge in the old courthouse seeking the warrant for the patient file. He subsequently had to return to treatment two more times. He was eventually defeated for the public office he held for forty plus years.

Oscar Mackey represented the board as our Attorney General assignee for one more year before retiring. Unfortunately, several years after retiring, at a fairly young age, he passed away from a heart attack.

I am not aware of the disposition of the motorist/trooper trial. Based on what I saw and heard of the trial, I suspect the motorist was found guilty of aggravated assault and spent several years at Parchman State Penitentiary. I hope so anyway!

CHAPTER 5

DOCTOR CAAN

Sexual contact between a doctor and a patient, even if ostensibly consensual, is strictly forbidden. In ethical terms, it's a never event. In a legal sense, it can be a crime. Physicians know it's a line that can't be crossed – it's a prohibition as old as the Hippocratic Oath. – The Atlanta Journal-Constitution, "License to Betray."

Dr. Caan (not his real name) came to the attention of the Mississippi State Board of Medical Licensure even before he had graduated from medical school. The Chancellor of the University of Mississippi Medical School (UMC), as it was known then, contacted Frank J. Morgan, Jr., MD, the executive officer at the board for assistance, in dealing with a fourth-year medical student. The medical student was known as a "late bloomer" because he had entered medical school in his early thirties. The student had been seen engaged in sexual relations with patients under his charge at the university hospital on more than one occasion. Dr. Morgan explained to the Chancellor that the board had no authority to deal with medical students since they were not yet licensed by the State of Mississippi. As the Chancellor provided more specific details of the incidents, it became clear that the patients were not able to have a consensual sexual relationship due to their condition. Although that would not have mattered, since the courts in almost every state had long recognized that sexual relations between a physician and their patients are outside the course of a legitimate professional practice even if the patient was able to argue that it was consensual. Dr. Morgan suggested to the Chancellor the best way in handling this type of situation was in-house by documenting the sexual encounters that had been observed, and then dismissing or refusing to graduate the student on ethical and/or moral grounds. However, that advice was ignored, and the university chose the path of least resistance and graduated the problem over to the Mississippi medical board. Dr. Caan was graduated from an accredited medical school (UMC) with a clean record, technically speaking, and passed the FLEX exam. He qualified for full licensure as a medical doctor. At that time, he officially became the problem of the Mississippi State Board of Medical Licensure. As the complaint information filtered in over a period of many months, I felt that this case would be open and shut because of the variety and seriousness of the information. I could not have been more wrong!

After Dr. Caan received his license to practice, we were informed that while in medical school Dr. Caan had also been a pastor at a local church. Several irate spouses informed us that Dr. Caan had engaged in sexual relations with several members of that church (i.e., their wives). In evaluating the complaints, clearly the medical board had no authority to investigate or charge a licensee with having consensual sexual relations with non-patients. Those complaints could not be pursued.

For several years, Dr. Caan practiced in various communities in Mississippi. It was in his last small-town clinic location that the medical board began to receive information and complaints indicating that Dr. Caan clearly had a problem with sexual addiction. The concept of sexual addiction was just beginning to gain momentum as a condition for medical treatment. Most complaints involved questionable practice techniques, suspicious prescribing issues, and inappropriate or compulsive sexual behavior with patients. The first significant complaint came from the husband of a female patient. He said that his wife had gone to Dr. Caan for treatment of female related problems. During the visit, Dr. Caan had made suggestive sexual remarks and even attempted to have sex with her in his clinic. Dr. Caan had locked the door to the examination room when he entered and was not accompanied by a nurse. His wife had expected Dr. Caan to be accompanied since all other physicians she had visited for her type of complaint had a nurse present during the exam.

The next complaint came from a local physician in the same community. This doctor actually took the time to travel to the offices of the medical board to discuss and present his complaint in person. One big rule to remember in the world of investigating doctors is that anytime a doctor complains about another doctor, it is best to take the complaint seriously. The executive officer and I met with the doctor, who I shall identify as "Dr. Callis." When we met, Dr. Callis told us that he knew something was not right with Dr. Caan from the first moment he met him. He described Dr. Caan as a con artist impersonating a physician. He said that he could not believe Dr. Caan had a bona fide Mississippi medical license because he never really seemed to care very much about his patients. Dr. Morgan confirmed that Dr. Caan did, in fact, have a valid Mississippi medical license.

Dr. Callis indicated he had a patient tell him that Dr. Caan had raped her in his clinic. She claimed Dr. Caan had given her an injection in her shoulder/neck area and raped her after the drug took effect. The patient was described as a sixty-six-year-old black female. Dr. Callis indicated his exam identified a probable injection site at the base of her neck and his examination of the genital area was consistent with recent rough sexual relations. She also presented a blouse that she said she was wearing at the time of the rape that had a large telltale stain on it. She said the stain was Dr. Caan's semen. This information and evidence were turned over to the local county sheriff's department resulting in Dr. Caan being indicted on a rape charge. The investigation revealed that the stain on the blouse was semen and the blood type from the donor of the semen residue matched the blood type of Dr. Caan, a rare blood type. DNA analysis was not available for final confirmation at the time. The investigation also revealed that the patient had a history of mental illness. As a result, the local district attorney decided to drop the indictment due to questions about the mental competency of the patient.

The publicity surrounding the rape allegations seemed to ignite a firestorm of additional complaints from various sources in the small community. Almost immediately, the medical board began to receive complaints of sexual misconduct from numerous women and other sources. Other complaints involved inappropriate prescribing of a diet pill regimen to primarily female patients who were not valid weight loss candidates. One complaint involved Dr. Caan delegating care of a broken wrist to his son who was not trained as a health care professional of any kind. This resulted in the patient losing most of the function in her hand. Finally, a complaint was received indicating Dr. Caan had attempted to surgically repair a female patient who had been through a very complicated and difficult delivery of a baby. Several vaginal and anal sphincter lacerations were noted but, instead of referring her to an appropriate specialist for surgical reconstruction, he attempted to make the surgical repairs himself.

The result was a severely infected patient who, because of such poorly mismatched tissue, was passing fecal matter through her vagina.

During the investigations, I used the local sheriff's department and local public library as a headquarters for contacts and interviews. The Sheriff graciously granted me the use of his chief deputy, Jerry Nickels, to help me with the sensitive female interviews. Without Chief Deputy Jerry Nickels to help me locate and track down witnesses and conduct interviews, the investigation could not have been successfully completed. Chief Deputy Nickels knew most of the witnesses and their families and, most importantly, where they lived. He also helped establish the integrity and veracity of the witnesses because he knew who could be trusted and who to avoid. The board truly owed him a debt of gratitude for his assistance.

The complaints from white and African American female patients, none of whom knew each other, concerning sexual misconduct, had several common denominators. All complained of sexual suggestions, inappropriate, unauthorized, or unnecessary touching of breasts or genitalia, locking the examination room door after entry, and not having a nurse accompany him during the exam. Many of the patients were young African American females living in a section of a town described at the time by several publications as the poorest area in the United States. It was not uncommon for a predator to select these types of patients for exploitation. One patient indicated that, after completing his exam, Dr. Caan said, "All you need is more sex, and I am going to fix you up." He began to unbuckle and unzip his pants. He only stopped because she got off the table and physically threatened him. One female patient said she went to him for a bad cold and cough. All Dr. Caan did was suck her breasts during the so-called exam. She left without treatment and never returned. Another woman indicated she went to him for female problems. During the exam, he fondled her breasts repeatedly, made sexual suggestions, and massaged her genital area as if he were trying to get her to have sex. Another went to him for treatment of female problems related to a possible infection. All he did was massage the genital area and ask her if it felt good. All these women provided statements and agreed to testify. Many other ladies were interviewed by us and admitted to the same or similar circumstances, but were afraid to get involved. Many acknowledged having sexual intercourse with Dr. Caan in the clinic but were too embarrassed or scared of their husbands to provide statements and testify. One even said her husband might kill her and/or the doctor if he found out about what happened.

During the sexual misconduct portion of the investigation, several current and former employees of Dr. Caan were interviewed. One nurse, a former employee, indicated she never saw or heard of anything inappropriate taking place in the clinic with female patients. She said she was always in the room when Dr. Caan examined female patients. However, she was not employed in the clinic during the time when most of the more recent complaints were generated. It was revealed that she had left the clinic's employment before the board started receiving complaints.

One nurse, Laura (not her real name), also a former employee of Dr. Caan's, refused to talk to us for a long period of time. She eventually agreed to be interviewed when I was finally able to track her down and contact her in person at her residence. She lived in a larger town approximately forty-five miles from Dr. Caan's clinic. Laura told me that she was reluctant to get involved in the investigation because of her previous involvement with Dr. Caan herself. She said that she had a long-term relationship with him and that her husband had caught them having sex together on more than one occasion. She had left employment with Dr. Caan because she did not want to lose her marriage. She did not want to bring up the past by getting involved in the investigation. I asked if her husband had been one of the spouses that threatened Dr. Caan. She said he had. On one occasion her husband had caught them together in their house. Dr. Caan, completely nude, had been found by her husband hiding in a closet. Her husband took a baseball bat and broke out every window in Dr. Caan's Cadillac. He then broke out all the lights and cut the tires. He put Dr. Caan, still completely nude, walking out on the road and told him that if he caught them again, he would kill him. I must admit, after hearing about the encounter, I began to hope her husband did not come home and find me interviewing his wife alone with Chief Deputy Jerry Nickels forty-five miles away.

I asked Laura to reconsider her position of not being involved. I told her it was important to know exactly what had been happening in the exam rooms with all the female patients. Dr. Caan had said that she had been with him in the room for every single female patient exam. Laura said she was aware of that because Dr. Caan had called her several times to have her corroborate his story that she was in the exam rooms during each exam. I told Laura that I just wanted the truth and to know what really happened. I reminded Laura that the patients told a very different story about what happened in the exam rooms. They all said that only the doctor was in the exam room with them and the door was locked.

It was obvious that Laura was stressed and very nervous because she had wrapped herself into a tight ball-like position in her chair. She put her head down between her knees and said without looking at me, "I want to tell you something that you might not quite understand. I am a person of a strong, certain faith. We might do a lot of bad things and I have done a lot of things not so good, but there are some things we do not do. We do not tell lies and I am not going to lie for Dr. Caan. No matter what Dr. Caan said, I was not in those exams with him and did not know what, if anything, happened because I was not there." She further added that she had repeatedly told Dr. Caan that she needed to be in the rooms, but he refused, claiming the patients told him they wanted privacy. Laura finally gave me a written statement to those facts and circumstances. Dr. Caan definitely had some explaining to do!

The investigation of the diet program operated by Dr. Caan involved borrowing agents of the Mississippi Bureau of Narcotics to go into the clinics undercover posing as patients. That portion of the investigation was conducted as a parallel investigation with the sexual misconduct investigation. All the agents selected were determined not to be in any way legitimate weight loss candidates. We first had them examined by our own expert doctor to determine that they were in no way obese or even slightly overweight. They did not need any kind of weight-loss treatment and at least one of the agents sorely needed to gain some weight. All the undercover agents in multiple visits were diagnosed by Dr. Caan as "grossly obese" and prescribed multiple prescriptions of controlled drugs along with a regimen of non-controlled drugs for weight loss. The regimen included thyroid pills, diuretics, vitamins, stool softeners, and Schedule IV diet pills. Many of the prescriptions were determined by expert witnesses to be contra-indicated to these patients because of their lack of any legitimate need for them. A review of the medical files seized pursuant to a board subpoena confirmed most of the patients had not even been weighed during their visits. The investigation documented literally thousands upon thousands of Schedule IV diet pills had been diverted by being prescribed for a less-than-legitimate medical reason.

Several regular weight loss patients also cooperated in the diet pill investigation. Dr. Caan had prescribed to these patients the same controlled and non-controlled medications as to the undercover agents. Many were inappropriate due to no real weight loss issues and potentially harmful because of very high blood pressure in some of the patients. Some of the patients were already being treated by their regular physician for thyroid problems and the thyroid prescribed by Dr. Caan was contra-indicated. Any medical history he did document, he ignored, placing the patient at risk of undesired side effects.

The investigation of the patient with the broken wrist and the patient with the poor vaginal repair surgery was simple. We simply monitored the progression of the lawsuits for inclusion in the board's charges. A subpoena for the files of the patients from their primary care physicians doing the corrective surgical procedures spoke where the patients did not have to. However, the patients were cooperative to the extent necessary.

Dr. Caan was charged in the medical board's summons and affidavit with multiple counts of administering, dispensing, or prescribing narcotic drugs or any other drug having addiction-forming or addiction sustaining liability otherwise than in the course of a legitimate professional practice. He was also charged based on the sexual transgressions with multiple counts of unprofessional conduct likely to deceive, defraud, or harm the public. The last charge involved performing any act which in any way assists an unlicensed person in the practice of medicine (the broken wrist patient).

The investigation had gone on for months. That was followed by several months of depositions, injunctions, and failed negotiations. It was after considerable legal banter when I was finally able to obtain the all-important statement from Laura disputing Dr. Caan's claim that she was in the exam room for every female patient visit. It was only then that Dr. Caan, through his attorney, entered into a consent order with the medical board. Dr. Caan agreed that his license would be suspended for five years. He would be allowed to practice only under direct supervision at a state or federal institution or within the confines of an American Medical Association approved residency training program. He could only examine or treat female patients with a female assistant present the whole time. He could only administer or dispense (not prescribe) controlled substances pursuant to the institution's DEA number and only for inpatient use. He could not perform any type of obstetrical or gynecological exam, treatment, or surgery until such time as he provided the medical board proof of successfully completing a surgical residency or residency in obstetrics and gynecology. He never completed the training.

Eventually, Dr. Caan obtained employment at a large state penal institution. He was never again investigated by me but there were constant rumors of problems, but no complaints were filed while I was employed at the medical board.

Jerry Nickels, who was so instrumental in helping to locate and interview many of the victims in this case, left the sheriff's department after a few years and went to work for Federal Express. He had a very successful career working in corporate security and as a training director before retiring. He currently resides in Mississippi and continues to work part time as a consultant in corporate security and training. You might find him one day eating lunch at the world famous Blue & White restaurant. One of our favorite places for lunch!

CHAPTER 6

CRAYON MAN

I will use treatment to help the sick according to my ability and judgment, but never with a view to injury and wrong-doing. – Hippocratic Oath.

The original call that came to the offices of the Mississippi Board of Medical Licensure was from a female who identified herself to the receptionist only as a health care professional. I will call her "Julie." She requested to speak directly to me by name. The call was put through to my office by the receptionist. When I answered, the voice on the other end was female, poised, clear, and confident. She identified herself to me and said she was currently treating a female patient that had been sexually abused by a psychiatrist and was willing to talk to me about what had happened. Julie said she was aware of the board's reputation and had convinced the patient that the Mississippi board was serious in dealing with these types of abuses. I thanked her for the comments and told her we would do the best that we could. I asked if she could provide any preliminary details to pass on to the executive officer.

Julie told me the situation was about as serious as it could get. It had taken her almost six months for the patient (who I will call "Valorie") to open up to her about the details and Julie suggested that I hear them from Valorie's own mouth. She described Valorie as a well-educated, but insecure, weak, and somewhat paranoid adult female who was much stronger now than when they first began therapy. She identified the psychiatrist as Dr. Colour (not his real name) and the location of his practice. We set up a tentative time to meet the following week. Julie then gave me her telephone number, address, and directions to the meeting place. (Remember there were no cellphones, GPS, or personal Internet access at this time!) The executive officer approved the meeting. I called Julie back and told her the meeting was on.

I arrived approximately thirty minutes early, hoping to have a few minutes to talk with Julie about Valorie before she arrived. Julie told me Valorie's full name, age, occupation, and how she came to treat Valorie. Julie described how difficult it had been for Valorie to talk to her about the "treatment" she had been given by Dr. Colour. She explained that it might take time for Valorie to be fully open to me. I asked Julie to remain in the meeting for its entire duration and she said she would. Julie had already obtained signed releases allowing her to talk to me about the situation. However, considering the fragile condition of Valorie, Julie thought it would be helpful if Valorie herself could describe what happened. She suggested I not overreact to what I might hear from Valorie. Valorie was upset with Dr. Colour and determined to see this through to the end.

Shortly thereafter, Valorie arrived for our meeting. Julie met with her briefly before introducing her to me. I identified myself to

Valorie, who responded a little nervously with her name, adding, "Well, I'm the patient." Surprisingly, Valorie seemed to be somewhat relaxed. Julie might have given her something to help her calm down before talking with me, but I did not ask. I told Valorie that before we got too far along in the interview, we needed to be sure that everyone was on the same page. I explained how I came to be involved in the possible case. Valorie acknowledged that she had signed releases for Julie to talk with an investigator from the medical board and that she also personally agreed to talk with me. I asked her to begin with when she first began to see Dr. Colour and to proceed from there and to be as specific as possible. I provided the usual reassurances we give to patients who are unaccustomed to speaking with strangers about the details of personal, intimate situations. I encouraged her to take her time and to talk with Julie alone if it would help her. All the introductory conversation is purposely designed to build confidence in the patient being interviewed. Equally important is establishing the reliability of the patient. When an investigator interviews a person, various techniques are applied to evaluate the truthfulness of that person. Eye contact is important in making such a determination. Generally, poor eye contact indicates deception, especially the type of eye contact before and after a comment or question. However, there are exceptions. A patient who is known to suffer from mental health issues, insecurity, or sexual trauma might have a problem with eye contact, but not necessarily truthfulness. Valorie had a real problem with eye contact during most of the interview.

Valorie said she began seeing Dr. Colour approximately two years earlier for problems she was having with paranoia, insecurity, and being fearful of everything. After approximately three months of therapy, she noticed that more and more of her sessions were moved to late in the day after most of the staff and patients were gone. Dr. Colour began to occasionally introduce wine and other alcoholic beverages into the sessions for what he termed "relaxation." This moved slowly to kissing and later to both of them disrobing in his office. Dr. Colour would make sure the door to his clinic area was always locked. All encounters/treatment took place in his office and at no other location. Valorie said Dr. Colour would at times comment how she must be getting stronger and more self-assured since she was strong enough to convince a trained psychiatrist to take his clothes off with a patient.

Several months of "therapy" sessions went by that included drinking, conversation, and disrobing, but no attempt at sexual intercourse. At one session, Dr. Colour introduced "toys" to the therapy. The toys, as he referred to them, were the jumbo crayons used by children for coloring books. Valorie said Dr. Colour would insert them into her vaginally and then have her insert them into him rectally. He contended that having her insert the crayons into him was making her a stronger, more self-assured person. After a couple of months of this "therapy," Valorie also began to visit Julie for help because she felt what was going on "was just not right." She slowly began to stop seeing Dr. Colour. It was only through the therapy sessions with Julie that Valorie began to realize how she had been abused and that what had transpired was "not right." She slowly began to talk with Julie about the specific "therapy" Dr. Colour had put her through. Valorie now realized that he was not treating her at all, just using her for his personal gratification. Valorie said she had not had any contact with Dr. Colour for quite some time and did not ever intend to again. She also said she was willing to provide whatever cooperation was necessary including testimony. I asked both Valorie and Julie if they knew of any other patients who might have had similar experiences with Dr. Colour. Both said they did not know of any other patients at that time.

I then explained, for the benefit of Julie and Valorie, the administrative process for bringing a licensee before the board. The initial step would be to submit all of the information from our meeting to the executive officer for review. If approved for investigation, we would proceed to a formal inquiry. I told them that MBML could only address the license of Dr. Colour and could not charge him criminally. The case could be referred to the local district attorney (DA) for charges, however, criminal charges rarely occur in cases of this type because DAs just do not like to prosecute a local doctor. Just to be certain Julie and Valorie were not caught off guard, I explained that if the case goes as far as a hearing to revoke Dr. Colour's license, Valorie and any other witnesses would be called to testify. They would then be subject to cross-examination by defense counsel. Valorie's identity would then be open to the public. Most media outlets do not identify victims of sexual assault, but I explained that I could make no guarantees. I assured them every attempt would be made to locate any other possible patients that may have had the same or similar experiences with Dr. Colour. The possibility of recorded telephone calls was briefly discussed but, unfortunately, ruled out because Julie and Valorie were opposed to any further direct contact with Dr. Colour. I did not mention the issue of credibility of Valorie as a witness, which I knew could be difficult to establish.

Everyone working in the health care business realizes it can be a close-knit community, not just locally but regionally and statewide. I can offer no other logical explanation for what slowly began to happen in this case. Some would call it coincidence, but investigators do not believe in that. Some may call it just dumb luck, but nobody is that lucky. Finally, the term "karma" comes to mind. Whatever it was, it was real, it was helpful, and it kept happening in this case.

Approximately three weeks after meeting with Julie and Valorie, I received a call from another health care professional concerning Dr. Colour. I'll call the second health care professional "Vickey." Vickey stated she was currently treating a patient that she felt needed to talk to an investigator from the medical board. Vickey told me she was married to a physician and when she told him what the patient had told her about her treatment by Dr. Colour, he strongly recommended that Vickey contact the medical board. A meeting was arranged with Vickey. Nothing was said to Vickey about my previous contact with Julie and Valorie. The meeting could not take place at Vickey's clinic because she was employed by a state government agency and she could not afford for the employer to be made aware of the referral. She said she just did not know how her supervisor or the agency would respond. A meeting was arranged at a motel well removed from Vickey's clinic for the next week. This provided a non-public venue to prevent Vickey's coworkers from accidentally seeing her meet with me. Vickey said that she would be there, but she would not introduce her patient into the conversation for now.

Before meeting with Vickey, I was very lucky to finally have hired a second investigator to work at the medical board. Previously, I had been the only investigator to cover the entire state of Mississippi. The new investigator was Charlie Moses. He had performed numerous criminal investigations over the years while working in his capacity as a deputy sheriff for Leflore County Mississippi. He had never had the opportunity to investigate a physician. In briefing Charlie before our visit, I warned him about what he might hear about the psychiatrist so he would be prepared. I called Charlie "rookie" even though he was not a rookie in the widest sense of being completely new to law enforcement work. Still, most people, even criminal investigators and some of our board members, could not believe some of the things we documented physicians doing with patients. I also made Investigator Moses aware of the first patient, Valorie, and her medical provider, Julie. I emphasized we did not want to mention them to Vickey.

At the meeting, Vickey described to investigators almost the same details that had been described by Valorie and Julie weeks earlier. Vickey's details included the late evening appointments, wine and alcohol, kissing, disrobing, no intercourse, and finally the jumbo crayons. After telling us what her patient had described happening to her, Vickey commented that she was as sexual a woman as any other and liked to have a drink on occasion, but this was the damndest thing she had ever heard anyone do to a patient! Vickey assured investigators she was not violating doctor/patient confidentiality because she had her patient's permission, in writing, to talk to investigators. I told Vickey we very much wanted to talk to her patient, who I will call "Ann." I also told Vickey that before we went any further, she needed to understand a few things about the process the board uses in handling a physician before the board. Since Vickey had explained that she did not want her employer to know of her contact with the medical board there could be a problem. I explained how hearings before the full board are public and that it was highly probable that her patient would have to testify. I told her that sometimes the media is present at board hearings and sometimes not. If the media were present for the hearing, that would likely reveal to her supervisor that her patient somehow encountered medical board investigators. I told her I could not make her any guarantees that would not happen. Vickey said that she started this party, so if her patient was willing to tell her story and testify, then she would just roll with whatever happens.

I wanted to see her patient as soon as possible, preferably while we were in town. A meeting in the same motel room was set up by Vickey for the following day. After the usual introductions and data collection on Ann, we explained our intentions to work with her to hopefully pursue administrative charges against Dr. Colour. In the interest of total transparency, I explained all the possible legal and personal ramifications for her if the investigation resulted in a hearing. I told Ann that I hoped working with us and her current practitioner would help her put her experiences with Dr. Colour behind her and she could then continue with a healthy recovery.

Comfortable talking with us, Ann described in significant detail the "treatment," i.e., abuse, that she endured from Dr. Colour. She described how she had been referred to him by another doctor for treatment of her emotional and other mental health problems. The facts and circumstances described were eerily like those from the previous patient, Valorie. Dr. Colour told her many times how she was gaining strength and courage by having him perform these acts. She now understood his comments were designed to make her feel guilty so she would not discuss what happened, or so he thought!

After hearing the details of her abuse, I assured Ann and Vickey of the board's interest in pursuing an investigation. I asked Ann if she was aware of any other patients that might have had the same experience with the doctor. Unfortunately, she said she did not. We still made no mention of Valorie. I discussed the possibility of recorded phone calls with Ann and the doctor discussing his treatment. However, Ann felt she could not talk with him again. At this point, the meeting ended. I told Vickey and Ann that we would be back in contact from time to time, and to contact us if they had any questions or new information. We now had two patients, with no knowledge of each other, telling almost the exact same story of abuse at the hands of the same psychiatrist.

After the meeting, Investigator Moses said he had never heard of anything so gross in his life and had no idea any doctor was capable of such conduct. I told him he was not alone, and that there were about two million other people in Mississippi that felt the same way. Our problem is proving it to them and our board!

There are a variety of investigative techniques that can be used during an investigation depending on the type of case. We now have at least two victims in the same circumstances with the same doctor and their stories match. What else can they tell us that might also match? What will they tell us, independently of each other, when describing the doctor's private parts or body markings? You might recall a certain President of the United States who had this happen to him. At separate re-interview sessions, they gave similar descriptions of the body and body parts of the doctor. These narratives can cover a wide variety of things on a body including scars, moles, birthmarks, tattoos, deformities, body hair, size, amputations, tan lines, etc. All their answers continued to add credibility to these patients. How else would they know if they had not seen for themselves? Why would patients have seen these things on their doctor if boundaries had not been crossed? The challenge for investigators in such a situation is to maintain the confidence and cooperation of the two patients without them becoming aware of each other. Hopefully, we would find other patients as well.

Circumstances again turned in our favor. Whatever exists with the investigation gods that help create and maintain investigative momentum is never fully understood; it just happens. Otto von Bismarck, who united Germany in the late 1800s, once said, "There is a Providence that protects children, drunks, idiots, and the United States of America." I felt medical board investigators could be added to the quote, however, some felt we already were included – in the idiot category! In an almost incomprehensible event, ten days later, a third patient came to our attention.

A male caller contacted the offices of the MBML and was referred to me. After the usual phone introductions, the caller requested investigators meet with him and his wife to discuss the treatment their daughter had received while under the care of Dr. Colour. To say the least, he had my attention. The caller and his wife requested to meet in person. They did not want to discuss details over the phone because of the serious nature of what they needed to discuss. They said they ran a business and would like to meet at their offices where it would be private. A meeting was set up for the following day.

At their office, Investigator Moses and I identified ourselves and asked them to provide as much detail as possible about Dr. Colour and to take their time. Before we got started, I asked the couple, just out of curiosity, how they came to find out about MBML and call us. They said they knew somebody had to license and regulate doctors because of the nature of their work (they were also licensed professionals), so they looked us up in the phone book. Simple as that! The stars seemed to be aligning.

They then began to describe the details of what happened to their daughter. Sally (not her real name) had been referred to Dr. Colour by their regular family doctor. She was described as having some mental health issues. They said she was not helped in any way by what Dr. Colour did with her and related to us the already familiar pattern of conduct by the psychiatrist. All the previous components described to investigators by the two other patients were present, including the crayons. The couple blamed themselves for what their daughter had gone through and became very emotional talking about it, requiring a brief break in the interview to collect themselves. They said that after several months of treatment, Sally did not seem to be showing any improvement and they asked her about her care from Dr. Colour. Sally then told them about his unusual “treatment” techniques. They were shocked and refused to allow Sally to go back to see Dr. Colour. That is when they decided to call the medical board. The couple told us that Sally would cooperate with investigators and would have joined us in the meeting but she had to work. They recommended we go to her place of employment to talk with her or set up a meeting after work. We asked for a picture of her or a brief description so we would recognize her and for them to call her at work to let her know to expect us. The father said a picture is not necessary. He looked me directly in my eyes and commented that when you see the most beautiful girl you have ever seen in your life; you will know that is Sally. We thanked the couple for their cooperation and assured them that the board would be interested in the case. We asked if there were any other patients, they knew about but, unfortunately, they only knew about Sally.

Now, the obvious response to the comment about Sally's beauty is, that is exactly what you expect from a truly loving father. However, when Investigator Moses and I arrived at Sally's place of business and saw her working, we had no doubt we had found Sally. She truly was Hollywood gorgeous and absolutely stunning! We identified ourselves to Sally and arranged to meet her in a nearby restaurant after she got off from work. At the meeting, we told her of our talking with her parents about Dr. Colour. They had indicated she would be willing to talk with us. Sally said she had spoken with her parents and was expecting us. As difficult as it would be, she would tell us what happened. Sally's description of events matched the already familiar pattern previously described by the other patients, including the jumbo crayons. During the interview with Sally, Investigator Moses and I, independently of each other, identified a potentially serious problem with Sally as a witness. Sally talked and acted with the maturity level of a twelve-year-old female. Physically, she appeared as a fully developed, beautiful adult female. Conversationally and emotionally, she was twelve-years-old, at best. While her information matched that of the other patients, we could not see a way to put her on the stand and offer credible testimony. We made an executive decision to end the interview and not put her or her family through anything further. Investigators asked Sally if she knew of any other patients that had the same experience, but she said she did not. We thanked Sally and ended the interview.

The very next day I was contacted by telephone by an attorney who identified himself as Sally's brother. He went into a diatribe about us interviewing his sister without him being present. He was extremely defensive and protective of his sister and denigrating both investigators and his parents for contacting the medical board. He said he would not allow his sister to cooperate with the board and that he would not allow her to testify. He stated he was aware of what had transpired between his sister and Dr. Colour and he was not going to allow her to be abused further by the board. I told the attorney the decision not to use his sister as a witness had already been made. It did not calm him at all, he kept repeating his disgust for me, the medical board, and his parents until I just hung up on him in mid-sentence. I was not going to waste time explaining to him that I was not going to put him on speed dial to get his permission to talk to a potential witness on an investigation. I do not know for certain, but I think he was upset at the possibility of us wrecking a lawsuit he was planning against the doctor and thus possibly causing him to lose out on a settlement for his sister and a fee for himself.

I contacted Sally's parents and advised them of our interview with Sally, our decision not to use her and why, and of the call from their loving son who had spoken of them in less than glowing terms. The father indicated they were aware of some "developmental" issues with Sally, which was why she was referred to Dr. Colour in the first place, but had hoped that somehow it would help address what the doctor had done. I assured him it would be very helpful, but it would not be in Sally's best interest to put her in such a stressful situation that she could not handle. He said that he understood and that he would be in contact with his son and personally address their feelings about his call to me concerning Sally.

Amazingly, as luck would have it, a fourth patient, who I will call "Beth," came forward on her own concerning Dr. Colour. Beth told Investigator Moses and I when we interviewed her that she simply had enough of Dr. Colour and his so-called "treatment." She exhibited real anger toward Dr. Colour. When asked about the possibility of recorded phone calls with Dr. Colour about his treatment, she said she doubted she could hold her emotions in check to talk to him again. She said she was not currently being treated by a health care professional and had no one she knew of to talk to. I recommended she contact Julie or Vickey for help and offered to set up a meeting if she wished. Without revealing any details, I assured her that they would understand the situation and could help her. She asked for and was given their telephone numbers and said she would probably contact one of them.

During the interview, Beth reported almost exactly the same facts and circumstances as the other three patients and, also like the other patients, said that she did not know of any other patients who were "treated" like her.

The statements and descriptions from the four women are strikingly similar and compelling. The health care professionals taking care of two of them believed they were completely truthful. The only question that remained unanswered was whether they were connected in any way other than all being abused by the same doctor. Try as we might, we could not identify a common denominator between the four patients to establish any possible collusion. The health care professionals knew *of* each other but did not *know* each other. They certainly had no way to know their respective patients.

The decision by the executive officer and board attorney was to proceed with the case. Stan Ingram and I drew up a subpoena to seize the files on Ann, Valorie, and Beth, along with a Summons and Affidavit charging Dr. Colour with the multiple counts of unprofessional conduct. Both documents could be served on Dr. Colour at the same time. Stan agreed that Sally could not be considered as a witness and the three patients should be enough for a conviction.

I went to Dr. Colour's clinic late in the day hoping to find him with a patient that might turn into another witness. No such luck.

While serving the subpoena to seize the patient files, Dr. Colour's manner and demeanor were like he knew this was coming and wondered why it took so long. He retreated into the back area of his office to retrieve the requested patient files. As we had been told by our three witnesses, he did not have any office staff or a nurse present in the clinic that late. While he was in the back area, I observed in his office several boxes of jumbo crayons but did not seize or touch any of them! When Dr. Colour returned, he saw me looking at the boxes of crayons and he commented how he had a large adolescent practice. He said he uses crayons to help communicate with the children. My only thought was, "Oh my God, how many children has he abused?" I did not comment, although I probably should have, however I did not want to do anything to hurt our case so I just let it drop. After obtaining the patient files and writing Dr. Colour an inventory receipt for the files, I served him with the summons and affidavit to a hearing. Dr. Colour took the documents and began to read them. I explained to him how the affidavit charged him with several counts of unprofessional conduct based on his "treatment" of the patients. The summons required him to appear before the board for a hearing on the evidence. I told him to have his attorney contact the board attorney if he had any questions. I then departed the office.

After all the pre-hearing motions and before the start of a hearing, Dr. Colour surrendered his medical license to practice in the state of Mississippi. He never succeeded in having his license reinstated in Mississippi, at least not while I worked at the medical board. He did obtain a full unrestricted license in a certain mid-western state that had a reputation of ignoring evidence from other states. I hate to think how many bad actors hide in that state and how many women and children have been abused.

Many have asked the question: Why was this doctor not thrown in jail? The main response is that most state prosecutors do not want to try such a difficult and costly case. Criminally, these cases would involve expert witnesses to examine the patients, requiring considerable time and money. Most importantly, the patient's welfare must be paramount. Most of these types of patients prefer not to have to endure the amount of stress, public exposure, and embarrassment that would be put on them. The state prosecutors simply prefer it to be handled by the medical board where the burden of proof is less stringent. The feds do not feel a case of this type or magnitude rises to the level of federal involvement and also feel it is more appropriate in the hands of the state medical board.

After completion of the case and the public made aware of the board's action on Dr. Colour, I received a telephone call from Sally's father. He stated he and his wife were glad to see what the board had done with Dr. Colour. He also said that Sally had been under the care of a new psychiatrist and had made significant progress. She had been accepted and was scheduled soon to enter training to be an airline hostess for a major air carrier. I never heard anything about a lawsuit on Sally's behalf or that of the other three women, but I hope it did happen.

I was informed well after the case concluded that Beth did make contact with a health care professional and was doing well. I know this because I received a call from the professional treating her who called me to confirm the "story" Beth had related to her upon initiation of treatment. She said it sounded so unbelievable that she thought the patient might be somewhat delusional. I assured her that she was not!

CHAPTER 7

DR. ELVIS and the CORRUPT COP

Nothing matters but the facts. Without them, the science of criminal investigation is nothing more than a guessing game. – Blake Edwards

Quite often, I had to drop or postpone one investigation after learning about a more egregious situation than the case I was previously working on. Such was the case involving Dr. Elvis and his sidekick, Corrupt Cop ("CC" for short), not their real names. This case got my attention, and the lessons I was taught by the evil Dr. Elvis and his sidekick have been shared with many of my friends to help them avoid suffering the same fate that Dr. Elvis and CC helped bring on many unsuspecting families who have no idea of the cruel, vicious nature of some people in authority. The evil practice involved in this case continues unabated, and no one is checking on the doctors doing the prescribing.

I was responding to a complaint and had begun pharmacy profiling of the drugs Stadol and Nubain, allegedly being prescribed in suspicious quantities to patients by a doctor in a medium-sized Mississippi town. What I found almost as soon as I began my original pharmacy profile was the prescribing of a most unusual combination of controlled substances by Dr. Elvis, a dentist. The controlled substance prescriptions were for 30 cc vials of Demerol injectable 100 mg/cc in combination with Ritalin 15 mg tablets. A pattern began to emerge indicating one patient, CC, was being prescribed these drugs. It is common for an MBML investigator to seek assistance from the pharmacist concerning a suspicious prescribing pattern in his or her store. Most pharmacists were very useful in helping us to understand a situation that looked bad at first but was appropriate for a certain medical situation. In this case, that did not happen. The pharmacist, whom I had known since college, came over and observed me documenting the prescriptions for Demerol and Ritalin. As he stood there, I noticed his increased interest and obvious nervousness. Without any prompting, he told me what I was looking at was not a problem. He knew both individuals and the situation well. He said Dr. Elvis was a nearby dentist and CC was a well-known state investigator assigned to the local district office. All the prescriptions were presented for filling by CC. He explained that the Demerol was prescribed because Dr. Elvis had to remove several impacted teeth from CC's mouth and the Ritalin was for a diagnosis of narcolepsy in CC. I thanked him for the heads up on the patient and commented how I just had never seen a dentist or any other practitioner write so many outpatient prescriptions for such large amounts of injectable Demerol over such a long period. Also, I had never heard of a dentist legitimately treating a patient for narcolepsy. The major medical indications for Ritalin are ADD (Attention Deficit Disorder), ADHD (Attention Deficit Hyperactivity

Disorder), and narcolepsy. The primary prescribers of Ritalin are pediatricians and neurologists, not dentists.

The pharmacist reiterated he was certain it was not a problem and that he had known both for years. I continued documenting the prescriptions without making any comment. I knew there was no possible way the prescriptions in any amount were acceptable as legitimate care despite the pharmacist's assertions, so I could not understand why he would insist they were. The dosage amounts in his pharmacy alone were clearly excessive. The second major red flag was that a dentist is not qualified or authorized under any circumstances, outside of third world medicine, to treat narcolepsy. The pharmacist knew full well the prescriptions as written were inappropriate. Therefore, I had to assume the pharmacist had more than a passing retail interest in whatever was going on and I intended to find out what. At that time though, I had no concept of just how bad it was going to be.

After leaving the pharmacy, I contacted the executive officer at the medical board and explained the situation. Based on the large quantities of Demerol and Ritalin, I requested approval to postpone the investigation I was previously working on and work on the newly developed information as a priority case. I suggested that I should expand the profile to include all area pharmacies to see if there were more prescriptions to document. The EO readily agreed to the change in direction. He, too, could not understand why a dentist would prescribe such large quantities of Demerol. Also, a dentist had no legal medical or dental authorization to prescribe Ritalin. The expanded pharmacy profile, while time-consuming, was productive. Not only did I document large numbers of additional prescriptions for Demerol and Ritalin to CC from Dr. Elvis in the original town, but also in many towns in the surrounding counties. The Demerol and Ritalin dosages were in the thousands. Somebody, possibly two or three somebodies, clearly had a serious abuse problem. Or so I thought!

At the direction of my executive officer, I contacted June Harris, the executive officer of the dental board to advise her of the situation. At the time, the dental board did not employ full-time investigators. They contracted with local investigators on an "as needed" basis whenever a problem or complaint was presented. After I briefed the executive officer of the dental board, I was authorized to investigate the dentist on behalf of the dental board and provide them with whatever updates and evidence I found. She, too, had serious concerns when she saw the drugs and amounts being prescribed by Dr. Elvis. At the time Dr. Elvis had not appeared on their radar for any reason; there were no recorded complaints or problems involving him.

I also contacted the internal affairs (IA) division for the state investigative agency that employed CC. I briefed them on the findings to date including the large amounts of controlled substances CC was being prescribed by Dr. Elvis. I also told them of the indications as explained by the pharmacist who vouched for both. They immediately expressed interest in joining the investigation and assigned Gordon Kennedy, one of their best and most experienced investigators, to join me on the case. Kennedy advised me that CC had some history with the IA division. He had several complaints filed against him for being pushy and fighting with people he had encountered during investigations. No one in the agency was aware of any diagnosis of narcolepsy, and there was nothing in his service record or background indicating any serious illness. Further, there was no information on his taking leave for dental extractions or illness. Kennedy was obviously concerned about the possibility of one of their investigators self-administering such large amounts of Demerol.

I suggested as an initial plan of action that we draw up an affidavit and search warrant to serve on Dr. Elvis. We needed to get access to CC's dental file to see what, if any, justification existed for the suspicious amounts of controlled substances prescribed. I suggested that we coordinate so that CC could be interviewed by IA at the same time I served the warrant on Dr. Elvis and interviewed him. All agreed that interviewing them separately at the same time, hopefully without prior notice, would obtain the best outcome. We assumed that Dr. Elvis and CC had already been alerted by the pharmacist that someone was snooping around looking at the pattern of prescribing, as in most cases someone usually alerts the prescriber that the medical board paid them a visit.

After completing the warrant and affidavit, I had Stan Ingram review, correct, and approve the documents. I, along with Gordon Kennedy and one other IA investigator, traveled in an unmarked state vehicle to the county where Dr. Elvis lived and worked. We needed to present the affidavit and warrant to a circuit judge to have it signed. We had previously called the judge and scheduled an appointment to meet with him. Unfortunately, when we arrived at his office, he was not in. His secretary said he had some issues come up and had to leave suddenly. She arranged a meeting for us for the following Monday and would call us if the judge could not see us. Conspiracy theories abounded. Did the judge get a call and disappear or was it just a coincidence? Investigators do not believe in coincidence. However, we had not revealed the name on the warrant to the judge's staff, so we figured we were probably still on solid ground.

On the return trip back to our offices, we planned the coordinated interviews for the following Monday, probably in the afternoon. Dr. Elvis would be in his clinic, so that would be easy. I would interview him after I served the warrant. Kennedy said he would have CC report to headquarters on Monday afternoon, and they could interview him there. We had a plan, we just had to coordinate the timing.

The ride back took place on a Friday afternoon. Southbound traffic on I-55 was extremely heavy due to the opening game of the

Ole Miss football season in Jackson against Memphis State University (as it was known then). The cars were bumper to bumper and moving at least seventy-five miles per hour! While we were talking about the case, we noticed two cars in front of us traveling side by side and seeming to talk with each other through the lowered windows. The cars, each with four occupants, merged closer and closer to each other. When the cars were practically touching, the people in the car in the left passing lane began handing six-packs of beer to the occupants in the car in the right lane that was just in front of us. We could not believe what we were seeing while traveling at seventy-five miles per hour! After several six-packs had passed, Gordon Kennedy said he had seen enough, that he did not usually make traffic stops, but this crossed the line. It was just too much! He pulled out his dash blue light and hit the light and siren. Both cars in front of us almost lost control. We signaled the car in the left lane to pull over to the right lane and waved both cars to the right side of the interstate. Once stopped we all exited the state vehicle. Gordon collected driver's license information from the two drivers while we observed the other occupants. Gordon asked all eight occupants to meet him at the back of his vehicle where he identified himself and commenced a dressing down that would make a Marine drill sergeant blush. Gordon told the young men that he would not arrest anybody or even ticket them if they allowed the search of the two vehicles and poured out all the beer and other alcoholic beverages they had. They agreed. Altogether, we poured out eight cases of beer and several fifths of whiskey bound for a fraternity party that weekend. To their credit, the students took responsibility for their foolish stunt and apologized profusely before they drove off. While we did not have a breathalyzer to test them, especially the drivers, none of the students appeared intoxicated. After Kennedy finished talking to them, I think they felt lucky to be leaving alive and not in jail. I bet to this day they remember his remarks well. A good man delivered a good message and I saw it. I told Gordon that by pulling over those students he probably saved about four or more lives! You just never know what is going to happen next.

As planned, the following Monday, I met with the judge in his chambers. He apologized for the problem with the Friday meeting but said it could not be avoided. He then proceeded with a detailed review of the probable cause and applicable state law for the warrant. After an exhaustive review, I finally obtained a signed search warrant. I called Gordon Kennedy to let him know I had the signed warrant and proposed serving it at approximately 2:00 pm. He agreed that would be a good time since CC was supposedly en route to HQ of the IA division as we spoke.

Surveillance of Dr. Elvis's clinic revealed he was seeing patients as usual. At 2:00 pm I entered the clinic, identified myself to the receptionist, and asked to speak with Dr. Elvis. She asked me what this was in reference to and when I told her it was a private matter that I could only discuss with the doctor, she said she would inform him. It is common and reasonable to expect delays when entering a doctor's office for a visit due to the nature of the operation of a clinic. When seeing patients, it is not always possible for a doctor or dentist to just drop what they are doing to meet an unscheduled visitor. It is also reasonable and good investigative technique not to announce the visit by making an appointment. Past case history revealed the target practitioner would delay and/or avoid the visit, tamper, destroy, or even create evidence. In the worst case, the target can plan an ambush. Desperate people do desperate things.

After an approximately thirty-minute delay, I met with Dr. Elvis in his private office. I identified myself to him and advised him of the reason for the visit. I then served him with the search warrant compelling him to provide the original dental file on patient CC. I told him he was at liberty to contact his attorney if he wished, but he declined. I suggested he read the warrant first and then make that decision. He read the warrant and fell silent for several minutes, just looking at me. I thought he might be trying to come up with some type of story, but he then said he did not feel he needed to contact an attorney. After another long pause, he admitted there was no treatment file on CC. He requested to see the pharmacy profiles referred to in the affidavit. After a review, he acknowledged that he had written prescriptions for injectable Demerol and Ritalin for CC, but he did not realize it was so many. This was not an unexpected response from Dr. Elvis. I have heard the same response many times from doctors who simply, because of the sheer numbers of patients and prescriptions with no file for reference, lose track of the prescribing amounts and frequency. That reason is one of the primary reasons to maintain a detailed medical file on all patients.

I then told Dr. Elvis that he would eventually be able to look at each original prescription that had been seized from the pharmacies to determine if any were in fact forgeries. He said that would probably not be necessary; he was confident he had written all the prescriptions. I then told him that I was here for one reason and one reason alone: on behalf of the dental board, I needed to obtain his explanation justifying the issuance of the prescriptions to CC. Since there was no dental file, I needed to hear the details from him. I cautioned him that he did not have to talk to me and offered again to allow him the benefit of legal counsel. Again, he declined. I suspected I would hear that both were chemically dependent and needed treatment. However, that was definitely not the case!

Very slowly he began to peel back the rotten onion and tell me a very sad and horrible story. It began approximately two years earlier when he and his ole friend CC began to enter the “wonderful world of dogfighting.” He said these were some of the meanest, cruel, most vile people he had met in his life. Many were so-called respectable law enforcement and business people in the local communities, by day living normal respectable lives, but at night turning into bloodthirsty killers of all kinds of dogs.

The reason they got into the business was for the money. Huge amounts of money were bet on the fights with the winners walking away with wallets full of tax-free cash and no questions asked. Most of the serious fights were protected by the local law enforcement, usually for a cut of the proceeds. He and CC housed and trained the dogs on some land he owns. They take the dogs to fights in the Port Gibson, MS area and in Louisiana. At this point, he fell silent with another long pause. I told him I appreciate the background, but that still did not explain the prescriptions. He then commented that I did not know much about dogfighting. I responded that gladly I did not. He then blurted out that the drugs are for the dogs. About ten to fifteen minutes before a fight they shoot them up full of Demerol and Ritalin. They become immune to pain, very aggressive, and will literally fight to the death with their guts hanging out. If your dog won, you walk away with several thousand dollars depending on the bets. The loser ends up with a dead dog torn to pieces. Truth is, the winner is often too injured to survive and usually ends up being shot.

I asked the "good" dentist how they managed to train dogs to be such killers. He said there is a rather large sideline in the dogfighting industry. Many of the dogs that turned up missing in neighborhoods across the state were not just missing. These friendly, older, trusting dogs, were frequently stolen by dog thieves to sell to fighters like them to train their dogs. Big or small, their fighting dogs can practice on them with little possibility of being injured. Depending on the dog, the dog thieves could make as much as $50 each. He said it happened all the time. People would let their pets out unsupervised. The pet would be picked up or even willingly get into a truck or car teased with food or just being friendly, never to be seen again, and die a cruel, unloved, inhumane, horrible, agonizing death.

I asked how many fights they attended. He said they went to approximately eight to ten fights a year with at least one dog to enter a fight.

I asked him, "Do you consider yourself one of the so-called respectable people that participate in this 'manly' sport?"

He said, "I can tell you do not approve."

I said, "You're damn right I don't approve and if I could I would pull out my gun and shoot your sorry ass right now! You can quote me anywhere, anytime – even in a hearing – and I promise I would not deny saying it."

I told Dr. Elvis I would be making a full report to the dental board for their consideration. I strongly suggested he seek legal advice because I was going to do everything I could to make sure he was going to need it.

The interview with CC at the IA division was a little more difficult at first. I was not present at the interview but was told by Gordon Kennedy that CC attempted to deny everything for a long time and demanded pictures of him attending any dog fight. CC was then presented with stacks of the copied prescriptions for Demerol and Ritalin in his name. Investigator Kennedy explained how each prescription was issued outside the course of a legitimate dental reason and thus obtained by fraud or subterfuge, a felony count for each prescription filled by him. He was also advised that the pharmacists had already identified him as the person filling the prescriptions. CC finally realized the hole he had dug for himself and confessed to basically the same information as Dr. Elvis.

All of the evidence, including prescriptions, the warrant, and interview reports, were turned over to the dental board and Investigator Gordon Kennedy. I added in my referral a recommendation that the investigation be sent to federal and/or state prosecutors to at least attempt criminal prosecution; however, neither were referred. The dental board decided to handle Dr. Elvis administratively. The head of the agency employing CC decided to handle it internally.

Dr. Elvis had his license revoked for three years but was permitted to return to practice after one year with restrictions. He was allowed to maintain his DEA number but was limited to administering or dispensing controlled substances on an inpatient basis. He could not prescribe any controlled substances on an outpatient basis. Any controlled substances dispensed, including samples, had to be accompanied by detailed records with justification and accountability.

CC was suspended without pay for several months, demoted two ranks, and transferred to a different district in the state.

The State Board of Pharmacy took no action against the pharmacist who filled most of the clearly inappropriate prescriptions. It was, and still is, my opinion that he was getting a cut of the cash for filling the prescriptions. To my knowledge, he was never interviewed by the pharmacy board Inspectors.

The crime of illegal dogfighting, at the time of this case, was rarely pursued for prosecution because it was just a misdemeanor. It has now been raised to the felony level but is still rarely pursued or investigated in Mississippi. The same goes for cockfighting where Stadol and Nubain are used to shoot up the birds for fighting.

During the remainder of my career, I had no further contact with Dr. Elvis or CC. When Gordon Kennedy retired from his state investigator position, I attempted to hire him to be an investigator at the medical board. Unfortunately for me, he declined. He went on to have a second successful career as an investigator with another state agency. He finally fully retired and continues to reside in Mississippi. You might find him eating one of the delicious hamburgers at the Blue Rooster restaurant in Flora, MS.

CHAPTER 8

NO LICENSE REQUIRED

Drug addiction has been a longstanding problem for the doctors, themselves. – William Stewart Halsted, MD, Father of modern surgery in America, who was himself addicted to cocaine and morphine.

The Mississippi State Board of Medical Licensure was very fortunate to have well-trained investigators. We were equally fortunate to work with well-trained investigators from the Mississippi State Board of Pharmacy, the Mississippi Bureau of Narcotics, and the DEA. We also enjoyed good cooperation from most local police departments and sheriff departments, but not all. Over years of working together on cases of mutual interest or concern, we developed real trust and confidence in each other. However, not all local, state, or federal narcotic agents like to work, nor do they understand how to develop pharmaceutical diversion cases. Diversion cases generally involve controlled substances that are channeled for use outside the legitimate medical indications normally intended for controlled substances. These cases usually require a large amount of time and paperwork to develop and a thorough working knowledge of pharmaceutical controlled substances, which can be difficult to learn, and for one to remain updated with all the changes and additions that occur. Also, these cases rarely carry with them the media headlines that seizing five tons of marijuana or twenty pounds of cocaine attract. Controlled substance diversion cases, even large amounts in terms of dosage units, rarely result in criminal prosecution. I feel that deliberate diverters, i.e., doctors, dentists, and other health care practitioners who prescribe, administer, or dispense controlled substances illegally, should face criminal prosecution in addition to regulatory action. However, local prosecutors rarely want to try a physician due to the difficulty of finding one guilty – not to mention the fact that they might lose a golfing partner. It took a certain type of investigator with a great deal of patience and perseverance to obtain a successful case resolution. Frequently, investigators had to endure personal attacks from politicians or even their own boards when maneuvering the difficulties and obstacles to complete cases. Trust among the various agents, investigators, and agencies in diversion work is critical to the success of each respective agency or department. Therefore, it was common to share information on a daily basis on cases or suspicious situations that more often than not developed into serious cases.

Such was the situation with a certain emergency room physician who I will call "Dr. Scofflaw,"[3] a man who never met a law he did not break. This doctor was like a bad penny: he never went away and kept finding unique ways to turn up somewhere in the state, always breaking the law.

---

[3] "Scofflaw" – A person who flouts the law. A person who flouts rules, conventions, or accepted practices.

This case started with a phone call in the summer of 1993 from a police detective from a suburb of Jackson. Dr. Scofflaw had been arrested for shoplifting at a local big-box clothing store after being caught by store loss prevention walking out of the store wearing seven shirts that he had put on in the men's dressing room. He had not paid for the shirts and was charged with misdemeanor shoplifting. The shirts were seized by the loss prevention department. Dr. Scofflaw was found guilty of shoplifting, paid a fine, and was banned from the store forever. The case was reviewed by the board, but since it was a misdemeanor, no action was taken.

The next part of the case started in September of 1993 with a phone call from a Board of Pharmacy inspector who I will call "Cliff." Cliff and I had worked on numerous successful cases over several years. Some state agencies in Mississippi call their investigative staff "agents," while others call them "investigators." At the time of our investigation of Dr. Scofflaw, the Mississippi State Board of Pharmacy referred to their investigative staff as "inspectors." Cliff told me of a situation he had identified with the help of a local pharmacist involving an emergency room physician. Dr. Scofflaw was writing controlled substance prescriptions using the names of patients and having them filled while posing himself as the patient. The local pharmacist who contacted Cliff worked for several different pharmacies in the town where this was taking place (some would refer to him as a traveling or contract pharmacist). Dr. Scofflaw had recently come into a pharmacy where the pharmacist was working and presented a prescription claiming to be the patient whose name appeared on the prescription. The day before, Dr. Scofflaw had come in with a prescription at a different pharmacy under a different patient's name. The prescriptions were always written for various hydrocodone products or hydrocodone cough syrups with the maximum of six refills. All forms of hydrocodone, at the time, were

Schedule IIIN controlled substances and could be refilled. Schedule IIIN controlled substances has a high potential for abuse but not as high as Schedule IIN drugs. In the 1980s, hydrocodone products were just beginning to grow in popularity with abusers and addicts. It was speculated by many in the business of drug enforcement that the intense monitoring of all Schedule II and IIN products caused abusers to change to hydrocodone. At the time, Schedule IIIN was less monitored and, as a result, prescribers wrote more hydrocodone prescriptions for the same reasons. Later, after the turn of the century, hydrocodone came into its own as a drug of primary abuse and was moved into Schedule IIN.

Cliff said that approximately two days prior, Dr. Scofflaw presented a prescription for hydrocodone cough syrup for filling at yet another pharmacy where the local pharmacist was working. The pharmacist realized, upon seeing Dr. Scofflaw again, that he had filled at least two prescriptions for him at different pharmacies under different names. This made the third one in just the last few days! The pharmacist filled the prescription but, suspecting that something was wrong, contacted the state pharmacy board the next morning. Cliff happened to be working in a town near the pharmacist and went by to talk with him the next day. After hearing his story, Cliff went to several local pharmacies and immediately began to see prescriptions on the local hospital prescription forms written by Dr. Scofflaw to numerous patients for the same hydrocodone products. The three names the pharmacist had identified to Cliff as being used by Dr. Scofflaw had also been found at other pharmacies on prescriptions for hydrocodone cough syrups written by Dr. Scofflaw. Cliff suspected he had identified a physician in difficulty with controlled substances and contacted me at the Mississippi medical board. I told Cliff to tell the local pharmacist to take no other action until I could obtain approval to investigate. Cliff asked what the pharmacist should do if Dr. Scofflaw presented another prescription? I told him to tell the pharmacist to fill it, business as usual. I did not want to alert Dr. Scofflaw that someone was on to him. I told Cliff to tell the pharmacist that I should be in the area soon and would talk to him and that the pharmacist could call me directly if he needed advice or help.

I immediately briefed the executive officer on all the details of the situation. The Mississippi medical board had long ago identified disabled or impaired physicians as posing the greatest immediate threat to the consuming patients or the public and thus warranting the highest investigative priority. After the briefing, the executive officer authorized an immediate response to the information.

The next day I drove to the town where the pharmacist was located. I was able to locate the pharmacy where he was working that particular day and introduced myself to him and thanked him for his cooperation. I assured him I would do everything to keep his name out of the investigation. He had no new information other than to say that there seemed to be a lot of Dr. Scofflaw's hydrocodone prescriptions in every pharmacy where he worked. I told him I would be working on the case locally and to please contact me if he heard any new information.

I began a pharmacy profile of all the pharmacies in the town and surrounding area and documented all of the controlled substance prescriptions issued by Dr. Scofflaw. Numerous prescriptions were found for hydrocodone products written by the doctor using the three patient aliases identified by the pharmacist. I also identified many other names and addresses of patients receiving the same drugs, all written by Dr. Scofflaw. It took approximately four days to profile all of the pharmacies in the area and to organize the information into discernable patterns. There were no computers yet for this type of work and, consequently, the organization of the data was done at night in the motel room manually and usually took several hours. What became immediately clear was that numerous names and addresses were found that closely matched each other, such as Bob Thompson at 409 Post Oak Road, or Bob Thomas at 404 Oak Dale Road, or Clair Thomas at 409 Post Oak Road. Most violators, whether drug abusers or bank robbers, follow human nature and frequently leave identifiable patterns of behavior. Most of the names and addresses on the prescriptions were determined to be fictitious. Unless the prescriptions are fraudulent, which most of these were, most legitimate patients use their real names and addresses.

I next contacted a confidential source employed at the local hospital who had been helpful in a previous investigation. I requested assistance to determine if any of the names from the prescription profile had been actual patients in the hospital emergency room where Dr. Scofflaw worked. I was told the following day that almost every name on the patient list I had provided was *not* treated or seen at that hospital. No records of any visits in the emergency room existed for any of those names. To say the least, the employee was concerned about Dr. Scofflaw seeing any more patients in the hospital ER under these circumstances. I told my friend not to worry because I would be briefing my executive officer immediately and, in all probability, I would intervene with Dr. Scofflaw when he showed up for his next shift at the emergency room.

I contacted the executive officer and briefed him on the investigation to date. He authorized me to immediately contact Dr. Scofflaw to offer him a chance to voluntarily enter a board-approved facility for an evaluation for chemical dependency. Otherwise, he would face a suspension and a possible licensure revocation hearing.

Most state medical boards, including MBML, want a physician in difficulty with drugs or alcohol to get help and hopefully return to a full, sober practice. This is possible only if the doctor enters and completes treatment in a facility that has been approved by the board for the treatment of physicians. The doctor must also participate in the physician's recovery program monitored by other recovering physicians as well as submit to monitoring by the medical board. Medical board monitoring includes random, unannounced, and witnessed blood and/or urine testing usually for a minimum period of five years.

I met Dr. Scofflaw when he came on duty in the emergency room the following night. I identified myself to him and told him I needed to talk to him about prescriptions he had written and picked up in the local pharmacies. In the interest of privacy, he led me into a lounge area reserved for doctors. I then detailed the information we had against him and advised him that several pharmacists in the area had identified him as picking up prescriptions written to fictitious patients. I told the doctor that I already knew those patients had never been in the hospital emergency room, thus, not only had he violated board regulations but also committed several felonies under state and federal controlled substances laws. I explained that the board's executive officer had sent me to offer him the opportunity to immediately enter an approved physician evaluation and treatment center to get help for possible chemical dependency. However, Dr. Scofflaw refused to cooperate with the board in any way. He denied he had a problem with drugs or alcohol and refused to go for an evaluation and/or treatment. I explained that his refusal to cooperate with the board could result in his being suspended from practice or having to undergo a full revocation hearing. Dr. Scofflaw continued to deny doing anything wrong or having any kind of a problem with chemical dependency. I then ended the interview and left the hospital.

After a phone call to the executive officer, an emergency suspension order was immediately prepared the following morning by the board's attorney, Stan Ingram. Dr. Scofflaw would be prohibited from practicing medicine in Mississippi until he entered and successfully completed a board-approved treatment program for chemical dependency. The following day, with a suspension order in hand, I returned to the hospital and met with the hospital administrator. His first comment when he saw me was, "Oh no, not again!" We were already familiar with each other from a previous investigation at the same hospital several months earlier. I advised him of the suspension order to be served on Dr. Scofflaw when he came in for his evening shift. The administrator did not ask a lot of questions since he knew the program fairly well. This heads-up briefing gave the administrator time to find a replacement physician so patients could be seen in the ER without interruption.

I was waiting for Dr. Scofflaw when he arrived in the emergency room that evening for his shift. In front of several nurses and staff, I served him with the suspension order in a loud and clear voice. Being discreet was no longer required since the doctor had his chance. Moreover, I wanted witnesses in the ER that observed him being served so there would be no doubt that he could not legally treat patients. He accepted the suspension order and quietly went into the doctor's lounge. I waited around in the emergency room to be certain he did not see any patients. When he came out of the lounge and left the hospital, I then contacted the executive officer and told him of the service of the suspension order. The hospital administrator had a physician on standby to take over the ER once Dr. Scofflaw departed the premises.

In most cases, after being served with an order of suspension, economic reality sets in fairly quickly, and the physician is off to an approved treatment center. The board provides the physician or his attorney a prepared list of approved treatment centers upon request. Upon being notified of the physician having entered an approved program, we notify the facility of the details of the case that led to the suspension order so that the treatment center gets the facts and not the physician's version of the facts. Dr. Scofflaw failed to enter an approved treatment program, choosing instead to enter an outpatient program that was not approved. He was informed by the executive officer in writing that the program he entered was not board-approved and therefore would carry no weight in the board's decision, and his license would remain in a suspended status.

In November 1993, after Dr. Scofflaw failed to enter an approved treatment program, the medical board entered a regular board order continuing the original suspension of his license until he completed treatment in an approved treatment program.

After almost two years of unemployment, in May 1995, Dr. Scofflaw finally entered a board-approved evaluation and treatment program. All information related to the board's investigation was provided to the physicians at the treatment program. As predicted, the doctor was diagnosed as being chemically dependent, requiring months of inpatient treatment and several years of board monitoring. However, Dr. Scofflaw failed to complete all stages of treatment and checked out "AMA" – against medical advice. Dr. Scofflaw's license remained in a suspended state in Mississippi. Since he was not licensed in any other state, he could no longer legally practice medicine anywhere. In July of 1995, the medical board issued an order prohibiting Dr. Scofflaw from practicing medicine until he completed all requirements of treatment and was deemed capable of returning to the practice of medicine.

Dr. Scofflaw disappeared from the medical board radar at least for a short period. In August 1995, the MBML received a complaint from DEA concerning Dr. Scofflaw attempting to order controlled substances from an in-state supplier without the authority of a license or DEA certificate. The supplier had done their homework and discovered Dr. Scofflaw did not have a current license or DEA certificate to purchase controlled substances and had notified DEA of the attempt. Shortly thereafter, a call was received by MBML from an employee in the emergency room of a fairly small hospital in Mississippi concerned about the poor manner in which a patient had been treated by an emergency room physician. The ER physician was identified as, you guessed it, Dr. Scofflaw! This was not the same hospital where he had been previously. The investigator who took the complaint did not reveal any of the doctor's history with our office to the complainant. As soon as he briefed me on the complaint information, we checked with the licensure division of the board and were advised his license status had not changed. It was still suspended. I immediately notified the executive officer of the complaint information. He authorized an investigation into the possible illegal practice of medicine by Dr. Scofflaw. If he had written any controlled substance prescriptions or inpatient orders for controlled substances, each prescription or order would constitute a felony since he had no legal authorization to handle controlled substances in any way. The Drug Enforcement Administration and the medical board allow a physician at a registered facility like a hospital to use the DEA number of the employer if his or her license is in good standing. However, since Dr. Scofflaw's license had been suspended, he was not allowed to use the hospital DEA number or his own DEA number.

Investigator Neil Breeland and I drove to the hospital. Upon arrival, we were told Dr. Scofflaw worked the night shift and would not be in until around four o'clock that afternoon. I decided to perform a quick profile of a couple of pharmacies in the small town just to see if Dr. Scofflaw may have been up to his old tricks of filling prescriptions for himself using fictitious patient names. Very few prescriptions of any kind and almost no controlled substances were found. Based on his history, I thought that to be just a wee bit unusual.

The delay also gave us time to take care of other very important business with the hospital administrator. The executive officer very much wanted to know, as did I, why the hospital administrator gave Dr. Scofflaw a job working in the emergency room with a suspended license. Despite this being somewhat of an impromptu visit, the administrator was available to meet with us. I have learned over the years after working often in hospitals, that hospital administrators are quite busy with their management and have little time for unscheduled meetings. I knew what I had to tell him was not going to make his day, and he needed to know just how much trouble he potentially was in. We introduced ourselves to the administrator and told him why we were there. When he heard that Dr. Scofflaw's license was suspended, and had been since November 1993, I thought we were going to lose him. I honestly thought he was going to have a heart attack. After he composed himself, he had his secretary bring him the hospital file on Dr. Scofflaw. The hospital application for privileges filled out by Dr. Scofflaw reflected his correct license number and that it was current with no restrictions. The application file data indicated Dr. Scofflaw had been practicing in the hospital emergency room for the last three months even though his license was suspended. It did not take long for the administrator to put two and two together. Although this was a fairly small hospital, it served a large area and had a very busy emergency room. Every patient seen in the ER by Dr. Scofflaw over the last three months was treated by a physician with a suspended license, and the hospital was responsible. Specifically, the administrator was responsible since it was his job to make sure each physician is properly licensed and qualified to practice and to have that confirmed in writing by the Mississippi medical board before he or she starts treating patients. Most large hospitals have a department that specifically performs the credentialing process, but this was a small hospital with no such formal department. The administrator had not followed up on his own credentialing process for health care professionals. I could read his mind: How many lawsuits were coming? How would he explain this to his board? No shade of white has yet been identified to match the pale color of his face!

The administrator admitted that he had taken the word of Dr. Scofflaw when he first applied and had not followed up on the application as he intended. I assured the administrator that we were there only to confront Dr. Scofflaw and to stop him from continuing to practice without a license. We did not intend to have him arrested for the illegal practice of medicine, which would be bad publicity for the hospital unless he refused to leave voluntarily. Nor did we intend for this to get out and create potential lawsuit problems for the hospital if we could prevent it. However, we did want to give him some advance warning that he was going to lose his ER coverage so he would have some time to find a replacement. I asked the administrator for permission to wait in the ER physicians lounge for Dr. Scofflaw and confront him there, out of sight and sound of most all the other staff. He approved the meeting location and thanked us for giving him an advanced warning of the situation. The administrator was requested to have his hospital security staff close by to escort the doctor out in case he refused to leave voluntarily. I suggested that having hospital security would be better than calling the local police – bad publicity and all that. The administrator agreed. While I had his cooperation, I also asked the administrator to check a few of the names on prescriptions filled in the pharmacies to see if possibly they had been patients in the hospital ER, or if they were fictitious as we had found previously. It turned out that all of the names had, in fact, been patients at the hospital ER. Again, I thought that strange considering Dr. Scofflaw's past behavior.

Shortly before four o'clock, Dr. Scofflaw appeared in the ER to begin his shift. As we approached Dr. Scofflaw, I told him, "Well, we meet again doctor. Remember me?" I then asked him to join us in the doctor's lounge for a meeting. I told him the board was aware that he had been working in the ER and treating patients for the last three months without a current medical license. I asked him if he recalled that his license had been suspended. He acknowledged that he was aware his license was suspended. I also told him that each patient he treated, could and probably would, eventually result in a charge of illegal practice of medicine. He was also told we were aware of his submitting a false statement on his hospital application for ER privileges by indicating that he had a license in good standing when he knew it to be suspended. That clearly established his intent to violate the law. I then told him that the hospital administrator was aware of his situation and that he would no longer be allowed to practice in the hospital. I suggested he leave quickly and quietly; if he did not, either hospital security would remove him or, if necessary, the police would be called to arrest him. Dr. Scofflaw said he would leave on his own and requested permission to collect his personal effects from the hospital lounge area. I told him he could but that he would be escorted, and every item he wanted to take would be inspected. As Dr. Scofflaw picked up his personal items, we noticed him putting large numbers of blank prescription pads in his carry bag. I asked him what he intended to do with the blank pads. He said he might need to write a prescription for a family member. I then asked him why I had to keep reminding him that he did not have a current medical license and could not prescribe, dispense, or administer any prescription medication to anyone! Dr. Scofflaw slowly began to remove the blank pads from the bag. I have no doubt that he intended to write controlled substance prescriptions only for himself and no one else. After he finished packing his bag, I requested his permission to inspect it. Dr. Scofflaw consented. Inspection of the bag revealed three additional blank prescription pads at the bottom that he "forgot" to take out. I removed the pads and decided to hold on to them until he departed. Dr. Scofflaw closed his bag and walked out of the lounge area. He was met by two hospital security officers in the ER and escorted to his car. As he was being escorted out, the hospital administrator told me he did not want to take any chances with him.

What could have been a catastrophe for the hospital turned out well. To my knowledge, not a single patient treated in the emergency room by Dr. Scofflaw filed any type of lawsuit against the hospital. This administrator was very fortunate! It would only take one to open the flood gates.

The decision was made by the executive officer and board attorney not to pursue multiple counts of the illegal practice of medicine against Dr. Scofflaw. While the case certainly would have been justified and easy to convict, it may have precipitated a deluge of lawsuits against the hospital.

In September 1995, the medical board entered another order continuing the suspension of Dr. Scofflaw's license and DEA certificate for another year or until he successfully completed treatment. However, Dr. Scofflaw was far from finished. He just would not let sleeping dogs lie!

As part of medical board investigations, we collect data from a variety of sources that handle controlled and non-controlled prescription medications. These include traditional pharmacies, hospital pharmacies, and distribution centers that ship medications to outside customers and health care providers. In October 1995, Investigator Charlie Moses and I were working in a remote area of the state on a case that had nothing to do with Dr. Scofflaw. We had to visit a small but successful supplier in south Mississippi that supplied pharmaceuticals and other products to providers in order to get information on the current investigation. We requested that the owner make a small computer run of all orders for only controlled substances shipped to Mississippi physicians over the last six months. He agreed to do so, and after about an hour, produced a green bar printout approximately one inch thick. We began a review of the printout focusing on the practitioner we were currently working on. What we saw caught us totally off guard! The printout revealed the most frequent large purchaser of controlled substances, specifically hydrocodone cough syrups, was none other than good ol' Dr. Scofflaw! I asked the distribution center owner to print out just the information on Dr. Scofflaw. A review of the printout revealed he had been ordering controlled substances for almost as long as he had been without a current license. No wonder he did not fill any more prescriptions when he worked in the last ER – he didn't need any! Dr. Scofflaw was ordering approximately four to six cases a month of generic hydrocodone cough syrup along with eight sixteen-ounce bottles of hydrocodone cough syrup. Each case contained forty-eight one-ounce bottles. These are commonly referred to as sample size bottles, the kind usually supplied by drug reps as samples to physician offices. The owner of the distribution center showed us the customer billing information completed by Dr. Scofflaw that reflected his DEA and license number correctly and indicated, you guessed it, that they were current. The required follow-up had not been performed by the supplier for verification that Dr. Scofflaw's license and DEA number were current. DEA later suspended the license of the supplier based on this case and, as it turned out, this was not the supplier's first compliance failure. We also later learned that the supplier had in fact been notified by DEA of the suspension of Dr. Scofflaw's license and DEA number but had as a matter of routine operation not acted on the information to prevent an order from being filled.

Fortunately, the owner of the distribution center did help the situation by noticing something on the green bar print out that turned out to be extremely helpful. There was a coded indicator reflecting a pending order from Dr. Scofflaw for four more cases of hydrocodone cough syrup. The order had been received the previous day and had not been prepped for shipping. The shipment data indicated that it was to be delivered to Dr. Scofflaw at his private residence in Mississippi almost 150 miles away. I requested the owner to delay the shipment of the order until I had time to coordinate with several other agencies to possibly set up a controlled delivery. He agreed to cooperate in any way. I contacted the executive officer and explained my plan to him. After obtaining approval, I contacted Randy Corban, a friend of mine who was a captain with the Mississippi Bureau of Narcotics and responsible for MBN operations in the same area and town where Dr. Scofflaw resided. I explained the situation and requested his assistance in making a controlled delivery of the hydrocodone to Dr. Scofflaw. A controlled delivery simply means that investigators control the drugs, in this case, the hydrocodone cough syrup from the supplier to its ultimate destination, Dr. Scofflaw. After taking possession of the drugs from an undercover agent, the doctor would be in illegal possession of a product he ordered using false information. He could then be charged with illegal possession of a controlled substance, obtaining controlled substances by fraud or subterfuge, and mail fraud. Captain Corban readily agreed to the plan with one minor adjustment. He suggested that we bring DEA in on the operation and take the case to federal court since the local state district attorney did not like to prosecute physicians. I totally agreed and very much appreciated the benefit of his local knowledge and experience.

Two days later, investigators from MBML, MBN, and DEA met at MBN offices in Dr. Scofflaw's town to plan the delivery. The shipment of hydrocodone cough syrup from the distribution center was delivered to MBN and DEA agents by MBML investigators at the meeting. The DEA had arranged to use a local UPS truck with MBI/DEA task force agent, Sam Aldridge, posing as the UPS delivery man. This was not their first operation of this type; therefore, they were quite familiar with the UPS delivery procedures. Field surveillance on Dr. Scofflaw's residence had been established the day before the delivery by MBN and MBML investigators. In the meantime, MBN and DEA agents had obtained a federal search warrant for the residence to be served after the delivery. On the day of the delivery, surveillance had observed the doctor going in and out of the residence several times. Finally, they reported him seemingly settled at the residence, thus creating an opportunity for delivery. The cough syrup was delivered to Dr. Scofflaw's residence via the undercover UPS truck driven by Agent Aldridge. Playing his role well, looking just like your friendly UPS man, Agent Aldridge calmly walked to the door and knocked. The door was answered by Dr. Scofflaw, who immediately signed for the shipment and took possession without incident, questions, or conversation. Agent Aldridge then left the scene as would any UPS driver continuing his deliveries.

In order for there to be "constructive possession," as determined by the court, a waiting period of approximately thirty to forty minutes must pass after delivery before agents could go into the residence, seize the contraband, and arrest the doctor. The reason for the delay is that the court allows the recipient of the contraband to have ample time to inspect the shipment, take possession, or call UPS to report a mistake. After a forty-five-minute delay with no call to UPS, agents knocked on the door. When Dr. Scofflaw answered, agents announced "police," entered the residence and then fully identified themselves and served the search warrant. The residence was immediately secured by MBN agents, DEA agents, agents from the local metro narcotics unit, and MBML Investigator Charlie Moses. After Agent Aldridge returned the UPS truck and changed clothes out of the UPS uniform, he returned to participate in finishing up the search warrant. No other family members or individuals were present in the residence. It was clear from what investigators found that Dr. Scofflaw had taken full possession of the controlled shipment. After arresting the doctor, he was personally searched, revealing two empty cough syrup bottles in his shirt pocket and two additional empty bottles in a trash can. All of the bottles were marked and bagged as evidence with information identifying the location they were found. Dr. Scofflaw admitted to drinking them immediately after receiving the shipment. Also found in the trash can was the shrink wrap and UPS labeling delivery data which were all retained as evidence of the delivery. Several more-full bottles were "chilling" in the refrigerator. A partially empty case was found stashed under the sink in the kitchen. The search of the entire residence revealed the other three cases hidden in the attic, all of which were seized as evidence. In addition to the shipment items found, agents also found various amounts of pills for morphine, meperidine, propoxyphene, forged prescriptions already filled out, and blank prescription pads from other doctors. The detailed search of the residence failed to uncover any of the required recordkeeping data concerning the ordering, administering, or dispensing of the controlled substances. Dr. Scofflaw admitted he did not maintain any records on the controlled substances.

The search of the residence also revealed something that surprised all of the investigators and solved a local mystery. The metro agents from the local police department and sheriff's office found several newly constructed bathroom and kitchen cabinets, construction equipment, appliances, construction supplies, and various expensive tools that were scattered around the garage, house, and backyard of the residence. The items looked totally out of place. When they ran serial numbers on some of the equipment, the items all came back as stolen from local construction sites. It turned out that several local residential construction site thefts had taken place over the past few months. They now had a pretty good idea who was behind the thefts. The doctor eventually admitted he had committed the thefts in order to sell the items to buy drugs.

I cannot say enough good things about the performance of Captain Randy Corban of MBN, the metro narcotics agents, task force agents, DEA agents, and others who helped complete the case in such a timely manner. They did a magnificent and completely professional job on extremely short notice, reflecting their skill and training, to bring this case to a successful conclusion.

The case on Dr. Scofflaw was ultimately presented to a federal grand jury. The interaction with the grand jury that issued the indictments is itself a story of human interest. I grew up in a mid-size Mississippi town where everybody knew everybody, or at least knew *of* everyone, including immediate and extended families. The local burger joint, which had the absolute best greasy hamburgers ever, was a popular hangout where young teenagers could purchase burgers and fries on credit. I do not mean the "daddy's credit card" type of credit; I mean the "note on an index card that had to be paid off at the end of the month or no more hamburgers on credit" type of credit. The joint went back a long time. On one occasion a no-name entertainer put on a concert in the parking lot on the back of a long hay trailer. His name was Elvis Presley (who, incidentally, died from a drug overdose, as did Michael Jackson). Had the respective state medical boards been doing their job, these senseless untimely deaths may have been avoided.

Many of the young people in the town while growing up, at one time or other, worked at a couple of factories located nearby, unless they were "connected" to other businesses, which I was not. Those better connected worked in a bank or the other businesses that did not require a lot of sweat. One friend of mine and one of the nicest guys I ever met or had the privilege to know was Johnny Stewart. He worked at the local theater, the only one in town. I always thought he had the coolest job ever, temperature and otherwise, because he was able to see all the movies and was paid for it! His aunt, Delores Carpenter, was the secretary at the Methodist church we both attended and gave me my first Bible. Even though Johnny and I were not "best" friends, probably because there was an age difference, we knew each other and each other's family well. It is impossible to predict when events are set in motion and someone from the distant past becomes a significant ally in the future.

I had been subpoenaed to testify before the federal grand jury in the case of Dr. Scofflaw. A grand jury normally consists of eighteen members located in the same district of the state where the case-in-chief occurred. After being introduced to the grand jury by the assistant United States attorney, Chad Lamar, I made a brief case summary presentation and answered his questions. After the presentation, the jury was encouraged to ask questions of me that they might have had about the case. The first question was from the back of the room from a male voice. The voice asked, "Where are you from?" The man who asked the question then stood up. It was Johnny Stewart! I had not seen him in at least thirty years and then out of no-where, there he was. Johnny was the jury foreman and commented to the jury how he knew me and my brother, a Secret Service agent. For about the next ten minutes, while the grand jury and Mr. Lamar, the AUSA, sat waiting patiently, Johnny and I caught up on family and friends. Finally, Mr. Lamar intervened to finish the case presentation. He commented how he could probably just go home, with Johnny as foreman of the jury and me presenting the case, he felt he was not needed. The jury had a good laugh over that.

Dr. Scofflaw was indicted by the federal grand jury on nine counts involving the illegal possession of controlled substances, obtaining controlled substances by fraud, mail fraud, and record-keeping violations. Mr. Lamar managed the case perfectly, resulting in Dr. Scofflaw eventually entering a guilty plea. He was sentenced to serve six months inside and one year of federal probation. After the conviction, Dr. Scofflaw's suspended medical license was revoked by MBML and remained that way when I retired from the board.

Legally, the outcome of this case reflects that justice was effectively served. However, from a medical board perspective, there is cause to feel some failure. A primary goal of the Mississippi medical board is to identify disabled or impaired physicians and hopefully persuade them to enter treatment, get into a good recovery, and return to the practice of medicine. Frankly, had Dr. Scofflaw listened to good advice, many his legal problems could have been avoided. During all of the encounters with Dr. Scofflaw, investigators attempted to convince him to enter an approved treatment program and obtain the help he desperately needed. He chose poorly every time! To my knowledge, he even refused treatment while in prison. This young, well-trained Emergency Room physician gave up everything he worked so very hard for!

Randy Corban had a long and successful career at MBN. After retiring from the state of Mississippi, he went to work for the United States attorney's office as Chief Law Enforcement Liaison.

Sam Aldridge had an equally successful career with the Mississippi Bureau of Investigation. After retiring he went to work as an investigator for the United States Department of Justice.

William Chadwick "Chad" Lamar continued to have a productive and successful career as a prosecutor with the United States attorney's Office. He was subsequently appointed as the United States Attorney for the Northern District of Mississippi.

Coincidentally, a few months after this case was presented to that grand jury, my brother, Pete Allison, made a case presentation on behalf of the United States Secret Service to that same grand jury. Johnny Stewart was still serving as the GJ foreman. Pete and Johnny also had an old hometown discussion. Sadly, several years later, Johnny Stewart, a fine man, passed away at a relatively young age.

CHAPTER 9

ABSENT PRACTITIONER

Outlier doctors have been gaming the system [for years]. Most doctors truly put patients' care first before profit. But there are a few who inappropriately use their medical degrees for profit. – Linda Girgis, MD, FAAFP, article in Physician Weekly.

In so many ways, investigations mirror life and people. All are different on so many levels and you never know what each might bring to the table. Such was the investigation of Dr. Kane (not his real name), who performed or caused to be performed a large number of abortions in the state of Mississippi and other states. This procedure was and continues to be very controversial throughout the nation as a whole. In 1973 the United States Supreme Court in a five-to-four decision in *Roe v. Wade* made abortion on demand the law of the land. There was very little any state could do despite the fact that many had specific laws banning abortion. So long as the procedure is performed by a licensed physician, meets the standard of care and other regulations, there is little to nothing that can be done.

Dr. Kane was famous to some and infamous to others depending on one's point of view about abortion. Suffice it to say he had a rather large and successful practice in Mississippi. However, he forgot one very important rule of living in the limelight or under the microscope (choose your own metaphor). Whichever you choose, Dr. Kane did not cross every "t" or dot every "i." He forgot or did not care that he was in the fishbowl.

This case was initiated by Sammy Webb (his real name, I will call him SW) a man obsessed with his love for all things children and determined to find a legal pathway to stop the practice of Dr. Kane in his town. SW recognized that he had an uphill battle and he came to the medical board offices mainly out of desperation. All other avenues had wilted under the Supreme Court decisions. When SW made his appearance at our offices, I met him and introduced him to other members of the investigative staff. SW was wearing riding heeled western boots and had a presence and passion as large as a ten-gallon hat. It was during the introductions that I learned that SW carried a badge and had been in law enforcement most of his career. He was currently employed as an investigator for a district attorney's office. Investigator Neil Breeland and I met with SW in my office to document his complaint. He exhibited genuine concern for what he perceived as the single major cause of the breakdown of the family unit in Mississippi. He expressed a great passion for the patients, their families, and for the welfare of the unborn. SW went on for several minutes often repeating himself in his expressions of how he felt about abortion being a violation of Mississippi law. For all of his strong personal beliefs, SW had not described any act by Dr. Kane that would be a violation of the Mississippi Medical Practice Act or a federal statute that the medical board could act on. I told him that technically some anti-abortion laws remained on the books in Mississippi as in other states, however, the United States Supreme Court had made those laws unenforceable. I explained that regardless of moral or religious beliefs the medical board could not and would not take any actions on this or any physician performing abortions. Because abortion is a legal procedure, unless he could provide information of harm to patients, diversion of controlled substances, or some other violation of law or regulation, there was nothing anyone could do.

I asked SW if he knew of any other area of the Medical Practice Act in which Dr. Kane might be in violation. I explained again that while the abortion procedure is controversial, it is legal and, as a medical procedure, it must be done by a trained and licensed physician following accepted medical practices. I asked SW if he had any inkling of information that Dr. Kane was not following proper medical procedures in Mississippi? He said he did not. I asked if he had any information that Dr. Kane might be diverting controlled substances to himself or others without legitimate medical justification or documentation? Again, he said he did not. SW said that all he knew was that Dr. Kane was one of the largest abortion providers in the South with clinics in Mississippi and at least one other state.

SW described a situation in Mississippi in his home county whereby Dr. Kane was accused of killing a baby shortly after delivery in his clinic but no evidence had been documented as of yet, but the investigation was ongoing. I told SW that the information he had provided would be documented and presented to the executive officer to consider for an investigation. SW asked me what was the realistic chances of the board performing an investigation? I told him that I did not make those decisions and that I had very little influence on those who did, but that I would not wager much money on a positive outcome. SW then became very serious and bluntly told me that if the board declined to deal with this physician, he would subpoena every board member and all the staff to a grand jury in his county to explain their inaction! Whether he could or would be able to carry out his threats, I did not know. I never got an answer to that question from the board attorney or our Attorney General assignee. In an effort to calm SW down, I assured him I would pass on to the executive officer the exact sentiments he had expressed and see what happened. I did not tell SW, at the time, that we had recently received information from an Arkansas police department that they had arrested one of Dr. Kane's nurses and in her possession was a 30-cc vial of injectable Demerol. The nurse admitted she had taken it out of Dr. Kane's abortion clinic drug room in Mississippi without authorization.

Although SW threatened me and the board, I still could not decide if I liked the guy or not. He turned out to be the most persistent person I think I have ever known, but there was something about his nature that made him likable. It may have just been his determination. Who knows?

I presented the information to the executive officer with predictable results. I could have guessed the result even without the threats. However, I did not want to completely write off SW as just another religious zealot for which the anti-abortion movement was known. While the executive officer did not approve a full investigation into the complaint information, he did authorize a preliminary evaluation of any information that might be of interest to the board outside the abortion procedure itself. A part of that decision was based on the Arkansas information.

I had explained to SW the complaint process and assured him I would be in touch as soon as a decision was made. I did not want to tell him a full investigation had been denied. Maybe his grand jury threats were a bluff, maybe not! I just knew I did not want to try and explain to my board members why they were subpoenaed to a grand jury to answer questions about a complaint/investigation that never took place. I also did not want to tell SW that I had been approved to look at some preliminary data on the periphery of the abortion procedure itself. I did not want any possibility of leaks to get out and alert the doctor in any way. Therefore, I had to delay and obfuscate for as long as necessary. When I explained to SW the complaint process, I also told him that we had numerous cases in the pipeline ongoing that took precedent over a new complaint and that unless there was some sort of reevaluation of the board's investigative priorities, it would be quite some time before an investigation took place, even if it were approved. This gave me the time I needed and was the truth.

Never one to give up, over the next several months I received several phone calls from SW checking on the status of his complaint. He frequently reminded me of the grand jury just so I would not forget. During this period, I began collecting information on Dr. Kane. As it turned out, there was quite a lot of information to be found. It appeared the good doctor had been attracting attention in another state for problems with patient care issues and possible violations of regulations. However, no formal charges or lawsuits had been filed that could be used in Mississippi. In one case Dr. Kane allegedly had a patient bleed to death in his clinic in another state. Supposedly, he refused to call an ambulance until it was too late. He allegedly said he did not want the public to see an ambulance at his clinic. A second allegation at his other clinics indicated that he had staff falsify records to reflect dates indicating he complied with the mandatory three-day waiting period requirements before an abortion could be performed. Again, no charges had been filed based on that information. While this was just the kind of information I was interested in, it was not current and not in Mississippi. More importantly, it was not the kind of information that would get me the probable cause to enter Dr. Kane's Mississippi clinic unannounced for a firsthand evaluation of the operation. However, now I knew that this guy was a rule breaker. I felt I was getting close!

At this point, I began to look at controlled substance purchases under the doctor's and the clinic's DEA numbers. I expected the amounts to be large due to the type of practice, but I was surprised at the amounts purchased. The purchase records that could be located indicated that during the past twelve months Dr. Kane had purchased huge quantities of Demerol injectable and Valium tablets. Demerol is a Schedule IIN narcotic for moderate to severe pain management. Valium is a Schedule IV Benzodiazepine for anxiety. Fortunately, the clinic did not have its own DEA number. Dr. Kane was at liberty to perform the abortion procedures barring any malpractice issues, however, he had to comply with all federal and state regulations regarding the process leading up to the procedure. Therefore, he had to have accountability records for every single dose of controlled substances he purchased. With this, I possibly had my way into the clinic unannounced!

A briefing with the executive officer and the board attorney resulted in tentative approval. Because of the anticipated political and legal turmoil such a case like this could and most likely would garner, they both wanted to involve the Executive Committee of the board before giving the final go-ahead. The Executive Committee of the board is made up of the President, Vice President, and Secretary. They are elected by members of the board and serve as the day-to-day governing body of the board when the board is not in session. The next day the executive officer polled the three members of the Executive Committee to brief them on the situation and get their input. All three of the committee members gave their approval to proceed. Their logic was as simple as it gets and that is usually the best kind. If any physician had ordered such a large number of controlled substances it would need to be audited for compliance, and it made no difference if the physician worked in an abortion clinic. The red flag had to be addressed.

Stan Ingram and I began working on the inspection affidavit and search warrant. Stan knew the affidavit, which spells out the probable cause, facts, and circumstances for the warrant would be challenged by the finest defense attorneys that Dr. Kane and pro-abortion supporters could buy. He was particularly careful to be certain every point of justification could be verified for the court. Once the warrant and affidavit had been completed an operational plan was put in place and the best day to serve the warrant was determined. The best day to serve the warrant was determined by headcounts identifying the busiest days patients were going in and out of the clinic. I preferred to enter the clinic when it was the least busy since it meant fewer interruptions. The day before the warrant was to be served, we met with the senior circuit judge recommended by SW in the county and presented the affidavit and warrant for his approval. Unlike the federal FISA (Foreign Intelligence Surveillance Act) courts in the news big time during the first Trump campaign and administration, where very little is asked by the judges of the presenting agents, we were vigorously challenged on every single point of law and our affidavit facts before the judge authorized serving the warrant. In this case, we spent almost two hours with the judge reviewing the law, the evidence, and answering his questions. He never once raised the question of the legality or ethics of performing abortions. SA had been correct in his assessment of the judge. The judge clearly knew what he was doing and that is the way it should be.

Before we served the warrant, I decided to have a little fun with SW, who to our knowledge had no idea of what we were on the brink of doing. I called him and requested that he meet with me at a local restaurant near his hometown to discuss the status of his complaint. He readily agreed. When he arrived, he saw me with four other MBML investigators sitting around one of the tables drinking coffee. As he walked up to us, he commented that we were a bunch of shady looking characters and that he probably needed to call backup and have us arrested. There had to be a bank that had been robbed around here somewhere. I laughed and told him to just shut up and sit down, I had something important to tell him. With a straight but serious face that was difficult to maintain, I told SW how over the last several months the executive officer, board attorney, and I had reviewed his complaint data and a considerable amount of other data involving Dr. Kane's clinic operation. We could find no justification to pursue any type of investigation into Dr. Kane's practice and considered the matter closed. The response was immediate and surprising from SW! He exploded from the table with a virtual flood of expletives directed at me and the board. Everybody in the restaurant saw and heard what was going on. The manager rushed over and threatened to call the police until we all presented our identification to him. He still appropriately demanded we quiet down or leave. I apologized for the disruption and assured him the situation was under control. With SW holding his breath, stomping around in his western boots, and about to pass out, I told him I had something I needed for him to read, if he knew how to read! I handed him the affidavit and inspection warrant. It took about five minutes and a couple of start overs before SW realized what he was reading and how he had just been played big-time. He leaned out from behind the warrant, just looked at me and said, "You dirty rotten S-O-B," and returned to reading. I said, "Well, I will disregard the fact that you knew my mother and, yeah, it takes one to know one." We joked that it would take three surgeons a week to remove the hook from his mouth! The other investigators were laughing uncontrollably. While he detoxed over a cup of coffee that I paid for, I brought him up to date on the situation. I think it was at this point he finally realized he really could trust us.

I invited SW to join us on the serving of the warrant. I told him I could justify his being there as a local law enforcement officer if it turned ugly and we needed backup. He felt he could not join us formally but would be on standby with others in the area if we needed help. I emphasized the need for absolute secrecy on the serving of the warrant. We wanted to catch the clinic completely unaware of anything going on. I asked him to not tell anyone including his boss until after the warrant was served. SW agreed and said he would not tell him until after we were in the clinic. At this point, I did not have a hint of the pandora's box of issues we would uncover the following morning.

I went into the clinic to serve the search warrant with Investigators Charlie Moses, Neil Breeland, and Mickey Robbins, along with two detectives from the local police department. We very much wanted the local police involved. If this turned into an abortion riot, we wanted backup immediately. What we found in the clinic surprised even the most experienced medical board investigators. I identified myself to the receptionist in the entryway and asked to see Dr. Kane. The receptionist took us to an office that had a view of a large treatment room area. The area contained several treatment tables lined on all sides with cloth blinds that could be drawn closed on all four sides. We noted that a few of the treatment table areas were completely closed off. A woman in a white nurse uniform came into the office and identified herself as the chief nurse for Dr. Kane. I introduced myself to her as chief investigator for the Mississippi medical board and requested to meet with Dr. Kane immediately. She told me he was out of town and was not expected to return that day. I requested she make every effort to contact him and suggested he might want to know that we were in his clinic. I suggested that she advise him that investigators from the Mississippi State Board of Medical Licensure were in the clinic and had a search warrant. We planned to serve the warrant whether he was there or not, but we preferred that he be present. She left the room and returned in about ten minutes. She could not get in touch with the doctor but had paged him to call the clinic. I told her I would have to proceed without him. I then presented the chief nurse – I'll call her "Faye" – with the clinic's copy of the search warrant and directed the investigative staff to secure the patient file area and the drug room storage area. We then began to interview staff. I told nurse Faye I was requesting her cooperation and hoped she would direct her staff to be fully cooperative. We would like to do our job and get out of her way as quietly and quickly as possible. She agreed. After the designated areas were secure, I requested nurse Faye to take me on a tour of the facility so I could become familiar with the entire clinic. After the tour, we returned to the centrally located treatment area. I asked her to explain why some of the treatment rooms were closed off, but I suspected I knew the reason. She confirmed my suspicions when she told me there were patients prepped for procedures. I then asked her if by the term "procedures" she meant an abortion? She said she did. I then asked her how the "procedures" could be performed when the doctor was not present in the clinic or expected to return. Nurse Faye began to tear up. I reminded her that she said she would cooperate and told her she really did need to talk to me. I assured her that she could only help herself by cooperating fully. The reluctant nurse acknowledged that procedures were done by nursing staff including herself when the doctor was away. Two other medical board investigators, Neil Breeland and Mickey Robbins heard the same story from other staff members. I suggested to Nurse Faye that she have the patients dress and leave the clinic. I was not going to allow the abortions to be performed in the absence of a physician. The patients were quickly ushered out of the clinic by staff.

While other investigators were interviewing clinic staff, I began the audit of the Demerol and Valium. I started with the Valium first.

The nurse responsible for the drug storage area was already cooperating with Investigator Charlie Moses. When asked for the drug ledgers indicating the inventory levels of the Valium and recording the usage, she indicated there were no such records maintained. Charlie told me that not only were no records maintained on the Valium, but there had been considerable amounts of Xanax in various doses that were also used in the clinic and no records on that either. She said most of the nursing staff had been helping themselves to the Valium and Xanax for various and sundry personal uses because the doctor was rarely in the clinic and no one monitored usage. When I interviewed the nurse, she confirmed what she had told Charlie and agreed to a written statement and testify if necessary.

While Investigator Charlie Moses continued his interview with the nurse and obtaining her statement, I began the audit of the injectable Demerol. The clinic had monthly ledger sheets that were available for use, but they had not been used correctly or consistently. Injections were logged intermittently and did not include the patient name, dose amount (1 cc, .5 cc, etc.), or the date, just the term "Demerol inj." on a line starting with the number 1. Rarely more than four or five entries were found for any single month during the twelve previous months. No purchases were reflected or added for new supplies received and only a few vials were found in the current inventory. All of the drugs were stored in an unsecured area with unrestricted access by the employees. I asked nurse Faye if it would serve any purpose to go through each file for the last twelve months and count the injections. She said probably not, since the drug injections were rarely recorded anywhere. I performed a sample review of approximately 100 files and verified her information. I then asked nurse Faye if the Demerol had been similarly taken from the clinic as the Valium and Xanax. She said the only person she knew that took Demerol out of the clinic was the doctor. He frequently would take numerous 30 cc vials on occasion and say he was taking it for use in another clinic. She did not know if it was true or not. To her knowledge, no records of the so-called transfers were ever made. Occasionally a note was entered in the file or ledger concerning a Demerol vial being broken. The entire drug room was carpeted. I asked nurse Faye how a thick glass Demerol vial could be broken on carpet area. She indicated she did not know of any that were in fact broken. Dr. Kane told us to enter the breakage notes to cover shortages. In summary, out of literally thousands of doses of Demerol, Valium, and Xanax purchased or acquired under Dr. Kane's DEA number, virtually none could be verified as used for legitimate medical procedures.

Investigators Neil Breeland and Mickey Robbins continued to engage other nursing staff in interviews of clinic operations. One nurse confessed to them that she and other nurses had routinely altered dates on most of the patient files to reflect compliance with the state three-day waiting requirement before an abortion could be performed. She told investigators that Dr. Kane had directed the staff to alter the dates to avoid a delay in performing the procedures. She said most of the patients were in agreement with what was done because they did not want to make a second trip to the clinic. She also provided investigators a statement and agreed to testify. Investigator Mickey Robbins, while searching an office area attached to the drug storage room, found a large cache of pre-signed prescriptions. They all bore the handwritten signature of Dr. Kane. One of the nurses admitted they were instructed to use them on patients when Dr. Kane was not in the clinic. Every employee in the clinic acknowledged they knew they were using pre-signed prescriptions, and everyone had access if they wanted some for themselves.

I told nurse Faye I wanted to have a serious conversation with her about what I expected to happen going forward and her role in that process. She could either be seen as helpful or become a target of the investigation like Dr. Kane. Thus far, we had collected evidence of multiple violations of laws and regulations concerning the operation of an abortion clinic in the state of Mississippi. We had also collected considerable evidence of violations of board regulations in the administering, dispensing, and handling of controlled substances in the clinic. Further, many of these actions were also in violation of federal and state criminal laws and regulations. I told her that I was aware of a certain investigator for the local district attorney that would probably jump at the chance to indict nurses in the clinic that failed to fully cooperate and testify against the doctor and that I hoped one of the nurses would not be her. She understood my meaning and again assured me that she would provide a written statement and be available to testify if necessary. She said she was pretty sure she was quitting as of today. I informed her that the Board of Nursing would have to be notified of the actions of the nursing staff in the clinic operation. I assured her pursuant to her full and continued cooperation I would be willing to testify on her behalf if it became necessary.

I told nurse Faye that based on the information provided by staff and her indicating the controlled substance medications were not securely stored, not properly accounted for, and were being diverted for unknown reasons or uses, we were going to seize the remaining controlled substances in the clinic and all DEA order forms to prevent any more controlled substances from being ordered. She offered no objection. We also seized a large sampling of patient files identified as having dates altered to reflect compliance with the three-day waiting period before an abortion could be performed, controlled substance records for the past twelve months reflecting little or no accountability, pre-signed prescriptions, and statements from nurses indicating that numerous abortion prep and procedures had been performed by them in the absence of Dr. Kane and that pre-signed prescriptions had been provided to patients when they left the clinic.

At this point, we had been in the clinic for almost five hours. I asked Nurse Faye if she or anyone else had heard anything from Dr. Kane. She said they had not. Over the next two to three weeks several attempts were made to contact Dr. Kane to obtain his side of the story. Through his attorney, he refused to talk to investigators. Who could have possibly guessed that such a quagmire of deceit and fraud could be perpetrated on such unsuspecting and vulnerable people by supposed professionals trained to help others?

As a result of the investigation and search warrant, Dr. Kane was charged in a summons and affidavit with thirty-six counts involving unprofessional conduct likely to deceive, defraud, or harm the public. Included were violations of the board's-controlled substance regulations, prescription regulations, and of the Mississippi Medical Practice Act including assisting individuals in the unlicensed practice of medicine. Dr. Kane's attorney agreed to accept process on behalf of his client partly because he did not want us to know where Dr. Kane was due to fear of harm to him. The attorney accepting process for their client has the same legal effect as serving the client personally.

It did not take long for the case to become public information. The MBML was besieged by both sides of the abortion issue and the media. Everyone in the investigative division knew the consequences of commenting to the media either officially or off the record. All media contact was only through the executive officer, board attorney, or board president. Many on both sides of the issue showed a complete misunderstanding of the legal issues by thinking that Dr. Kane was going to jail. Charges by the MBML are administrative, not criminal. Had the DEA or the local DA been so inclined, there were plenty of criminal charges that could have been filed. However, the number of controlled substances diverted did not rise to a level that would make the case a realistic DEA case. The local district attorney clearly supported the efforts of the

MBML in the investigation. However, his investigative focus was on a more serious allegation indicating that Dr. Kane had terminated a live birth in the clinic during a late-term abortion procedure.

Routinely with high profile cases, the defense attorneys are granted about as many delays or continuances in hearings as they request. The defense wants all the time in the world to review evidence, develop a realistic defense theory, and hope prosecution witnesses become intimidated and/or just disappear. The prosecution agrees to most of the requests for delays to refute any arguments of not having enough time to prepare if the verdict is appealed. Fortunately, during all of the delays, Dr. Kane could not practice medicine in Mississippi. Part of the agreement to the multiple delays was that Dr. Kane would not practice medicine or operate a clinic until the hearings were completed. Still, there was no way the MBML could win. After each continuance was granted, SW would call me just to be certain the board was not getting cold feet and stress how he wanted a front-row seat each day at the hearing. Individuals from the other side would call to complain about how the board was denying women their constitutional right to an abortion. At times during the months of waiting for the hearing to commence, the two groups would get rowdy with each other in the parking lot at our offices. Assistance from the Jackson police, supervised by Assistant Chief Jim French, was required to prevent any kind of violence.

During this period, several radical anti-abortionists shot and killed doctors and staff at abortion clinics throughout the country. There also had been bombs planted in cars and dumpsters at clinics. Dr. Kane was well-known in his chosen field and had numerous threats made against him and his staff. We were responsible for and committed to protecting Dr. Kane and his staff. Regardless of how one may feel about abortion, we did not want anyone killed or injured as a result of our actions or inactions. The continuances gave me time to put together a security plan. This included limiting access to the hearing room, securing equipment, including metal detectors, obtaining extra security personnel, and obtaining bulletproof vests for certain individuals if they wanted them. The security plan allowed only twenty seats in the hearing room for the public. Everyone, including the media, had to submit a request for seating, be vetted, and agree to a lottery for seat selection. Attendees also had to agree to a full search of themselves and their bags. No matter how large or small, the bags had to be emptied, searched, and along with the person, pass through a sensitive metal detector system provided by the local U.S. Marshals office. Investigators Charlie Moses, Neil Breeland, and Mickey Robbins were responsible for seeing that no one got into the hearing room with a weapon of any kind. They searched everybody and everything!

Three locations in the room were provided for television media, but the cameras and/or audio recording equipment could not be on once the hearing commenced. I am happy beyond words this hearing took place before cell phones came along! All parties participating in the hearing as members of the defense team or Medical Board members and staff, were required to wear a lapel patch, clearly visible, in order to gain entrance to the hearing room. The lapel patch was changed daily to prevent duplication by unauthorized individuals that might attempt to gain access to the hearing. Anyone who entered the hearing room could not leave once the hearing started. During a break, if anyone left the hearing room area beyond the restrooms, they were not allowed back in. These individuals were escorted by security staff until they left the premises. The only exceptions were defense attorneys or their identified staff and certain medical board personnel. Everyone who was allowed back in had to go through the metal detector again before re-entry. All restrooms were searched before people went in and after they came out. Any purses or bags of any kind had to be emptied and re-searched before re-entry. Anyone who made an unsolicited comment during the hearing would be removed and not allowed to return. Individuals who attempted to disrupt the hearing process would be removed and not allowed to return. The building and parking lot were continually searched for unusual packages. Vehicles could not be parked in proximity to the offices of the medical board. Fortunately, all of the other tenants in the area were cooperative during the time of the hearing. No one wanted to be a victim of a car bombing. Dr. Kane and his entourage were escorted into the building by uniformed officers and medical board investigators and escorted out similarly. Dr. Kane, his attorneys, and staff were all offered bulletproof vests, but they declined.

Once the hearing started the room held approximately forty to fifty people. This count included board members, board staff, assistant attorney general, defense attorneys and staff, prosecutors and assistants, court reporter, media, the public, and extra security staff. During the hearing I was one of only three board staff members with unencumbered access to and from the hearing room. On the first day of the hearing while doing a security sweep I encountered a large man wearing a western-style hat sitting on the ground next to the main entrance to the hearing room. He had not attempted to make entry into the hearing. As I approached him, he stood up and said to me, "You don't like me very much, do you?" I quietly looked him over and responded, "I do not even know who you are. Why would you say something like that?" Before he could comment I then said, "Listen, I don't really care who you are, but if you start any trouble here or even look like you might start any trouble, I am going to have you locked up. Is that clear?" Fortunately for me, he just turned and walked away. He was a large man and I really did not want to tangle with him at all! Thankfully, I never saw him again. I later learned he was a professional protester at abortion clinics nationwide and in Mississippi.

The hearing lasted for two full days and very late each night. On the second day, one of the board members was removed from the hearing for making a comment about abortion "killing babies." The defense raised an objection and made a motion that the doctor was prejudiced in the case and had to be removed from the hearing. The assistant attorney general assignee sustained the motion. As I was escorting him to his car, he commented, "I guess I made a mistake by saying what I said."

I responded, "You spoke your feelings. I just wished that you had waited until the board was in executive session and not in an open hearing." Medical board investigators never knew how the board was going to rule on a case regardless of the evidence. I felt we truly needed this doctor in the final deliberations. A few years later, the doctor was honored in his hometown for delivering over seven thousand babies during his decades of practice.

I learned early in my investigative career that just because a witness or investigator/agent says they will do something does not mean that they really will when the case heats up. As in most cases, the defense aggressively attempted to have all of the evidence from the search warrant suppressed or thrown out using various legal maneuvers. It did not work! They then attempted to find the slightest error or mistake in the affidavit or warrant and repeatedly attacked and harassed investigators and other witnesses with allegations of incompetence or outright corruption. Fortunately for the medical board investigators, all of the nurses that provided statements and agreed to testify stayed true to the case. They presented clear and convincing testimony of the shabby operation of the clinic. They described the altering of the waiting period dates in the patient files as instructed by Dr. Kane and detailed the complete lack of any accountability of the thousands upon thousands of doses of Demerol, Valium, and Xanax. Finally, the nurses testified how the nursing staff was instructed and trained by Dr. Kane to perform procedures. They described how they performed procedures that should only be done by a licensed physician, frequently in his absence. Investigators testified how, on the day the warrant was served, Dr. Kane was not in the clinic, but patients were found prepped for procedures. Testimony was presented on the numerous unsuccessful attempts to contact Dr. Kane by nurse Faye. One of the nurses testified he spent the majority of his time, when away from the clinic, in various casinos in Mississippi.

The defense primarily consisted of questioning the intentions and integrity of the nurses and investigators. They reminded everyone that *Roe v. Wade* provides a constitutional right for women to have an abortion. After closing arguments and summations, the board, minus one, went into executive session for deliberations. After several hours, the board indicated it had reached a decision. It took some time to screen everyone who wanted to re-enter the hearing room. After everyone was seated in the hearing room, the board announced a unanimous decision of guilty on thirty-four of thirty-six counts as charged in the summons and affidavit. The two counts he was found not guilty on related to his conspiring with staff on violations of the medical practice act. The decision was to suspend the medical license of Dr. Kane for five years with four suspended. That meant he could not practice for at least one year from the date of the suspension. He also had to complete courses in medical ethics and controlled substance accountability and submit proof of successfully passing the training before returning to practice.

After the hearing concluded late that night, a very large crowd of people gathered in the parking lot outside the main entrance to the offices of the medical board in anticipation of Dr. Kane leaving. The media wanted interviews. The anti-abortionists wanted blood. Occasionally shouts of “bring the killer out” or “baby killer” were heard from the crowd. My security plan called for almost everyone involved in our security to act as if Dr. Kane would be leaving through the main door that had previously been used. Almost all of the investigators, police, and extra security were converging in the front area, creating a barrier between the crowd and the walkway. In the meantime, I had a second stretch limo parked by a back entrance to MBML offices that very few except medical board staff knew about. The back access to our offices was frequently mistaken for an employee entrance to an attached bank branch office. Dr. Kane and staff were quickly shuttled into the waiting limo and whisked away into the night before anyone in the crowd on the other side of the building knew what had happened. As Dr. Kane walked out of the building past myself and Assistant Chief Jim French, he must have then realized he would not have to face the rowdy crowd on the other side of the building because he leaned toward us and said, “Thank you.” Those were the first and last words I personally ever heard from Dr. Kane. He was alive and gone into the night! We could finally relax! As the limo rapidly drove out of the parking lot and made a left turn on to Lakeland Drive, a flood of frustrated media and radical anti-abortionist rounded the corner of the building. Along with me, they watched the taillights of the limo as it sped toward I-55. I could not have been more thankful for all of the help from the medical board staff, JPD, and especially Assistant Chief Jim French, along with many others. I suddenly felt the urge for a drink of scotch, a double!

I have often wondered about the outcome of this case many times. Had Dr. Kane been present in the clinic when we first presented the search warrant or if he had shown up later at the clinic, would we have been able to convince the staff to cooperate with us? Quite frankly, in my own mind, I do not think they would have cooperated. We did not have a magic wand to wave and make people talk. I feel we were just plain lucky or guided to be there on the right day at the right time. What happened to the patients that were discharged? Did they go elsewhere, or did they become mothers and raise a child that I somehow know today? I will probably never find that out.

Sammy Webb, who by his efforts alone started this pressure cooker case, left the district attorney's office to become a successful chief of police in a mid-size Mississippi city. He was later appointed director of a youth court program in one of Mississippi's most populous counties. He retired with thirty-eight and a half years of service within the criminal justice arena in the northern half of Mississippi. After retiring he was later called back into service in the youth court area and serves in that capacity to this day. All of the investigators that worked this case still consider him a friend and, at times, a few other things!

I received information after I retired from the medical board that Faye, Dr. Kane's chief nurse, went on to bigger and worse things. She was later convicted of capital murder in Mississippi. She allegedly had her best friend hit in a contract killing related to an insurance scam. I met such nice people when I was working for the medical board!

Assistant Chief Jim French, who was instrumental in helping us keep Dr. Kane and the defense team safe and alive throughout the ordeal, later retired from the Jackson Police Department. He became a manager in the security division of a major bank in Mississippi. However, before he retired from the police department, we would work together again on a health insurance investigation involving a Jackson police officer who attempted to defraud Blue Cross and Blue Shield of Mississippi. The police officer lost his job.

As to the question of Dr. Kane having possibly deliberately killed a live birth baby in his Mississippi clinic during a late-term procedure, none of the clinic staff that cooperated with the MBML investigation indicated they had any knowledge of that happening.

Dr. Kane did not appeal the suspension of his medical license. After his license was suspended in Mississippi, his license in another state was revoked based on the Mississippi action. After his license was revoked in the other state, the Mississippi board revoked his suspended license based on the other state's revocation. He never attempted to have his license reinstated in Mississippi.

CHAPTER 10

MOTEL MAN

Never underestimate or overlook the advantage offered an investigator who is underestimated or overlooked by a perpetrator or adversary. – Richard Allison, MBML Chief Investigator.

Small towns are the backbone of Mississippi. If a problem is documented in a small town, it is magnified in the bigger towns. It just might not be identified yet. I remember when I would hear from school administrators, "We do not have a drug problem at this school." They did not want to have students move to other schools and lose state education money based on the student census. What they should have asked instead was, "What can we do to identify and address the problem before it becomes like a big town problem?" A lot of time and lives were lost because "leaders" buried their heads in the sand.

This specific case, like many others, developed out of the monitoring program started by the medical board in the early 1980s to address an opioid problem in Mississippi and nationwide involving the drugs Dilaudid and Percodan. We were trying to avoid the big town problems other states were dealing with. Dilaudid is chemically known as hydromorphone HCL, a Schedule IIN controlled substance primarily used for severe pain management and is highly abused. Percodan is oxycodone, also a Schedule IIN controlled substance for the treatment of moderate to severe pain. Both are intended for short-term use unless the patient is terminal. "Short-term use" is generally defined as no more than a week to ten days.

As part of the board's area development proactive monitoring program, I was profiling pharmacies in several small towns in south-central Mississippi looking for suspicious patterns of prescribing for Dilaudid and Percodan. It did not take long to identify a suspicious pattern of long-term prescribing of these drugs to several female patients by one physician. Most of these females I knew as well-known "doctor shoppers" or "professional patients" from previous cases. These people make a good living by obtaining controlled substances from dishonest or duped doctors. The physician had not appeared on the board's radar before and was probably being duped, as was sometimes the case. Anyway, on the first encounter, we try to give the benefit of the doubt to the doctor. Most of the time this works, but not always. Unfortunately, there was more to this situation than met the eye, as I would later learn the hard way. There is also a "first" rule involved that goes something like this: "No good deed goes unpunished." In life, never forget the first rule! After completing a good sample profile of the prescribing, I put together a briefing for the executive officer for the following day. After the briefing, he authorized a warning visit to the physician. A warning visit was meant to be educational only and not adversarial. During such a visit, we lay out the profile sheets showing the patients had visited multiple physicians and explain their well-documented history. We offer suggestions about evaluating the prescribing to these patients based on their history including referring them for treatment. If the professional patient fails to follow the recommendations of the doctor, which most do, the doctor is under no obligation to continue treating them. These types of visits to physicians were carefully choreographed to be very benign. I trained investigators to have the heart of a teacher during these visits. The visit was followed up by a formal warning letter from the executive officer. Most of the time the problem was resolved, and we never heard from the physician again. Not this time! Try to be nice and the first rule kicks in.

The physician, who I will call "Motel Man," contacted the executive officer and expressed his appreciation for the visit from the medical board and said he did not like to be taken in by these types of people and would be more careful in the future. Someone not familiar with investigations might get the idea that investigators are cynical. Well, we are not cynical – we are *very* cynical, and you are about to learn why.

The executive officer told me about his telephone call from Motel Man concerning the visit and follow-up letter. He directed a follow-up profile to be scheduled without fail on Motel Man in six months just to cut the cards and see what was going on. Neither of us was convinced that Motel Man was entirely sincere.

About six months later, I began a follow-up profile of Motel Man's prescribing in the same general area of the state. At first, there was little to indicate a problem. It appeared that maybe Motel Man had taken the visit and letter to heart and had ceased the suspicious prescribing. There were few Dilaudid and Percodan prescriptions found and those that were found were determined to be for legitimate cancer patients, many of whom had already passed away. I decided to cut the cards again and expanded my profile area to include a couple of major towns on the fringe of the original profile area. After only a few pharmacy visits I started finding prescriptions issued by Motel Man for Dilaudid and Percodan to most of the same female patients. The number of prescriptions and the amounts on the prescriptions were greater than before. It took several days to complete the profile due to the large number of pharmacies to visit. It took several more days to organize the profile and prepare a briefing for the executive officer and board attorney.

Before meeting with the executive officer, I received a call from a contact of mine who worked in a treatment center. I will call her "Marilyn." Marilyn had been a "professional patient" for years until pressure from one of our investigations finally convinced her to get help. She had been sober for several years and working in a treatment center that specialized in treating prescription drug abusers like herself. She had been working with a female patient that was just finishing treatment and wanted to talk to somebody about a doctor that she had been providing sexual favors to in return for prescriptions for narcotics. Marilyn identified the physician as Motel Man. Marilyn knew as well as I did that time was important. After being released from treatment the patient may or may not continue to be so cooperative. After I heard the doctor's name, the sense of urgency was immediate. I set up a meeting through Marilyn for the following day. Investigator Charlie Moses and I traveled to the halfway house where the patient was currently living. Marilyn introduced us to the patient, Mae, not her real name. Mae was a tall, attractive blonde who described herself as a long-term prescription drug abuser. She, like so many others we had interviewed, started using marijuana at a very young age and quickly graduated to prescription drugs. She described almost two years of providing Motel Man sexual favors for prescriptions. Many of the encounters were in his clinic, others were at his residence, and, most recently, at a motel in Jackson well-known for being used by politicians and other government executives. She said she frequently saw the doctor on Sundays. He told her to call him or have him paged on Sundays at approximately ten o'clock in the morning so he could tell his wife he had an emergency and would not have to go to church with her. Conveniently, there were no staff members at the clinic on Sundays, so they would not be disturbed. Mae told us that even though she was in treatment, Motel Man had been in contact with her to try and see her again. She identified several other females who she knew traded drugs for sex with him. To her knowledge, none of them had entered treatment and all of whom were probably still involved with him.

Mae said she had no desire to return to the drug-seeking life and did not plan to see the doctor again because she knew exactly what he wanted to do. I asked Mae if, by "what he wanted to do," she meant he wanted to continue trading drugs for sex. She said it was. I asked her if she would be willing to work with investigators on a case to catch Motel Man in his little scheme? She said she would. I asked her how far she was willing to go to nail down an airtight case against the doctor. She said that if I meant having sex with him in return for prescriptions, she was willing to do that if necessary. She added she had already "done it" with him hundreds of times, so a few more times for good measure would not be a problem. I told her it may not be a problem for her, but it might be a big problem for us. I told her it would probably involve federal agents to accomplish such an operation because there was no chance a state prosecutor would be willing to take such a case to court. She said she did not care and she was willing to cooperate and help.

When we returned to the offices of the medical board, I briefed the executive officer and board attorney on the developments. I suggested we contact the Mississippi Bureau of Narcotics and DEA for assistance. They both approved the plan. When I spoke with a friend who was an agent at the bureau, he readily agreed to involve the DEA because of continuing problems with local DAs refusing to prosecute doctors, especially in the county where this case would take place. A meeting was set up with all agencies to brief them on the developments and to work on an investigative plan going forward. Time was of the essence because Mae was due to be cut loose from supervision at the halfway house soon and we needed to keep her close and sober. At first, DEA said they would not be able to work the case because the US Attorney's office would probably not go along with allowing Mae to perform sex acts in return for prescriptions. The liability was just too great and a jury could find the tactic morally objectionable. A meeting with the local US Attorney resulted in a "maybe." He said he would have to get approval up the line for such an operation. In the meantime, he wanted to meet the informant, Mae, and evaluate her for himself. A meeting was arranged for USA staff and MBN agents to interview Mae. After the meeting, they were convinced she was a willing participant and had credibility. However, they still doubted the Department of Justice in Washington would approve such a seedy operation. Surprisingly, in approximately two weeks, approval was granted, by the big man himself, but with conditions. By "the big man," I mean the United States attorney general. The conditions were reasonable and did not vary from standard investigative procedures. Mae had to sign consent agreements before commencing the operation. Every contact between her and the doctor had to be recorded and transcribed, including the sex acts. All the prescriptions and tape recordings had to be turned over to the agents immediately after each encounter. A minimum of three encounters was required to establish intent on the doctor's part. Mae agreed to continue the operation.

All had been approved and the case was set into motion. Immediately after Mae was released from treatment, she was contacted and directed to meet with MBN, DEA, and MBML investigators to initiate contact with Motel Man. The first phone call, which was recorded in its entirety, resulted in a meeting date and time between Mae and Motel Man to take place at their favorite local motel. Motel Man jumped at the chance to see Mae again. He indicated he would be in town for some meetings and for Mae to come to his room at approximately 8:00 p.m.

So, how do you record a person when they are having sex in a room when access to the room before the sex is not possible? Mae cannot wear a "body" recorder/transmitter for obvious reasons. The answer? Put a very small, sensitive but effective tape recorder in her purse with a remote microphone carefully attached and concealed in the purse strings. The technology of the time provided for approximately two and a half hours of recording time. Surely, that would be enough. Mae said that based on past experience, ten minutes would probably be enough. We all secretly hoped so, but did not comment, just kind of laughed. Most of the recorders had an end of tape alarm that had to be disabled. DEA and MBN had ample supplies of this type of equipment readily available. Several tests of the arrangement were completely successful.

On the night of the rendezvous, investigators met with Mae at approximately 7:00 p.m., just around the corner from the motel to rig her purse and test the recording device. Investigators also had to record, at the beginning of the tape, the case agent's name, date and time of the recording, location, people present, and case number. Mae was told not to cut off the recorder under any circumstances. Surveillance had already been set up around the motel. At precisely eight o'clock, Mae turned into the motel parking lot. She exited her car and walked noisily on the concrete floor up one set of stairs to Motel Man's room. She was observed knocking on the door and immediately disappeared through an opened door. A little over an hour passed before she exited the motel room. She walked to her car, got in, and exited the motel parking lot. She met with investigators at the designated site for debriefing and retrieval of evidence. Investigators removed the recording device, reversed it, then hit play. The recorder worked to perfection. All the audio was completely audible. From the case agent's establishment comments, her getting into her car to drive to the motel, radio in her car, exiting her car at the motel, walking to the motel room, knocking on the door, getting reacquainted conversation, the sex act itself, conversation after the sex, and her leaving the motel and meeting up with investigators where the recorder was cut off. There were only two minor background noise issues, but the tape was still clearly audible. Mae had been told to cut off the television in the motel room, if it was on and it was, she forgot. Although the tape was perfectly clear, it also gave us, in the background, approximately one hour of the movie "Hamburger Hill." Also, the bed made a loud screeching noise during the highlight of the sex act but not enough to conceal the intimate back and forth conversation. The noise from the bed was probably because Motel Man was a big man weighing at least 280 pounds. There was a bonus toward the end of their conversation. While writing prescriptions to Mae, Motel Man commented how careful she had to be when filling the prescriptions. He wrote her several for Dilaudid 4 mg and Percodan with various post-dates for filling in the future. On the tape, he could be heard telling Mae to go to various pharmacies a long way from his clinic location and not go to the same pharmacy twice. He told her about the medical board's visit with him and that he had to be careful to tell everyone to really spread out the prescriptions at various pharmacies. Now I knew why I found few prescriptions in the original profile area in my follow-up. Motel Man's conversation established his intent to commit a crime involving the issuing of controlled substance prescriptions outside the course of a legitimate practice. Motel Man was not practicing medicine; he was swapping controlled substance prescriptions for sexual favors.

Mae was good as her word. Over the next two months, she completed two more visits with Motel Man. The two encounters were carbon copies of the first. The recorder worked well with the audio being legible, and she received numerous post-dated prescriptions from Motel Man. Motel Man also kept reminding her about being careful where she got them filled. The case was nearly complete. All that was left was the preparation of the transcripts for presentation to the federal grand jury. I had accepted the responsibility to have all the tapes transcribed for court. Literally every sound recorded on the tapes must be explained. A project of this kind is not complicated, just time-consuming. During the transcribing, radio background must be identified, television conversation must be explained as separate and apart from case conversation, and loud screeching noises from the sex act in the bed must be explained. Investigator Charlie Moses was helping me with one of the tapes. When he came to the bed noises on the tape, he came into my office and asked me how to spell screech, screech, screech, the continuous bed noise. The word screech really does not capture the actual sound. I told Charlie I did not know because I never had to do that before. In between laughs, we did the best we could! We completed the transcription and turned all the tape evidence over to the case agent.

Motel Man was indicted by a federal grand jury. In a deal worked out with prosecutors, he pled guilty to one count of prescribing controlled substances outside the course of legitimate professional practice. He was sentenced to approximately three years imprisonment and specifically banned by the court from ever having a DEA number again. He was also placed on three years of probation. The Mississippi State Board of Medical Licensure revoked his medical license based on the conviction. After being released from prison, Motel Man petitioned the medical board for the return of his medical license. After being tested and determined to be competent to practice medicine with reasonable skill and safety, he was granted a license with conditions that also included a ban on handling-controlled substances and other substances that were similar to controlled substances. Motel Man was divorced by his wife while he was in prison. Once relicensed, he relocated his practice to a different small town in Mississippi and started a new practice.

During the process of obtaining his new license, Motel Man had to visit the offices of the medical board to complete paperwork. During these visits, he and I had the opportunity for short conversations in my office. Motel Man admitted he had made many mistakes that had cost him a lot in money, family, and career respect that he would not wish on his worst enemy. He said one of those mistakes was underestimating me, and to some extent, the board. He then said, "I thought you had given up on my investigation and I was in the clear." I told him that neither I nor my investigators ever gave up on an investigation. We tried to work low-key and to be as invisible as possible, which was how I was trained. During the course of monitoring of Motel Man's new practice, I became more acquainted with him and eventually, we became what I would call friends. At least we became friendly enough for him to have sufficient confidence in me to become an excellent source for information on problem doctors he occasionally ran across. Motel Man never again came to the attention of the medical board from a negative perspective.

Shortly after this case was settled in federal Court, MBML was advised by DEA agents that the Department of Justice had issued a memo advising that in the future, the use of females to perform sexual acts with a doctor to obtain controlled substance prescriptions would no longer be approved. Go figure!

CHAPTER 11

DOCTOR WARDEN and the GAMER

I have always been very interested in the issue of drugs because as much as illegal drugs are prosecuted, if you think of it as a health issue, the real killer [is] prescription drugs, [like] the over-prescribing of opioids. – Pedro Reyes, Mexican artist known for fighting drug problems in Mexico.

The case of Dr. Warden and the Gamer (not their real names) fits perfectly and clearly establishes the purpose and premise of why we label certain drugs "controlled" and seek to limit access. This was not a complicated investigation. It was a fairly short-lived case that plainly demonstrated a primary way that pharmaceutical opioids were inserted into every community, no matter the size and population.

This case was initiated by what was commonly known to diversion investigators, in my day, as the "ARCOS" report.

Diversion investigators are investigators whose primary responsibility is to investigate the diversion of pharmaceutical controlled substances by health care practitioners. They do not investigate drugs like cocaine, meth, marijuana, or heroin. ARCOS is an acronym for Automated Report and Consolidated Order System. In the 1980s and 1990s, this report was instrumental in helping the Mississippi medical board identify large numbers of over-prescribers and impaired physicians. The report compiled controlled substance orders and purchases by individual DEA numbers in each state and could even be broken down by zip code. I am giving away a few trade secrets here. Using this report, we, at the medical board, could identify all the orders and purchases of controlled substances made by every single physician in the state with a DEA number. This included samples given to physicians by drug reps. The Drug Enforcement Administration, at my request, sent me a copy about every six months. It was a very thick (several inches) print out and occasionally it was late being compiled. Sometimes we only got the report annually, but we were happy just to get it because the data was spot on. Every time I reviewed a report, I was able to generate several new cases. The question you may ask is, why did DEA not use the report for identifying problems or targets like the medical board? The explanation is "number of dosage units." DEA established targets based on the number of dosage units diverted and the target had to divert huge quantities to attract any attention from them. For example, to be classified as a DEA class III violator (small-time by their standards), a physician would have to be diverting at least 50,000 dosage units monthly. Class I and II violators for DEA involve much larger numbers. Not so with the individual medical boards. A single impaired physician, even though he or she may divert a large number of controlled substances for themselves, does not approach 50,000 dose units a month. During my entire career with the medical board, we did not have a single investigation that even reached the DEA class three category. DEA looks only at numbers, nothing else. For example, a physician sexually abusing patients may divert some controlled substances but would not qualify as a DEA target. They would prefer the medical board handle the case. I am not suggesting that the New Orleans DEA diversion division that covered Mississippi was not helpful. They were always responsive to us whenever we asked for assistance. There are several cases in this publication where the DEA provided critical assistance on the case. The ARCOS report was just one of many tools they helped us with, and they really did not have to do that. They did so because they were good agents and good people.

The ARCOS report was also helpful in identifying the prescribers. If a pharmacy in a certain town was ordering unusually large quantities of Percodan or any other controlled substance, it was usually because a certain physician was prescribing that amount of the drug. A pharmacist is not going to order a huge amount of a drug and hope he can fill enough prescriptions to use up that inventory. That is not a good business model. He cannot afford to carry a large amount of speculative inventory. The drugs are ordered based on prescriptions written and for no other reason. Once we figured out how to apply the data, it was easy peasy to identify a case rich environment and address the problems quickly.

Most doctors purchase only a few 30 cc vials of Demerol injectable 100 mg/cc for clinic use. Demerol is a Schedule IIN drug for short-term, severe pain management. It is for short-term use because it is highly addictive, abused, and only relieves pain for short periods. A review of one of the ARCOS reports identified Dr. Warden as having purchased approximately fifty 30 cc vials of 100 mg Demerol for his clinic during a previous six-month period. 1,500 or more doses, depending on the amount given, were off the chart in terms of purchases for a small-town clinic operation. A 200-bed hospital might buy that many vials in that period, but not a single physician. I presented the suspicious purchases to the executive officer and was approved to schedule an audit. According to the same ARCOS report, suspicious amounts of Percodan were being purchased by pharmacists in that same zip code area. Percodan is a Schedule IIN controlled substance primarily prescribed for pain management. Before the Demerol audit, I planned to perform pharmacy profiles in the small town to see what, if anything, could be developed concerning the Percodan. I suspected the two drugs might be related. I did not believe in coincidences. What I found in the profile helped me connect the dots.

The small town only had six pharmacies. In each pharmacy, we found large numbers of prescriptions for 100 Percodan each to Gamer. The prescriptions were all written by Dr. Warden and no other physician. Dr. Warden was the same doctor ordering the Demerol. One of the pharmacists told us that Gamer was a "gun-toting" state law enforcement officer assigned to the local area. None of the pharmacists knew any medical justification for the Percodan prescriptions, which was an unusual circumstance by itself. Personally, I think they knew, they just did not want to say and incriminate themselves. The individual pattern in each pharmacy was of interest, but when we put all of the pharmacy profiles together, we had a nightmare of a problem! Still, some of the profiles had date gaps in them. So, we expanded the profiling to two other towns in the area and quickly picked up a pattern that more than filled in the gaps. Once the completed profiles were finished, the profile indicated Gamer was receiving an average of almost 100 Percodan daily from Dr. Warden. Percodan is normally prescribed in small doses of approximately twelve to twenty-four tablets at a time for very short periods. The directions are usually to take one tablet every four to six hours as needed. The profile indicated Gamer was taking almost 100 tablets daily! That amount of oxycodone at 4.9 mg per tablet, not counting the 325 mg of aspirin in each tablet, would be fatal to the average person or drug abuser. Yet, Gamer was getting these prescriptions for months and still somehow functioning as a gun-toting state law enforcement officer. In my opinion, there was no possible way he could be taking them. He clearly had something going on the side. In addition to the audit, the executive officer approved an immediate preparation of a warrant and affidavit to seize Dr. Warden's medical file on Gamer and confront him for an explanation of the Demerol orders and the Percodan prescriptions. The only possible reason for such an outrageous amount of Percodan on an outpatient basis would be a diagnosis of terminal cancer. However, Percodan is not the drug of choice by most physicians for such a diagnosis. I began to suspect, based on the amounts, that the physician and Gamer were in a tit-for-tat arrangement. Both individuals or others probably had an abuse problem and Gamer was bringing a split of the Percodan back to the doctor in return for the injections of Demerol. It was just a theory.

Once all of the paperwork was completed and approved, Investigators Neil Breeland, Mickey Robbins and I traveled to Dr. Warden's clinic to serve the warrant and interview him. Dr. Warden refused to talk to us. He told his nurse to cooperate and provide any information requested or required in the warrant. The medical file provided on Gamer was woefully deficient of any documentation justifying the huge numbers of Percodan. It only contained two pages and most of that was initial personal and insurance data, with nothing in the way of medical exams, diagnosis data, or prescriptions.

The audit documentation was equally deficient. Of the fifty 30 cc Demerol vials ordered by Dr. Warden, during the previous approximately six months, only two and a half vials remained in the clinic and were stored in an unsecure cabinet drawer. The nurse did tell us there was another physician in the clinic with Dr. Warden and he did on occasion use some of the Demerol for patients, but no files, ledgers, records, or inventories were maintained. I point blank asked the nurse why Dr. Warden ordered so much Demerol

(100 mg) since there was no obvious explanation nor reason for its use. She said a patient, Gamer, comes by the clinic several times a day for an injection. Dr. Warden had a verbal standing order to give him the injections. I then asked her if the doctor, himself, has a problem with controlled substances. Did he need some help or treatment? She responded in an almost shocked manner that she did not know of any type of problem. We seized the medical file and audit records, such as they were, along with the remaining Demerol vials. We provided the nurse a copy of the receipt of the items taken and departed the clinic.

Since Dr. Warden would not speak with investigators, we could not ask for a surrender of his DEA certificate. With no other options available, the executive officer decided to call him to a full license revocation hearing.

Gamer was equally difficult and refused to talk with MBML investigators. We contacted the supervisor of internal affairs (IA) for Gamer's employer and advised him of the case. We told him we had attempted to interview Gamer concerning his side of the story, but he refused thus far to talk with us. We also told the agency's IA investigator that we were planning to subpoena Gamer to the hearing but seriously doubted he would appear. The IA supervisor offered very little in the way of cooperation. According to our attorney general assignee, the employer could order Gamer to present to us and cooperate in an official state agency investigation or face additional internal action for insubordination. The supervisor refused to compel Gamer's cooperation. He did ask that we keep him posted on the hearing because he wanted to send an agent to the hearing to hear Gamer's testimony. I told him not to hold his breath on that request.

Investigators Neil Breeland and Mickey Robbins attempted to locate and serve Gamer with the subpoena to the hearing. Considerable surveillance was necessary on his residence, a $300,000 – $400,000 (1980s money) fortress. Because of the nature of his work, he worked out of his home and did not have a formal off-site office location. He was not seen for several days. The residence was protected by a large security gate on a multi-acre plot of land surrounded by a high, well-built steel decorative fencing allowing limited access. Investigators could easily identify approximately eight to ten security cameras and lights around the property. We all concluded that Gamer had assets and a lifestyle well beyond anything close to a state journeyman employee level. He either had vast family wealth or a large income from another source. We felt we knew where his money was really coming from. Investigators were finally able to make personal contact off the property with Gamer and served him the subpoena. Gamer still refused to comment or be interviewed.

On the hearing date, approximately two hours before the hearing, Gamer, escorted by a female officer from the same agency, came to the medical board offices. The female officer indicated Gamer was willing to talk to investigators concerning the prescriptions. When interviewed he was vague, uncooperative, and, in my opinion, untruthful. He said that he got all of the prescriptions from Dr. Warden and took them mostly for headaches. I asked him to explain how he took 100 Percodan tablets a day for headaches. He said he did not take all of them. A lot were "stole" out of his truck and many were eaten by his dog. I asked him if his dog was still alive. He said it was. I said that was unlikely if he ate anything close to 100 Percodan. I also asked him if he ever heard of locking the doors to his truck. He said "they" always broke in. I asked him if he ever reported the break-ins to the local sheriff or police. He said he did not because it would be too much trouble. I asked him if his state agency that owns the truck did all of the repairs on the break-ins. He said he paid for some of the repairs and the agency paid for some of them. I then asked him about the four to five Demerol injections he had been receiving from Dr. Warden daily for the past six months to one year. He said he only got those when the pills did not work. I commented, "100 Percodan every day, plus four to five Demerol injections daily and you can still function and drive a state vehicle!" I told him I thought he was a liar and completely untrustworthy as a law enforcement officer and a disgrace to his uniform. I told him that I had heard enough, and I hoped and prayed for one thing. I looked straight into his eyes when he would look at me and I said, "I hope you go into that hearing room and tell that board exactly what you have told us. Promise me you are going to do that. If you don't tell them, I am. You will put a noose around Dr. Warden's neck so tight he will scream about your role in this situation." Gamer got up and immediately left the interview and walked out of the board's offices never to return. The female officer stayed for the hearing.

Investigators gave testimony during the hearing in which they presented the facts of the case. The board attorney had admitted into evidence all of the pharmacy profiles, Demerol orders by Dr. Warden, Gamers' so-called medical file, the lack of accountability records on the Demerol, and Gamers' comments just before the hearing. The attorney for Dr. Warden presented very little in the way of a defense or cross-examination. Dr. Warden took the stand and denied knowing he was responsible for documenting every prescription he wrote and felt they were all justified in his opinion. He testified he had no knowledge of any requirements to keep records on the Demerol. He denied he had a personal problem and asserted that all of the medication was for Gamer. The board questioned Dr. Warden at length about his treatment of the patient and why he did not have him evaluated for chemical dependency or just plain cut him off as a substance abuser. It was about this time when Dr. Warden had had enough. He then told the board that he was the doctor and nobody should be telling him how to treat his patients – or words to that effect, anyway. That was a very wrong comment!

After closing statements, the board went into executive session for deliberations. After approximately twenty minutes of deliberations, the board returned a guilty verdict. Dr. Warden had his license "permanently" revoked by the board. The board used the term permanent in its verbal sentence but by state law, it was not enforceable. State law provided that Dr. Warden could apply for reinstatement of a revoked license after one year. It did not mean the doctor would get his license back, but he could petition. He could also appeal the decision of the board. He did neither. To my knowledge, he sold what was left of his practice to his partner and never returned to the practice of medicine.

The female officer reported the hearing events and the interview to her superiors. I was informed that Gamer was given the choice of resigning, retiring, or being fired. He chose to retire.

This case resulted in an ugly political backlash. After Dr. Warden was charged by the board, the executive officer and I were summoned to the state capital for a meeting. In the meeting we had a state senator and two-house members. One of them, a very high-ranking house member, basically threaten to disband the medical board or cut the agency budget if we did not stop our investigation of the doctor. I told the "gentlemen" that the last thing any state agency wanted was problems with the legislature. However, we were going to continue with the case and present it to the full board because the number of controlled substances that had been diverted by the doctor was way too large to disregard. I then pulled out my pocket tape recorder and just held it in my hand. Everyone could see it was running. One of the "gentlemen" then commented that if drugs were involved, then by all means the case needed to go forward. They all seemed to agree, and the meeting broke up. I found out once I returned to my office that unfortunately, there was not a microcassette in the tape player! To my knowledge, that executive officer never got another call from the legislature about one of our cases during the remainder of his tenure. Unfortunately, we also observed that over the next two legislative sessions, while the very high-ranking member of the House remained in his position, no legislation on behalf of the medical board ever made it out of committee for a vote. Payback can be hell!

To return to my opening comments about the diversion of controlled substances, it should be noted that this case was a classic example of the prescribing and administering of controlled substances gone haywire. Just substitute the drug OxyContin for the drugs Demerol or Percodan and you have the same scenario, only it is 2020. The doctor in this case lost touch with his practice, control of his patient and considered himself to be not accountable and untouchable. The patient was controlling the doctor and controlled substances were flooding that small town. Controlled substance epidemics are created and perpetuated by the failure of medical boards to not properly police the unscrupulous over-prescribers. No other single factor causes the diversion of controlled substances more.

CHAPTER 12

DR. ADAMS and EVE

Anything is easy to the man who sees [what is going on]. The open eye of the open mind – that has more to do with real detective work than all of the deduction and induction and analysis ever devised. – Samuel Hopkins Adams, American investigative journalist and author.

The complaint came to my home on an unusual day, a Saturday morning, from the police department of a suburb of Jackson, MS. Specifically, the call was from the captain of the narcotics division of the police department. He provided me some details and requested assistance because the primary perpetrator was a medical doctor, Dr. Adams (not his real name). He said the police had received a call about a residential break-in in progress. The captain told me that once the police had arrived the owner of the house told them that Dr. Adams had attempted to break into her house to retrieve what she said was drugs that he used in his practice, many of which were later identified as controlled substances. The officers then called the captain of the narcotics division because it involved controlled substances and he called me because it involved a doctor. So, what does the medical board have to do with a doctor committing a "B and E" (police jargon for breaking and entering)? That's a local police issue. I was asking myself that same question until I heard about the controlled drugs, amounts, and some of the circumstances. I quickly became very interested!

The scene of the crime was a nice, upscale, residence with a beautiful view of a large lake and an estimated property value of approximately $400,000 (in 1990s dollars). The doctor was being detained at the scene until a basic understanding of the facts could be made. The captain and I decided to first interview the homeowner concerning her complaint and to find out how the controlled drugs, including injectable Demerol, Valium, Xanax, hydrocodone, and Tylenol with codeine came to be in her residence. I will call the female "Eve." A strikingly beautiful, twenty-five-year-old woman. She said she had been in a long-term relationship with the doctor, but they were not married. They had been living together in the house for over two years and had planned to marry at one time. During their relationship, Dr. Adams began treating Eve for various medical complaints. He stored the drugs at the residence because his primary practice location was approximately seventy-five miles away. When he traveled to his work, the nature of the practice required him to remain at a hospital for up to a week at a time. Eve stated that almost a year earlier he had put the house in her name. She produced the warranty deed and title confirming her ownership of the house with no liens on the property. Recently, Dr. Adams had become difficult to live with or be around. He was making demands on her and acting out of control. She had consulted an attorney and, per his advice, told Dr. Adams she wanted him to leave. Once he left for his work, just a few days earlier, she had all the locks changed to keep him away from her and out of the house.

That morning, Dr. Adams had finished his shift at his practice and had come to the residence trying to get in. When he realized the locks had been changed, he began to bang on the door, shout at her, and threaten her. He then broke the glass to the front door and was trying to enter when she called the police. I asked her to show me where the drugs were being stored. She led me to a closet in the master bedroom where she slept and to a closet in a guest bedroom. I collected all the controlled drugs I could find and carried them to a large dining room table to inventory. Eve then went with one of the officers and waited outside the house until we interviewed Dr. Adams.

The narcotics detective and I invited Dr. Adams into the house, and we all sat down around the dining room table on which I had put the controlled drugs. I introduced myself to Dr. Adams and showed him my credentials as chief investigator for the Mississippi State Board of Medical Licensure. The detective introduced himself to Dr. Adams and advised him he was not under arrest, but he was going to mirandize him anyway just to be legally safe and to be certain Dr. Adams understood his rights. Once the Miranda warnings had been read, Dr. Adams signed a waiver and agreed to answer questions for investigators. I also advised Dr. Adams that he was not under any obligation to speak with us, but I considered it important that he be interviewed so the medical board could clearly understand what had transpired. Dr. Adams agreed again to be interviewed. He told basically the same facts and circumstances as Eve had said earlier. He had originally bought the house before he met Eve. They had been living in the house together for over two years and had planned to marry. He had, at her insistence, transferred the house into her name to convince her he was serious about marrying her. The transfer was accomplished approximately eight or nine months previously. Dr. Adams admitted he had been treating Eve as a patient due to various common illnesses and at times chronic pain due to female issues. He did not consider any of them serious enough to refer her for specialty care or evaluation. He acknowledged he gave her injections of Demerol for pain along with Valium and Xanax pills for anxiety. He also said he provided her with hydrocodone or Tylenol #3 for pain. He ordered the drugs using his personal DEA number and stored them at the house for ease of access. He explained his primary practice location was in a hospital approximately seventy-five miles away. He worked a weekly schedule (on a week, off a week) at the hospital. He was not aware of a problem in their relationship until he got to the house this morning and could not get in. He admitted he had become concerned and then angry and had tried to force entry into the house. I then asked him if he had access to his personal DEA certificate issued to him by DEA. He showed me a copy. The copy indicated his DEA registered location address was at his place of employment and not the residence in which the drugs had been stored. The only place a Doctor can legally store controlled substances is at their DEA registered practice location which is usually their primary practice location. Doctors are allowed some small leeway to carry an emergency bag with very small amounts of controlled substances. This allowance was a carry-over from when doctors made house calls. The true emergency bag has gone the way of the Edsel. Dr. Adams again insisted that he stored the drugs at the house only for convenience. I told Dr. Adams that we potentially had some real problems. I advised him he might want to consult an attorney before we proceeded. He said he had not intentionally done anything wrong and did not feel he needed legal counsel. I continued by reminding him that both he and Eve had acknowledged that he was treating her as his patient and that they were not married. Dr. Adams acknowledged that was correct. I advised him he could tell me to stop whenever he felt the questioning had gone far enough. He was asked to produce the complete patient file on Eve indicating his examinations, diagnosis, and treatments. He paused, then quietly responded that there was no file maintained on her. I requested ledgers or other inventory records documenting the purchasing, administering, or dispensing of the controlled substances he had acquired for Eve's treatment. Again, he paused, then he said he had not maintained any records. I asked Dr. Adams if he was aware that by regulation, he could only store controlled substances at the registered location on his DEA certificate. He said he was not aware of that. Finally, I told him the last issue was that of his engaging in sexual relations with a patient. He said he had not even considered that a problem because of their relationship. I then inventoried the controlled substances. Altogether, the amounts came to several thousand dosage units. I explained to Dr. Adams that I was seizing the controlled substances based on them being stored at an unregistered location, in an unsecured manner, with no accountability provided for their use. I completed the inventory and made out a receipt for Dr. Adams with a copy for the police department file. I told him I would be making a full report to the executive officer of the board the following Monday. If he or his attorney had any questions, they should call the executive officer or the board attorney.

Eve traveled to the local police headquarters to file charges against Dr. Adams for breaking and entering. She was met there by her attorney who reached an agreement with Dr. Adams and the police. In return for him gathering his belongings and departing the residence, never to return, she would not file any formal charges. He agreed to do so. It turns out most of the furniture was included along with the house. Eve had cleaned him out!

After the executive officer and board attorney reviewed all the data from the Saturday encounter, they authorized a full investigation for charges against Dr. Adams. I identified the primary suppliers for the controlled substances and obtained updated amounts. The orders identified much larger quantities of controlled substances that Dr. Adams could not account for.

The executive officer authorized a visit to Dr. Adams to discuss a voluntary surrender of his DEA certificate. Other restrictions on his medical license would include an evaluation for chemical dependency with treatment if recommended, submitting to random, unannounced, and witnessed drug testing, and assuring compliance with any and all other regulations dealing with the maintenance of patient files and record-keeping for controlled substances.

A meeting was arranged with Dr. Adams at the offices of his attorney. Since he wanted to meet with his attorney present, the executive officer authorized the board's attorney, Stan Ingram, to accompany me to the meeting. The meeting deteriorated into somewhat of an adversarial event. Dr. Adams and his attorney decided to go to a full hearing before the board. Stan prepared the summons and affidavit that identified the specific charges against Dr. Adams including unprofessional conduct likely to deceive, defraud, or harm the public by ordering and storing controlled substances unsecured at an unregistered location, failing to maintain proper records and accountability of the controlled substances, having sexual relations with a current patient, and, finally, failing to maintain a file on a patient being treated with controlled substances.

In preparation for the hearing, the board attorney wanted to interview Eve and get an idea of her testimony. I strongly urged against using her as a witness for the prosecution. I told Stan Ingram that she was nothing but an extremely beautiful but evil con artist and drug abuser that had completely conned Dr. Adams out of his house and was the cause of the lapse in good judgment in his professional life. Dr. Adams had been completely blind to what was happening to him due to the siren call of Eve. Stan said he did not understand my reluctance. I painted him a clearer picture. I told him in no uncertain terms that this absolute knockout of a woman had screwed Dr. Adams, literally and figuratively, out of his life. I must admit to using language that was a little cruder, and which is not necessary here. Any man could and probably would fall for her scheme, especially one like Dr. Adams, who was single, much older than she, with plenty of money, and in need of an ego boost. I told Stan that she was so beautiful but absolutely evil that if the board saw and heard her in the hearing room, they would feel sorry for Dr. Adams and vote not guilty. I even felt sorry for him and I knew he was guilty. I could read her, and I knew she had played him, and he fell for it. Stan took my advice and decided not to use her in the hearing.

I testified to all the events of that Saturday and the follow-up investigation. I described the large amounts of controlled substances that Dr. Adams had ordered, the amounts in the inventory and the even larger amounts missing for which no records or patient file existed. I described the unsecured storage of the drugs in the residence, how Dr. Adams was gone five days a week at work, leaving the patient with unfettered access to the drugs, and emphasized that a large amount of the controlled substances that were purchased were missing. Finally, all the information of the doctor/patient relationship was described, including the living arrangements and sexual relations of the two over the past two-plus years when Dr. Adams admitted he had been treating her.

During my cross-examination, something happened that was an all to common occurrence and was always in the favor of the prosecution's case. Although we felt we had a very strong case to present to the full board, the defense attorney representing Dr. Adams made the case that much easier. The defense attorney, in an attempt to defend his client, would shout questions to me, interrupt my answers to his shouted questions with inappropriate comments and make accusations of unlawful or corrupt allegations about myself and the investigation, or about the local police. He would ignore objections by the prosecutor and rulings by the board and just continue his inappropriate behavior. The attorney made the board so angry, the client had to be in real trouble. This was not an isolated event. Many of the attorneys appearing before the board just did not get it. They would present their defense in such an obnoxious manner and show such disrespect for the board or its staff, the outcome was almost predictable. From my perspective, it happened much too frequently but, was fun to watch. It was difficult to imagine the attorneys did not realize they were not helping their clients.

Dr. Adams' testimony did not dispute or refute any of the previous testimony. His main defense was one of ignorance of the laws and regulations governing the handling of controlled substances and his lack of good judgment in the handling and management of Eve as a patient.

At the conclusion of the hearing, the board unanimously found Dr. Adams guilty on all twelve counts in the summons and affidavit. Dr. Adams' license was suspended for one year with all but three months suspended. He was required to surrender all but Schedule V of his DEA certificate, undergo evaluation for chemical dependency, and submit to random, unannounced, and witnessed blood and urine testing for three years. Dr. Adams immediately completed the required evaluation for chemical dependency and was not found to be dependent.

After one year, Dr. Adams petitioned the board for the return of all privileges, lifting of all restrictions, and full restoration of his DEA privileges. After a hearing, in which it was determined Dr. Adams followed all requirements of the board, the board authorized only a partial lifting of his DEA certificate. Once again, the attorney chimed in way too many times and in a tone that clearly was reminiscent of the original hearing. Thus, all other restrictions and requirements remained in place! The board allowed Dr. Adams to have only Schedule IV of his DEA certificate back with the stipulation he could return in one year to petition for the further lifting of restrictions on Schedule II and III. Dr. Adams appealed the decision to Chancery Court in Hinds County. The appeal to Chancery Court by state law is based on the record only, no hearing is required. The Chancellor, Patricia Wise, ruled in favor of the board.

Dr. Adams was monitored for the required period with no problems in his practice. He eventually regained full unrestricted practice privileges. All blood and urine samples were clean.

No formal follow-up was done on Eve. However, approximately two years later I received information from an MBN friend of mine in one of Mississippi's larger cities that Eve had pulled the same scheme on a local, single, older, multi-millionaire businessman living in that town and got his house, the furniture, a new car, the whole kit and kaboodle! Eve was obviously good at what she did and none of her targets could see her coming.

CHAPTER 13

PERFORMANCE BY PAPAVERINE

Overprescribing of opioids is not limited to just a few bad apples. – Stanford Medicine, December 14, 2015.

Part of what makes an investigator's job interesting is the myriad twists and turns an investigation can take. In this case, the initial telephone call came from the mother of twin girls who had a definite sense of urgency in her voice. After introductions, she told me her twin girls (over the age of eighteen) had just been released from a treatment center after having successfully completed the chemical dependency program. They were continuing to maintain their sobriety, at least for the moment. The girls were willing to cooperate and talk to investigators about a doctor (I'll call him "Dr. Shotz") who was supplying them with drugs. She was anxious to meet soon because she did not know how long the twins' mood to talk would last. In other words, she could not say how long they would be sober. She said their sobriety, in the past, had not been maintained for very long. The twins' primary drug of choice was marijuana along with Percodan and Dilaudid. Percodan (oxycodone and aspirin) and Dilaudid (hydromorphone HCL) are Schedule IIN controlled substances primarily used for moderate to severe pain management. They were obtained usually by prescription from a physician. The Percodan is taken orally and Dilaudid is usually cooked down and injected when taken on the street. These drugs were in Schedule IIN because they are classified as narcotics with a high potential for abuse and addiction. Marijuana was in Schedule I because, at the time, it had no generally accepted medical use.

A meeting was arranged for the following day in a conference room at the mother's business. Upon arrival, I met with the mother and identified myself to her. Whenever an MBML investigator interviews female patients or witnesses, an effort is made to have a female employee from the board present. Hopefully, this accommodation helps the witness build a rapport with the investigator and protects the investigator from accusations of untoward activity. Since the interview was taking place over 100 miles from the MBML offices, a female employee was not able to be present. MBML did not employ any female investigators at the time and all efforts to hire any had resulted in zero applications.

I invited the mother to join the interviews if her daughters did not object. One twin did object emphatically, stating she would rather her mother not be in the room. The other twin did not object. This early in the investigation, I had no idea what was coming!

The first interview was with the mother present. At first, Twin 1 was open and forthcoming without much prompting. Sometimes, even with an individual cooperating in the interview, obtaining information is like pulling teeth. Investigators frequently must be very patient with some witnesses in order to give them time to develop confidence in what they are doing and in whom they are confiding. Sometimes it takes months before this bridge is crossed. Investigators do not rush an interviewee, accommodations are made for breaks, and in this case, we even provided the twins with a chance to talk privately with their mother if they thought that would help.

Twin 1 told the following story with a little bit of anger. She indicated she and her sister had been serious drug users since they were sixteen years old. They started by smoking marijuana at first but quickly moved up to pharmaceutical drugs. Unfortunately, this graduation to more serious drugs was a theme I had heard many times before in my career. The crowd of girls and boys they ran with were all drug users and were always looking for reliable sources. Twin 1 identified three other females as involved with her and her sister. She refused to identify any of the other abusers especially the males in the group. She said she did not feel right talking about the boys but did not have any problem talking about the girls. The girls were doing exactly what she had done to get the drugs they all used. In an effort to reassure Twin 1, I told her the names of the boys were not necessary. I was here to talk about the doctor.

After a short time gathering courage, Twin 1 slowly proceeded to tell how she and Twin 2, along with the three other girls, began to go to Dr. Shotz for prescriptions. Dr. Shotz was originally picked to visit just as a part of their overall drug-seeking efforts. Twin 1 admitted to going to a lot of doctors in the area. The visits began slowly with the five girls taking turns seeing a doctor at his clinic for prescriptions that were split with each other after filling. As the visits became more frequent, most doctors cut them off because they knew what they were doing. It was different with Dr. Shotz. As he became more and more comfortable with the girls, he began to make suggestions about having sex with them. Twin 1 said they all realized that the doctor knew they were just seeing him for the drugs because he had never really performed a real exam. He just would have them disrobe. Dr. Shotz seemed to enjoy seeing the Twins together at the clinic. At one visit he informed them that future visits would have to be off-site away from the clinic. His staff knew the girls were just seeking drugs and were getting suspicious, insisting he cut them off. Dr. Shotz told the twins to tell the other three girls that all five would have to see him at his farm on certain days. He said it would be easier if they all came at the same time.

When the visits at the farm took place, Dr. Shotz would take the girls to his barn behind his house. This barn was not your typical old rundown rattletrap Mississippi farm barn. Twin 1 described it as a well-built structure with an office with heating, cooling, and lights. He always brought a medical bag that contained injectable drugs, Valium, and Xanax in pill form. Valium (diazepam) and Xanax (alprazolam) are Schedule IV controlled substances with significant potential for abuse. They are prescribed mainly for anxiety. Both drugs are in the benzodiazepine class of drugs.

At the barn, Doctor Shotz would have the girls disrobe all at once and then give them injections of Dilaudid along with pills of Valium or Xanax, whichever they preferred. The girls knew that Dr. Shotz was an older man, but they did not know how old and were not familiar with the term erectile dysfunction (ED). It did not take long for them to become educated. Once all the girls were high on the drugs Dr. Shotz would disrobe. He then would take a syringe out of his bag and, with the girls watching, give himself several injections in his penis (about three, as best as Twin 1 could remember). Shortly thereafter, he would achieve an erection that would persist long enough for him to sometimes have sex with all five girls. Twin 1 was not certain of the drug injected but said she was fairly sure it started with the letter "p." Investigators determined that the drug used was probably papaverine. Papaverine is used in some surgical procedures as a vasodilator, and when injected into the base of a penis, causes blood vessel dilation. It is not a controlled substance and comes in injectable, pill, or gel form. This was one of the pre-Viagra meds that worked but had to be injected for maximum effect – not a popular option for most men. The pill and gel form was slow-acting and had considerable undesirable side effects, and thus they were not commonly used either. The visits with Dr. Shotz occurred approximately two to three times a month. At the end of the visits, Dr. Shotz would then issue them prescriptions for the drugs they wanted. He always told them to be careful where they were filled. Twin 1 indicated the prescriptions were filled in multiple pharmacies spread out over several counties to avoid suspicion. The encounters continued with the doctor for over a year until the twins went into treatment. Twin 1 was not certain if the relationship with Dr. Shotz was currently going on with the other three girls, but doubted it because she was certain Dr. Shotz knew the twins had entered treatment. He had probably cut off relations with the other three girls. During treatment, patients usually talk a little about where they get their drugs but never reveal all their sources. Treatment centers hear about most of the physicians that are easy marks. Sometimes the information comes from the patient, sometimes from the patient's family. Many treatment centers' staff worked confidentially with the medical board to help the board identify and investigate these irresponsible prescribers. However, not all treatment centers would help, maybe because the more people on drugs, the more treatment was needed, and the more money they made.

I then interviewed Twin 2 without the mother present. The two versions of events were remarkably similar. Maybe the twins colluded, maybe they did not. Twin 2 said she did not mind talking to us even though she knew her mother knew what they did, she was just uncomfortable with her mother present, which was not hard to understand.

I then met with the twins and their mother together and briefly explained the legal/administrative process to address the ability of the doctor to continue to practice medicine. This process included the possibility of a public hearing if the doctor was not willing to cooperate. Both girls said they would be willing to testify if a hearing was necessary.

Upon return to the board offices, I briefed the executive officer and board attorney of the interview details. I was authorized to continue the investigation with profiles of the area pharmacies for prescription patterns on the five females. A pharmacy profile of approximately forty pharmacies in the area documented a pattern of suspicious prescriptions by Dr. Shotz to the five girls and many others not previously identified.

Based on the results, the executive officer and board attorney authorized the service of an administrative inspection and search warrant to seize patient files for possible board action. After going before a circuit judge and getting the warrant signed, I served Dr. Shotz at his regular clinic location during normal business hours. The doctor and staff provided the patient files listed in the warrant. The analysis of the files found almost no indication of real medical exams, diagnosis, or proper treatment. Some files had complaints of menstrual or migraine pain but few if any of the prescriptions issued were entered into the records. No follow-up or referrals for specialty evaluation or consults regarding the frequent pain issues were found.

Before serving the warrant, the executive officer told me that if the patient files were as inadequate as expected, I had the authorization to seek a voluntary surrender of his medical license. The alternative would be to face a full board hearing. When advised of his options, Dr. Shotz said he would not surrender his license and refused to talk any further. I told him that I was aware of his on-going sexual relations with female patients for prescriptions. Dr. Shotz said he had nothing to say. I then collected all the patient files authorized to be seized by the warrant, prepared an inventory of items taken from Dr. Shotz's records, and departed the clinic.

A full report of the interview at Dr. Shotz's clinic was provided to the executive officer and board attorney. Preparation began for a summons and affidavit to be served requiring Dr. Shotz to appear before the board for a full licensure revocation hearing. Before I had an opportunity to serve the summons, the board's attorney was advised by an attorney for Dr. Shotz that he would surrender his medical license. In Mississippi, physicians who have surrendered their license may reapply for reinstatement of their license after as little as one year. Dr. Shotz never attempted to obtain reinstatement while I was employed at the medical board and to my knowledge never returned to the practice of medicine.

Approximately one year after this case ended, I was told by an MBN agent that the twins were again using and up to their old tricks. I attempted to contact their mother to let her know we would again work on any doctor supplying the twins, but she did not take or return my calls. I guess she finally just gave up.

CHAPTER 14

DOCTOR SOP[4] and the INFORMANT

Doubt, indulged and cherished, is in danger of becoming denial; but if honest and bent on thorough investigation, it may soon lead to full establishment of the truth. – Ambrose G. Bierce, 19th-century journalist and author.

Cases involving sexual abuse are a challenge to win due to one primary issue: credibility. How does an investigator make a patient (victim) who alleges to have been sexually abused by their doctor credible in a hearing before nine other doctors? Even under ideal conditions with strong evidence, this is a difficult proposition. Why? One answer is that there are so many gold-digging "victims" who look for an opportunity to abuse the system, especially targeting a doctor. The other answer lies in the legal system, where

[4] *Sop – noun – A conciliatory or propitiatory bribe, gift, or gesture.

a few corrupt lawyers will knowingly file frivolous lawsuits to try and gain a quick out of court settlement. They know they have very little chance of winning on the merits, but they file anyway.

One must also consider that many of the nine doctors on the Mississippi State Board of Medical Licensure have faced this legal situation personally or know a colleague who has. Because of the unscrupulous actions by a few, any fair-minded sane person could, unfortunately, be skeptical when dealing with people claiming victim status.

One patient testifying against a very successful physician is a David vs Goliath situation and, if the patient cannot be made absolutely credible and the evidence does not support guilt beyond a reasonable doubt, they do not stand much of a chance. Now take the simple word "informant." This word conjures up the same uncomfortable feelings in most people like crude language or the word "Gestapo." It goes without saying that informants usually do not hold a high degree of esteem in the investigative field, usually somewhere below fungus level, even by those who depend on their information. Informants are generally just not believable without considerable evidence to support them.

So, how does a medical board investigator make an informant credible in a complaint when the informant claims to have been sexually abused by a well- known, respected physician with considerable influence? It is in these situations that I am reminded of a conversation with my previous boss who, when he hired me at the Mississippi Bureau of Narcotics, told me, "Boy, you can make more money selling shoes than being a narcotics agent and have a lot less stress." I should have listened because I learned later in life that he was right!

This case started when I was contacted by a friend of mine who was an agent with the Mississippi Bureau of Narcotics (I'll call him "Will"). Will said he had an informant (I'll call him "Archie") who had allegedly been sexually abused by a doctor (I'll call him "Dr.

Sop*") while he had been a patient under Dr. Sop's care at a local hospital. I asked Will about Archie's reliability. Will said he was a coded and paid informant and had always been reliable. Being a coded informant simply means the informant has proven himself with his ability to penetrate criminal operations in the state and is assigned a code to protect his identity. All communication references and payments to Archie were done by using the assigned code (never his real name) to avoid identification. However, not all the news was good. Will then told me there was a "tiny" complication. Archie had been arrested and was currently residing in county jail. As best he could determine, the charges stemmed from a check forgery charge. I commented to Will how he was just making the situation easier and easier! Will emphasized to me that despite the hardships presented he had used the informant numerous times and never found him to be deceptive. In other words, he thought the informant was truthful and the abuse really took place.

When asked about the specifics of the sexual abuse, Will related the following facts and circumstances. Archie went into the hospital for what Will thought was to have his appendix removed, but he was not absolutely certain. The day after the procedure, Dr. Sop came by to check on him. While checking the surgical wound, Dr. Sop suddenly began to perform oral sex on him. To say the least, Archie became very upset and shocked. Caught by total surprise, he desperately tried to separate from Dr. Sop. However, he could not effectively move much to escape the situation due to the pain from the surgery. When he finally persuaded Dr. Sop to stop, the doctor evidently came to his senses and realized he had made a mistake and began to apologize. He repeatedly asked Archie not to report him to anyone. Will acknowledged the bizarre nature of the information but again emphasized the reliability of the informant.

I told Will that I would document the information in the form of a complaint but that he should not be surprised if the executive officer denied assigning it for investigation. I also told him that if the complaint went forward for investigation, I seriously doubted MBML would approve any payment to Archie. Will said if the case had a successful conclusion, he could probably pay him something through MBN.

The complaint information with all identifying data was presented to the executive officer and Stan Ingram, the board's attorney, for consideration. Surprisingly, they both authorized, without much fanfare, pursuing the investigation as far as possible.

I contacted Will and advised him of the approval to pursue a formal investigation. Will was requested to introduce the MBML investigators to Archie. This would help MBML investigators' credibility with Archie and, hopefully, he would speak freely with us about the case. The following day, Investigator Neil Breeland and I traveled to the county lock-up where Archie was being held and, along with Will, interviewed him on the details of his complaint. All the information relayed to us by Will was repeated by Archie. Archie said there had been minimal contact previously between him and the doctor and, most importantly, there had never been any previous sexual contact with the doctor, ever! Dr. Sop had been the primary family doctor for his family members. Archie agreed to work with investigators and provide any and all information that might be needed to complete the investigation. In order to be tranparent, fair, and open with Archie, we told him that it would be highly unlikely that the medical board would authorize any payment for his assistance in the investigation. Will told Archie that MBN might be able to help in that area.

Investigator Breeland contacted the police department holding the charge against Archie and requested their permission to use him in an undercover capacity under close supervision in the investigation of a doctor. The police department agreed to allow Archie to work with the medical board on the case.

A very important point, one that can be an elephant in the room, but cannot be discussed by MBML investigators with any witness or victim, is the possibility of a civil suit resulting from a successful investigation. However, Archie was told with a successful investigation, MBML investigators would be able to testify on his behalf in his current check forgery problems. Archie expressed his appreciation for any help he could get and agreed to begin work with MBML on the case as soon as he could get out of jail. Fortunately, the possibility of a civil suit did not come up during the interview. Archie was told to contact me as soon as he was released from jail and not to talk with anyone, not even his family, about the case. Contact with Dr. Sop was to be avoided until he was out of jail and under the supervision of MBML investigators. He was also told that his family could keep Dr. Sop for their family physician if they still wanted to. That might be best so that Dr. Sop would not be concerned or suspicious about a possible problem.

Now, back to the important issue of credibility. How could we make Archie credible in his testimony in the event of a full board hearing? We had one witness with a questionable background residing in jail testifying against a highly respected physician. I would rather try to refloat the Titanic!

The following week Archie contacted me and said he had made bail and was finally able to go to work with the medical board. While waiting for Archie to be released from jail, we had been formulating a plan that we hoped would establish his credibility and prove the allegation of sexual abuse. Archie's testimony about a physician before nine board members who were also physicians had to be clear, strong, and completely true, leaving no room for doubt. At the time, we thought the plan was a good one. The way it played out shocked and surprised all of us!

As planned, we had Archie place a secure landline telephone call to Dr. Sop. Investigator Neil Breeland set up the equipment to place the call and record the conversation. The equipment was tested several times. The conversation between Dr. Sop and Archie discussing the oral sex at the hospital would be critical to the case. The landline call would not ID the caller or the origin of the call. There are always variables that are beyond the control of investigators in working any case. The most important variable here was simply whether Archie could contact Dr. Sop at his clinic on a busy workday or, for that matter, if Dr. Sop would talk with him at all. He was instructed to tell the receptionist that he was returning a phone call from Dr. Sop. Surprisingly, luck was with us and Dr. Sop took the call. A summary of the conversation follows.

Archie told Dr. Sop who he was, to which the Doctor replied he hoped he had recovered well from the surgery. Archie said he thought he had but was concerned and upset about him performing oral sex on him in the hospital and wanted to talk about it. Dr. Sop apologized again for the incident and requested to meet in person with Archie to settle the matter. After a brief back and forth about where to meet, a meeting was agreed to in a parking lot behind a popular local restaurant at two o'clock the following afternoon. Archie gave the doctor a brief description of his vehicle. The ease of setting up the meet was a second unexpected break. It was right about this time when we began to be concerned about how Dr. Sop planned to "settle" the matter.

Time was short, so investigators immediately had to get to work setting up video and audio recording equipment in the informant's car and for remote use. It had to be tested and retested for operational integrity. One rule an investigator learns early in their career about recording equipment, whether it is audio or video is, "what *can* go wrong *will* go wrong." That meant replacing and testing batteries, power sources, angles, and mounts to be certain that all the equipment was fail-safe and impossible to detect.

Investigator Breeland was setting up almost all of the equipment used in the surveillance. MBN agents who were assisting us provided him with a miniature tape recorder far superior to anything we had at MBML. It would work perfectly inside Archie's car and was easy to conceal. Investigator Breeland visited the meeting site to determine the best location for Archie to park to obtain the best possible remote video surveillance and audio reception. As backup, Archie would be wearing the standard code-10 transmitter, which he had worn many times before, to send the conversation to receivers used by the investigators to monitor and record the conversation between Archie and the doctor in real-time. The restaurant location turned out to be a perfect site. There was plenty of parking within a direct line of sight from several remote locations. The surveillance vehicles would be hard to detect even by experienced countersurveillance agents. The time was also perfect because most patrons at the restaurant would be long gone.

Archie was instructed to arrive at the meet location forty-five minutes to an hour early to be certain of getting the parking spot investigators had selected and to have time to wire up. Archie was instructed to back his car into the parking slot for the remote surveillance cameras to have a direct, unobstructed view into the front seat. We also told him to make sure that the doctor got into Archie's car when he arrived, and to cut off the engine, car radio, and air conditioning. We knew we were preaching to the choir – Archie had done operations like this more times than we had – but we did not want any background noise to distort the audio recordings. During the set-up, other investigators were conducting countersurveillance of the area to determine if the doctor had anyone watching Archie. None were detected. It was always possible that the way the doctor intended to "settle" the matter was to have Archie killed, but we did not verbalize that to Archie.

Desperate people, including doctors, do desperate things. Once everything was in place, we waited.

It is common in meetings of this type for someone to get cold feet and not show up. It is also a real possibility that a doctor might have a medical emergency and be unable to meet, even if he wants to. Thankfully, none of that occurred. Dr. Sop was spotted by surveillance driving his gray Tahoe into the restaurant parking lot at almost two o'clock. He was alone. He drove around to the back area, parked by Archie's car, and was waved over by Archie. Dr. Sop got out of his vehicle and into Archie's on the passenger front side. Luck was still with us! After the usual exchange of greetings, Dr. Sop again expressed his apologies about what happened at the hospital. He expressed hope that Archie would not be discussing the incident with anyone, ever! Dr. Sop made a comment about being attracted to the informant and had simply made a mistake when he saw him in the hospital bed. Then, the biggest shock of all occurred when out of the blue, Dr. Sop offered Archie $1,000 if he would agree not to discuss the incident with anyone. Another major surprise occurred when Dr. Sop said, as a condition of payment, he wanted Archie to sign a contract that he had written agreeing never to discuss the incident with anyone. All of this was totally unexpected and unplanned. Fortunately, Archie, thinking fast and clear, told Dr. Sop he was not signing anything and that "we do not want anything in writing that this ever happened." Archie took the contract out of Dr. Sop's hand and read it, unfortunately, not aloud. He then went through the motions of ripping it up, only tearing it into a few pieces, and put it in his coat pocket. He knew that if he gave it back to Dr. Sop, MBML would lose the evidence and that we could always reassemble it after the fact. Experience is always a helpful tool. Dr. Sop insisted Archie take the money as a show of good faith and with the understanding nothing was ever to be said about what had happened. Archie verbally agreed to take the money and to total silence. All of the investigators breathed a collective sigh of relief since we were more concerned about the doctor wanting to have Archie killed to keep him silent.

Dr. Sop counted out ten $100 bills, gave them to Archie and thanked him for his understanding as they shook hands. Dr. Sop then got out of Archie's car, got into his SUV, and departed the parking lot. Investigators followed the doctor until he was well away from the area and certain that he was not following Archie. Other MBML investigators followed Archie to a designated location away from the restaurant and recovered all the evidence. Investigators put all the money and the torn-up contract into separate evidence bags and carried them to the offices of the medical board, where all the equipment was removed from Archie's vehicle. The audio and videotapes were played and found to be of excellent quality. Dr. Sop and Archie were identifiable in the video and all the audiotapes were clear. All the information was provided in a briefing to the board's executive officer and the board's attorney. To say the least, they were speechless at the surprising developments. Will at MBN was also advised of the successful progress of the case. There could be no doubt as to the credibility of our informant.

Investigator Breeland had one major assignment remaining: to assemble the torn-up contract without damaging or tampering with the evidence. If fingerprints had to be recovered, we did not want to alter them in any way. If we had to use handwriting analysis as part of the forensic evidence, we did not want to alter it in any way. DNA had not yet arrived on the scene for use. Investigator Breeland had quite a challenge. He consulted with the state crime lab on the procedures, techniques, and forensic type sticky paper to use to avoid any alteration to the evidence. The crime lab was the best possible choice to perform the reassembly of the document, but they would not be able to get to it for weeks or months and we could not wait that long. They told him he had to wear surgical gloves at all times and to handle the torn pieces only with tweezers. It took some time, but he succeeded in the assembly of the contract pieces on a special type of forensic sticky paper the crime lab supplied. When finished, it was legible and secure. All of the evidence had been carefully sealed and marked properly to protect fingerprints on the money and the contract as well as the handwriting.

At this point, the case was referred to Stan Ingram, the board's attorney, and prosecutor. Stan was one of the best legal minds in medical regulatory law in the south, if not the whole country. He reviewed all the evidence to be certain it supported bringing formal charges against Dr. Sop. He then prepared a summons and affidavit that spelled out the specific details and charges based on the Mississippi Medical Practice Act. In this type of case, the charges usually involved unprofessional conduct likely to deceive, defraud, or harm the public. Performing oral sex on one of his hospitalized and unwilling patients certainly fit that description.

Once the documents were prepared, investigators were instructed to contact the doctor to serve him with the documents and to see if he had any response to the charges. This was the doctor's chance to explain himself and get his side of the story.

Dr. Sop was contacted by telephone by me and told that investigators at the board needed to talk with him concerning a serious violation of the Medical Practice Act and/or board regulations by him. When he was told it would be inappropriate to discuss the matter over the telephone, Dr. Sop agreed to meet investigators at the offices of the medical board. He was told he could and probably should have an attorney present. A meeting was agreed on for the following day. When Dr. Sop arrived at the medical board, he was greeted by me and Investigator Neil Breeland. He did not bring legal representation. He was again reminded he could have legal counsel present, but he declined. I informed Dr. Sop of the details of the investigation from start to finish. The oral sex in the hospital, the meeting behind the restaurant, and the money and the contract sealed in evidence bags were all detailed and presented for his review. He was also told about the audio and video recordings. A somewhat stunned Dr. Sop understandably said he did not wish to discuss anything until he had time to consult his attorney. I then served him with the summons and affidavit and briefly explained them to him. Dr. Sop took the documents and departed the office.

Anticipating a full legal challenge to the case, the board's attorney instructed investigators to begin making copies of the videotapes and to prepare transcripts of the audiotapes for the defense. All defendants in a criminal or administrative case have a legal right to all evidence that will likely be presented at trial or in a formal hearing. A motion for discovery must be filed by attorneys representing the doctor in order to obtain copies of all the evidence.

Several days later, I was contacted by Stan Ingram and told he had been contacted by Dr. Sop's attorneys. They requested an informal viewing of all the evidence, including viewing the video and audiotapes. In addition, they wanted to inspect the contract and the cash. I was instructed to set it up. Since there was not a formal motion for discovery, copies or transcripts were not necessary. A time was agreed upon to meet with Dr. Sop's attorneys at the board offices. When the two attorneys arrived, they were taken to the conference room to inspect the evidence. The attorneys requested to be able to review and inspect all the evidence in private. Their request was denied. I explained that, although I did not suspect they would do anything untoward, I was solely responsible for safeguarding the evidence and as long as the evidence stayed in my presence, the chain of custody remains intact. I assured them that the appropriate copies of everything would be provided promptly when they made a formal discovery motion. The audio and video recordings were then played for them and they were allowed to view the cash and the contract that was all sealed in clear, tamper-proof evidence bags. They also requested identifying information on Archie, which was provided, then left the office.

Approximately one week later I was contacted by another doctor and current board member as well as a close friend of Dr. Sop. The board member requested to personally view all the evidence in the case. The board member was advised that any viewing of the evidence before a full hearing might preclude the board member from participation in the hearing. The board member said it was necessary to view the evidence to remove any possibility of bias on the part of the investigators. I told the board member that the evidence was compelling, to say the least, and no bias of any kind existed. The board member still insisted on seeing the evidence personally. I advised the board member I would have to obtain approval from the executive officer and board attorney and call back. The meeting was approved. The board member reviewed all the evidence, in my presence, at the board's offices. Apparently satisfied and more than a bit shocked, the doctor exited the board's offices without any comment, not even a thank you!

In the end, this case was resolved with a consent order, no hearing required. At the direction of the executive officer, Investigator Neil Breeland and I met with Dr. Sop at the offices of the medical board. We presented him with a consent order that provided for a five-year suspension of his license with all but one year stayed. He also was required to undergo evaluation and treatment, if necessary, for chemical dependency and/or sexual addiction. Following his attorney's advice, Dr. Sop agreed to the terms and signed the consent order. The order was formally approved by the full board at the next board meeting.

A second patient came forward just after the consent order had been approved by the medical board. The executive officer decided that no further action was likely to be taken against Dr. Sop and that information was not pursued.

It took several years for Dr. Sop to comply with the myriad of reinstatement requirements such as treatment and training. However, after one year, he had completed the required evaluation portion with no treatment necessary, so the board granted a lifting of the suspension on his license. That allowed him to return to the practice of medicine, but with considerable restrictions. No additional complaints were received, or any other problems identified concerning his practice during my remaining tenure with the medical board.

Another issue for Dr. Sop was the possibility of a civil lawsuit. As medical board investigators, we cannot and did not advise anyone concerning filing a lawsuit. However, in this case, Archie did file suit against Dr. Sop. I was told that it was settled for an amount in the area of a medium five-figure number. I did not ever determine if the second patient filed a similar suit. In most lawsuits of this type, involving sexual abuse or assault by a practicing doctor, the case is usually not considered malpractice, therefore Dr. Sop's malpractice carrier is not responsible or involved in the defense of the case or the final settlement. The payment is the responsibility of the doctor alone.

Information concerning payments to informants is confidential, therefore I do not know if the Mississippi Bureau of Narcotics paid Archie or not, but I suspect he got his usual fee, and he earned it as far as I was concerned. I sought approval from the board's executive officer to authorize a payment to Archie on behalf of the medical board, but it was denied. The criminal charges against Archie based on the check forgery, to my knowledge, were settled with Archie making restitution.

CHAPTER 15

DR. EXCALIBUR and BENEDICT

I am not the law, but I represent justice so far as my feeble powers go. – Sir Arthur Conan Doyle.

Throughout the career of an investigator, various agencies (such as DEA, MBN, Federation of State Medical Boards, and others) offer training to improve investigation outcomes and collaboration in joint operations. In January of 1991, the board's executive officer and I were invited to attend a seminar on asset forfeiture in Destin, Florida, sponsored and paid for by the New Orleans Office of DEA Diversion. The training focused on a new United States Justice Department and DEA initiative to help state medical boards and other investigative agencies work with DEA to seize assets of doctors and other practitioners found in violation of controlled substance laws or regulations. Basically, the investigation had to clearly establish that the prescriptions or purchases of controlled substances were not for a legitimate medical reason. They had to originate from the practitioner, be issued in a property (clinic, office, house, etc.) owned by the practitioner, and, most importantly, the property had to be lien free.

After the training conference, on the return drive, the EO and I discussed at length the potential for using this new tool in our investigations in Mississippi. Several questions came up. Would there be any conflict with Mississippi law? Would the full board allow investigators to participate in a seizure process? Could the board take possession of a seized property? What would the board do with a seized clinic or property? I must admit we concluded the training would probably not be very helpful and the opportunity to seize a property would probably never occur. Never say never!

Another distraction to just about any logical thought process at the time was the Gulf War. During the drive back from the Destin training, the radio interrupted normal programming with the announcement that bombs had started falling on Baghdad beginning the effort by the US and our allies to kick Iraq out of Kuwait. We forgot all about our little problems. All we wanted was a quick victory and no American casualties.

Meanwhile, life went on. I had barely unpacked from the training trip when Investigator Charlie Moses came to me with a complaint, he had received from a pharmacist indicating a Dr. Excalibur (not his real name) had been prescribing Vicodin, Valium, and Xanax to several young female patients in suspicious amounts for quite some time. Dr. Excalibur was not previously known to the medical board. His licensure file indicated he was a general surgeon and practiced in one of Mississippi's larger cities. At one time he had a large surgery practice, but it had faded in recent years, primarily due to his age. Surgeons have a legitimate need to prescribe pain medication for short periods of time to patients while they are in convalescence after a surgical procedure. Most patients are given a prescription for twelve to twenty-four dosage units after surgery for any complaints of pain. After the convalescence period, patients are referred to their primary care physician for any necessary follow-up. By that time, most patients are fully recovered from surgery and no longer require any pain medication. The information that Dr. Excalibur was prescribing to several young women was not that troubling. The concerning part of the information was that it had been going on for quite some time.

After a review of the complaint information, the executive officer authorized an investigation to assess Dr. Excalibur's prescribing patterns. We conducted profiles in all the pharmacies in the city and surrounding areas. Numerous prescriptions for Vicodin, Valium, Xanax, and other controlled substances were documented to the eight females identified in the original complaint, all prescribed by Dr. Excalibur. At the time of this investigation, Vicodin was a Schedule IIIN controlled substance containing 7.5 mg of hydrocodone and 325 mg of acetaminophen. It was a popular painkiller and just beginning to be highly abused. Vicodin and all other hydrocodone products were put in Schedule IIN by the DEA in 2014. Several other suspicious profiles on patients were also documented for the same or similar drugs, again, for long periods. It appeared Dr. Excalibur's practice had deteriorated to basically a prescription mill.

During the pharmacy profiling, information was received from several pharmacists indicating one of the female patients, Diane (not her real name), was living at Dr. Excalibur's residence. Dr. Excalibur was married but his wife was confined to bed and non-ambulatory due to serious medical problems. The sources also indicated that most of the other females were apparently friends with Diane. On certain days when Dr. Excalibur's clinic was supposedly closed, the girls would bring in prescriptions signed by Dr. Excalibur. When the pharmacists questioned the girls about the prescriptions and how they got them, they said from Diane at the residence or from the mailbox at the doctor's house.

Surveillance on Dr. Excalibur's residence verified that patient Diane was, in fact, residing at the home. A check of the mailbox on several occasions by me confirmed prescriptions in the mailbox written for the females identified in the profile. On occasion, Diane was observed by investigators placing prescriptions in the mailbox to be picked up. The residence was a large two-story split level with an estimated value of at least $350,000 (in 1980s money).

All the above information was passed on to the executive officer and board attorney Stan Ingram. They authorized the service of an inspection warrant for the medical files on the patients to determine justification. The amounts prescribed and long-term pattern indicated probable drug abuse. The only question was whether any of the drugs were being returned to Dr. Excalibur for his personal use. The inspection warrant was prepared and served on Dr. Excalibur and the patient files were recovered and analyzed. The files contained very little in the way of medical justification. It appeared that Dr. Excalibur was just supplying prescriptions for controlled substances without any legitimate medical reasons. The first reaction was to seek a voluntary surrender of Dr. Excalibur's DEA certificate, but I suddenly recalled the training with DEA on asset forfeiture. A review of the city land/property land records indicated the residence appeared to be free and clear of any liens. The executive officer authorized me to contact the supervisor of the DEA diversion office in New Orleans, LA to see if there was any interest in pursuing the case as a seizure opportunity. The diversion supervisor at the time was Harold Neuman (not his real name). The MBML had worked numerous successful diversion cases with him and his staff over the years. I contacted him by telephone and briefed him on the case to-date. He said he wanted to meet with us to take a further look at the situation. The following Monday, Harold traveled to our offices for a detailed briefing on the case. After the meeting, he indicated this case was, on paper, a classic case for asset seizure. The evidence seemed to meet all the criteria set by the Department of Justice. Harold said he would meet with his supervisor to brief him on the case and, if approved, he would present the case to the US Attorney's office that was responsible for that portion of Mississippi. We provided Harold a copy of all the case information for his presentation. Harold said he was going to follow up on our review of the lien data just to be able to tell his supervisors that he had also confirmed the property was lien free.

In approximately two weeks I was contacted by telephone by Harold and informed that DEA Washington had approved pursuing the seizure case as a violation of DEA controlled substance regulations based on the improper prescribing. Since the residence was being used to facilitate the improper prescribing, it was subject to seizure. Harold would be presenting the case to the US Attorney in Mississippi the following week. He contacted me after his meeting with the US Attorney and told me they had agreed to pursue the case. Harold said he recommended the process be fast-tracked due to the age of the physician. He might decide to sell the property before the government could place a hold on the property. It took about six to eight weeks for the USA's office to prepare the necessary paperwork and place the hold on the property. After the hold was placed on the property, Harold called me with some bad news. He said, that shortly after the hold was placed on the property, the Assistant US Attorney handling the case (I will call him "Benedict") was contacted by an attorney for the doctor. The attorney advised he was informing the US Attorney that the property was not lien-free as previously indicated in the seizure order. The doctor had made a home equity loan using the house as collateral a month earlier. The amount of the lien was $150,000.

I could not believe what I heard, and I do not believe in coincidence. I told Harold that this sounded just a tiny bit suspicious. I asked Harold who was the AUSA handling the case. He identified him as Benedict and described him as a senior attorney who had multiple years in prosecutions. I asked if he had any family or personal connections with the doctor. No one knew that answer. I knew no one in my office knew the doctor. No one with DEA New Orleans was from the area so it was extremely unlikely anyone there knew the doctor. That left only the US Attorney's office. I began asking questions of the pharmacist in the city where Dr. Excalibur practiced. One of the pharmacists informed me that he knew Benedict and that Benedict grew up in the same town where Dr. Excalibur practiced. I passed on this little factoid to Harold in New Orleans. He said he was reporting this to his supervisor and hopefully up the chain to Washington.

Since the asset seizure case had fallen on hard times, the executive officer sent me to seek a voluntary surrender of Dr. Excalibur's DEA certificate. I met with Dr. Excalibur in his office in a small medical complex. He did not have a nurse or secretary staff primarily due to his shrinking practice. He admitted he did not do any more surgeries due to his age. I provided the doctor copies of the pharmacy profiles on the females receiving the prescriptions from him. He acknowledged that he wrote the prescriptions for the patients. I then advised him that an analysis of the previously seized patient files failed to establish any medical justification for the long-term prescribing patterns. I asked if he had any explanation for the lack of documentation. Class I and Class II for DEA The doctor admitted that he failed to keep any files or documentation. He also acknowledged that patient Diane was living with him. He said he had not had any kind of relationship with his wife for several years due to her poor health. I inquired about the nature of his relationship with Diane. Dr. Excalibur refused to discuss that but agreed to surrender his DEA certificate to avoid a license revocation hearing. After all the paperwork was completed, I took custody of his DEA certificate and a small number of controlled substances he had in the office. I reminded him he could no longer administer, dispense, or prescribe any controlled substances until he was allowed to reregister for his certificate. After I left the office, I contacted Harold to advise him that Dr. Excalibur's DEA certificate had been surrendered and I was mailing the document to him for processing.

Approximately two months later, Harold brought me up to date on the latest with the seizure portion of the case. The Department of Justice (DOJ) had sent a representative from Washington to handle the possibility of a leak from the local USA office. Benedict, the Assistant USA handling the seizure, when interviewed, had confessed that he had leaked to Dr. Excalibur that a seizure order was being planned on his residence. He said members of his family had been patients of the doctor. The AUSA was allowed to quietly resign from office. Harold told me he had gotten into a lot of trouble and almost terminated because he had raised so much hell since the AUSA was not criminally prosecuted. Benedict, the AUSA, had obstructed justice by compromising the case, placing investigators in harm's way, conspiring with the doctor to prevent the government from seizing his residence, and got away without being charged!

Whether or not this case had anything to do with it, Harold was transferred to Washington D.C. approximately one year later. Washington D.C. was not an ideal office to be assigned.

Information was received by investigators several weeks after Dr. Excalibur surrendered his DEA certificate that Diane had moved out of the doctor's house. Wonder why? Could it be that she did not want him since he could no longer supply her with a steady source of controlled substances? Yet another example of classic diversion of controlled substances by a prescriber. Also, we received information that approximately six months after Diane went out on her own, she won two million dollars in the Louisiana Lottery. We never heard from her again. Imagine that! Can't we just be friends?

I have no idea what finally happened to the AUSA who caused this conflagration and could care less. All of this was kept very hush-hush, until now.

The Mississippi State Board of Medical Licensure never again entered a joint seizure investigation with DEA during my tenure. The entire process had left a bad taste in everybody's mouth. I was later advised that the program was just another DOJ government failure.

Dr. Excalibur never sought the return of his DEA certificate during the remainder of my tenure at the medical board.

CHAPTER 16

DOCTOR CLARK

Addressing physician prescribing practices is critical to addressing the nation's opioid abuse problem. – "Waismann Method Advanced Treatment for Opioid Dependence," Mortality Morbidity Weekly Report.

There are several things in life that cannot be controlled or changed, such as one's skin color or one's parents. Little can be done to alter those two basic facts about one's life. So, you will appreciate the difficulty of the situation I found myself in with a doctor that I will call "Dr. Clark" (or "DC" for short), who was my uncle by marriage. My father had a sister who married DC, but my father disowned her sometime after the marriage. I suspect it had something to do with money since that is usually what breaks families apart, but I never really learned why. I did not even know about the aunt or uncle situation until I was in my twenties. My father had never mentioned it. My mother told me shortly before she died from a probable drug overdose but suggested I not discuss it with my father. He truly did not want anyone to know about the marriage and became upset when people asked him about the situation. DC and his family lived in a town not far from where I grew up, but family get-togethers were out of the question.

I had pretty much forgotten about the family issues until at least twenty years later. I was profiling pharmacies in DC's hometown when I noticed a significant pattern of mainly Schedule IIIN drugs, Tylenol #3, #4, hydrocodone products, and Valium to a name that I recognized, for some unknown reason, as my aunt Carol (not her real name). The prescriptions were all written by DC, her ex-husband. I found out from one of the pharmacists that DC and Carol had divorced several years earlier. However, prescribing or treating family members, even ex-family members, is strongly discouraged, especially with controlled substances. Although it was not prohibited by regulation or law, the concern was about being able to say with any certainty who was getting the drugs – the patient, the doctor, or both. The pattern documented was seriously concerning because the amounts were excessive and went back for more than two years.

At the regular staff meeting the following week, I briefed the executive officer on the profile and recommended a visit to DC to determine what was happening. The executive officer agreed and told me to strongly recommend to DC that he refer his former wife to another doctor for any further treatment. He also recommended that she be referred for an evaluation for chemical dependency. In the interest of transparency, I explained to the executive officer my relationship with DC. He offered to have another investigator handle the case, but I insisted it was in my assigned area and should not be a problem. The truth is that I probably should have relented and let another investigator pursue the case. At the time, I did not have a clue what was coming.

The following day I traveled to DC's clinic. At the clinic, I identified myself to the receptionist and asked to speak to DC concerning a patient. By now, I had learned not to identify the patient or purpose of a visit except to the doctor. After approximately a one hour wait, I was taken to his office. When he came in, I introduced myself to him and presented my identification as chief investigator for the medical board. I told him I needed to talk to him about his prescribing to his former wife, Carol. He asked what I needed to know. I explained to him how long-term prescribing of controlled substances to any family member, past or present, is of concern to the board because of the possible loss of objectivity. I requested to see her patient file to verify the diagnosis or indications justifying controlled substances over such a long period. DC said he did not maintain a patient file on her. He said she still works for him part-time and he occasionally treated her for various pain issues from time to time. He said that he recognized that he probably should not treat her, but he was able to monitor her closely and felt the situation was under control. I asked for specific information on her diagnosis that justified such long-term prescriptions for controlled substances. DC said there were different things such as female problems, headaches, but nothing too serious. I noticed he failed to provide any specific diagnosis. I suggested to him, on behalf of the board, that it was strongly recommended he no longer treat his ex-wife. He should refer her to another doctor to ensure total objectivity in her management.

I also told him the board recommended that in situations of this type, the patient be evaluated for chemical dependency as soon as possible. Since my father had long been an alcoholic, I strongly suspected his sister probably had the same predisposition for chemical dependency issues but said nothing about that to DC. DC then told me the board was overreacting to a situation that he knew was under control. He said he was very comfortable with his former wife's medical condition and chemical dependency was not a problem. I stated that the board was also concerned about his situation. DC paused for a minute, then asked what I meant by that comment. I told him there was always the possibility that they both had a problem. I explained that just because the prescriptions were in her name, it did not mean some or all of the drugs were not coming back to him. It would not be the first time that had happened. DC then said, "Tell Frank Morgan (the executive officer) that I have the situation under control and I do not need the board to tell me how to treat my patients." DC made it clear that he considered our meeting a nuisance and it ended abruptly. DC was acting like he was one of the "untouchables." I specifically did not mention our family relationship and if he knew who I was, he did not let on.

The next day I related the details of the meeting to the executive officer. He said he would follow up my visit with a strong warning letter and for me to plan a follow-up profile of the situation in six to twelve months.

Unfortunately, due to a heavy caseload, it was longer than twelve months before a follow-up profile could take place. In fact, it was closer to two years. The follow-up profile documented few prescriptions to Carol and most of those were non-controlled. Maybe the visit and warning letter had done some good after all. The only suspicious prescriptions I found written by DC were for approximately 300, one cc vials of injectable Demerol, 100 mg per cc. The prescriptions were found in one pharmacy for fifteen different patients. The names on the prescriptions were legible but the addresses were not. Due to caseload requirements, I had to assign the laborious process of identifying and locating the patients to Investigator Charlie Moses. The pharmacist was not cooperative and reluctant to help to the point of convincing us something was amiss. All he would provide was that he too could not read the addresses and did not personally know any of the patients. He knew that DC had written the prescriptions, so he filled them. At that time, little in the way of identifying information was collected by some of the pharmacists on their patients. Investigator Charlie Moses used city and county cross-reference indexes, phone books, and talked to local authorities in an attempt to identify the patient names on the prescriptions. Only three names matched with a local address, but we did not know if they were the actual patients because the addresses were not legible. Those three individuals were contacted and all three denied any knowledge of the prescriptions. During the profiling and investigation of the prescriptions, Investigator Moses received information that DC had remarried to a much younger local woman. I will call her "Abbey." According to the sources, Abbey was known to be a serious drug abuser. After hearing about the history of the new wife and DC's history of prescribing to family members, we felt we knew where the Demerol prescriptions were going.

After briefing the EO at the next staff meeting, a second visit to DC was authorized to discuss the prescriptions for the injectable Demerol. The executive officer told me to seek a surrender of Schedule II, IIN, III, and IIIN of his DEA certificate if DC could not or would not produce proper patient identification, patient files, and medical justification for the prescriptions.

The second visit to DC was as contentious as the first, if not more so. After once again identifying myself, I met a barrage of disparaging comments about how I was wasting his time. After he finished, I told him I was investigating several prescriptions for injectable Demerol he had written to patients that could not be located or even identified and asked to see the medical files on each patient to determine the identification, indications, and justification for the prescriptions. I handed him a copy of the profile sheets with a copy of the prescriptions attached. After reviewing the prescriptions and profiles he commented how he was tired of being visited by the board for such nonsense and considered the visits to be just harassment. He said he wrote the prescriptions to have the injectable Demerol for his office use. He said on occasion they run short and needed the medication for use in his clinic for patients. Since the time period was over several months, I asked why he could not order the drugs through his normal supplier using his DEA order forms? DC said it was more convenient to write the prescriptions and send a staff member across the street to fill them. That answer explained why the pharmacist had been acting snarky and difficult. He knew the staffer picking up the Demerol and had to suspect the prescriptions were not for a real patient. I then asked DC how he came up with the patient names. He said he just made them up. I then told DC I needed to see the drug ledgers to inventory, audit, and establish accountability and use of the drugs. I reminded DC that state and federal regulations required him to maintain ledgers accounting for the use of every single cc of the Demerol injectable. DC said he did not maintain any records on the use of the Demerol. I told DC if that were true, he was in violation of several laws and regulations. I advised him that state and federal regulations specifically prohibit the writing of prescriptions for the purpose of resupplying a clinic or office with controlled substance inventory. Moreover, using fictitious names on controlled substance prescriptions for the purposes of obtaining controlled substances, for any reason, is a felony under state and federal law. Another way we describe that practice is to call it "obtaining controlled substances by fraud or subterfuge."

The fact that DC intentionally failed to maintain accountability records to reflect proper use established criminal intent to any reasonable thinking person. Also, this was the second time we had to visit him for writing controlled substance prescriptions improperly and violating state and federal regulations and laws in the process. I then requested to see the remaining inventory of Demerol for counting and to inspect the storage container for security. DC refused my request stating it was unnecessary and just more harassment, becoming angrier by the minute. After his refusal, I told DC that under the circumstances I had been directed to seek a voluntary surrender of Schedule II, IIN, III, and IIIN of his DEA certificate. If he refused, he would face the consequences. DC said he was not going to surrender anything to the board. I told him that his failure to surrender could force the board to summon him to a full revocation hearing. He said to do whatever needed to be done because he was not surrendering anything. This meeting also ended abruptly. On the way out, DC told me to "tell that sorry ass son of a bitch Frank Morgan not to send me another one of his silly ass letters." I told DC, "I will quote exactly what you said, word for word," and I did just that.

After hearing the exact quote from DC, the only comment from the executive officer was, "That sounds just like something he would say." He authorized a summons and affidavit requiring DC to appear for a revocation hearing before the full board. The summons and affidavit were prepared by myself and the board attorney, Stan Ingram, charging DC with multiple counts of unprofessional conduct based on his issuing the Demerol prescriptions in violation of regulations and failing to provide proper accountability records documenting the use. I personally delivered the summons and affidavit to him in his clinic. We never had to sit down or even say hello. I just gave him the documents and told him that he was hereby served to appear for a licensure revocation hearing. If there were any questions, he should call the board's attorney. "Have a nice day," I said, before turning around and walking out.

Just before the hearing, DC, through his attorney, offered to surrender Schedules II, IIN, III, and IIIN of his DEA certificate to avoid the full revocation hearing. Before the executive officer agreed to accept the surrender of the DEA certificate, I suggested we proceed to the hearing. I felt DC needed some time off to reflect on his overall attitude toward the board and the cavalier way he handled controlled substances. The executive officer agreed to accept the surrender of the DEA certificate but required DC to appear before the full board for them to see and hear what he did and to present his case on why the board should accept the surrender. After hearing a summary of the facts and circumstances, and DC's response, mostly through his attorney, the board agreed to accept just the surrender of the portions of his DEA certificate. Through his attorney, DC stuck with his story that the Demerol was used for just office/clinic inventory purposes. I do not think the entire board believed him and I know the investigative staff did not. Somehow, I felt we had not heard the last of him. I guess experience can be a good teacher.

Approximately ten months later, Investigator Charlie Moses had been assigned to investigate complaints against a physician on the Mississippi Gulf Coast. While profiling pharmacies on the original complaint, Charlie began to find numerous prescriptions written by DC for injectable Stadol, Nubain, and Dalgan to a man and woman with an address in a small town near where DC practiced. The coast area is at least 250 miles from the practice location of DC. Also, the town and address on the prescriptions for the two patients was over 250 miles from the coast. I will call them John and Joan Smith (not their real names). Even more suspicious was the fact that the time period for the prescriptions covered almost the entire ten-month period since DC had surrendered portions of his DEA certificate. It was hard to picture patients receiving prescriptions locally, then driving 250 miles and back just to have them filled unless something was not quite right. Stadol and Nubain were, at the time, non-controlled synthetic narcotics similar to Demerol. Dalgan, also known as dezocine, is an opioid narcotic, that was also not controlled. All three drugs had shown significant potential for abuse statewide. Unfortunately, it took several more years, thanks to one particular state senator resisting the move, for Stadol and Nubain to be added to Schedule IV in Mississippi. Dalgan was never placed on a controlled substance schedule. The finished profiles indicated a large amount of injectable Stadol, Nubain, and Dalgan had been prescribed by DC to the Smiths. We suspected that Mr. and Mrs. Smith would turn out to be fictitious patients and that the drugs were intended for DC's young wife.

The investigation of the names John and Joan Smith identified a couple by the same name that matched the address on the prescriptions in a small town near where DC practiced. Investigator Neil Breeland and I traveled to the town to locate and hopefully interview the couple concerning the prescriptions.

At the address, as we were walking up to what appeared to be the main entrance to the house, I met a pit bull head-on. The dog did not sound or look very happy. When I saw the dog I froze, ready to pull my weapon, if necessary. Now, this is not what you want to happen. What is the chance of getting the couple's cooperation on the prescriptions if we had to shoot their dog? We were in a bad spot. Suddenly, Investigator Breeland came walking up behind me. I turned around and shouted, "Dog!" to Investigator Breeland and took off in the other direction. He claimed I left him in the dust to deal with the dog and he was absolutely correct! Mama did not raise a complete fool. We have all heard the cliché a hundred times, I do not have to be fast, just faster than the other guy. That situation was upon us and a decision had to be made. Fortunately, the dog must have been fed or just gentler than it looked because he did not come after us. That was not my first time confronting a pit bull face-to-face during an investigation. On both occasions, the dogs turned out to be fairly tame. Thank goodness!

We quickly went back around the house in the opposite direction away from the dog, eventually finding the real front door. I knocked. When it opened, I identified myself and asked to speak with Mr. John Smith. The man who answered our knock said he was John Smith. I then presented my credentials to him and asked if we could talk to him and his spouse concerning some prescriptions. He led us into a living room area where we were introduced to Mrs. Smith. We had three large stacks of prescriptions that we sat down on a coffee table. We explained that each stack contained prescriptions for three different drugs. One stack contained injectable Stadol written in both of their names, the other was for injectable Nubain and the last stack was for injectable Dalgan. I asked them to personally review the prescriptions bearing their respective names to see if they could verify the prescriptions were for them and that they had received the medication. Mr. Smith immediately spoke up and said that they did not have to look at the prescriptions. He said they had not received any of the prescriptions and did not know what the drugs were. I asked Mr. Smith if he or his wife had ever been treated by DC for any reason. He said neither his wife nor he had ever been a patient of DC. He then dropped a bombshell. He said their daughter, Abbey, was DC's wife. It caught Neil and I totally by surprise. I know that I must have turned a bright shade of red from embarrassment. I told Mr. Smith, "I had no idea of the relationship and, truthfully, had no way to know." I told them that I was sorry but, through no fault of their own, DC had brought them into the world of illegal prescriptions. I emphasized to them that they were not in trouble of any kind. However, DC had used their names as a conduit to divert the prescriptions to a person or persons as yet unknown. About this time, I begin to wonder if the prescriptions were forgeries, written by Abbey without DC's knowledge. It did not seem likely, because if she was going to forge the prescriptions, she would probably make them out for the real drugs that she wanted, instead of substitutes. The more I thought about that, the better I began to feel. It is funny how fast your mind works when your back is to the wall. Also, by this time, I was an expert on DC's handwriting and signature. They both looked legit. My confidence was high.

Mr. Smith then said, "They were probably for Abbey. We know she has a drug problem. We were not wholly supportive of her marrying DC, but there was nothing we could do." I then told the Smiths that we needed their help in the form of a statement from each of them that they did not seek or receive the prescriptions bearing their names. I suggested they call an attorney and explained that we would understand if they did. I told them I would be happy to talk to their attorney in their presence to answer any questions they might have. Fortunately, they said that was not necessary. They were very cooperative, providing detailed statements and agreeing to testify if necessary. Once again DC was in hot water. I was beyond glad I did not have to shoot their dog. Before we left, I asked Mr. Smith about his rather fierce-looking dog. "He just looks bad," he said. "He really is gentle." I felt better on the way out and relieved in more ways than one!

The executive officer made an executive decision, and it did not take long. The decision was to summons DC again, to a full revocation hearing. The board attorney, Stan Ingram, did not even suggest I go and try to obtain DC's side of the story. The Smiths had agreed to testify and one of the pharmacists that Investigator Charlie Moses interviewed indicated he had called DC's clinic to verify the prescriptions were valid before he filled them. There was nowhere for DC to hide. Once the documents were prepared, I traveled to his clinic to serve him. This time he refused to meet with me, so I could not serve him in the clinic. I patiently waited for him to leave the clinic. Later that evening when he exited, headed for his truck, I caught him in the parking lot and personally served him with the summons and affidavit. Again, not much was said. I told him, "I am serving you with a summons and affidavit requiring you to appear for a license revocation hearing. You know the routine by now." I did not wait for a response. I also knew that doctors were known to carry weapons on them when leaving their clinic late at night. I walked backward to my car, not wanting to turn my back on him, got in, and drove away.

Two hours before the start of the hearing, DC and his attorney requested a pre-hearing conference with Stan Ingram to discuss the case. Stan requested the executive officer and I join him in the meeting. In the meeting, DC, through his attorney, emphatically denied writing any prescriptions to Abbey's mother and father. What the attorney and DC did not know, because they had not requested discovery, was that we had done our homework on the handwriting on the prescriptions. We considered fingerprints but that turned out to be unnecessary because of the results of the handwriting analysis. For the handwriting analysis performed by the Mississippi State Crime Lab staff, we provided all of DC's handwriting from completing his licensure file and numerous recent prescriptions for non-controlled drugs to other patients that were known to have been written by DC himself. The expert at the crime lab compared the known DC handwriting samples to the prescriptions written in the names of Abbey's mother and father. He prepared a report that established that the same person had written all of the items presented for analysis.

After DC had denied writing the prescriptions to the parents, I requested if DC could review all of the prescriptions and just pull out the ones he did not write. He and his attorney agreed. I had several stacks of prescriptions that included the prescriptions to the mother and father and the other patients. I requested he look carefully at all of the prescriptions and just pick out the ones he did not write. It did not take an expert to see that the handwriting and signatures all matched but we went through the process. After a brief scan of the prescriptions, DC admitted he had, in fact, issued the prescriptions in the names of the mother and father. Stan then provided the report from the crime lab to the attorney that established, by an expert who was available to testify in the hearing, that the documents were all written by the same person.

Although the report could not identify that person, we all knew, including the attorney, that it was DC. The attorney for DC then ended the meeting.

In the hearing, DC did not challenge the validity of the prescriptions and admitted he wrote them for his wife to help her deal with her chemical dependency problem. He felt he had legitimately treated her and did not need the board to keep interfering or monitoring his prescribing. He also admitted that he had used his in-law's names in a misguided effort to help their daughter. During an administrative hearing, the board is allowed to question witnesses and defendants. DC was reminded by the board that he had two previous encounters with the board and had ignored the appropriate recommendations to remedy the situation. DC said he was acting out of frustration and from the difficult problems he was having treating his wife. One board member said he was not treating his wife, just supplying her with what she wanted. The hearing did not go well for DC and the board revoked his license to practice medicine.

Approximately eight months after DC lost his license, Abbey divorced him. If DC could not get her the necessary drugs, she did not need or want him around. Shortly after the divorce, she married a law enforcement officer from a neighboring county. Abbey continued to descend further into chemical dependency. She began to inject whatever she could get her hands on including a drug called Mepergan Fortis. This is a capsule form of Demerol that is definitely not intended for injecting. As a result of the injections, she began to have pieces of her hands and fingers surgically removed. Mepergan Fortis does not dissolve well for injections. The undissolved particulates, when injected into the bloodstream, collect in the capillaries of the hands and feet and prevent proper blood flow. The tissue dies from lack of blood flow and becomes necrotic requiring removal. Some say she did this on purpose, another form of Munchausen syndrome to be able to get more drugs from the surgeries.

Abbey became more and more desperate and began visiting emergency rooms for prescriptions or injections of narcotics. On one particular visit to an emergency room not very far from her hometown, the ER doctor on duty recognized her from previous visits at other hospital emergency rooms. He told her that she was not going to get anything stronger than extra-strength Tylenol so she might as well leave now. Abbey said she would go but she would be right back in just a little while. Abbey left the emergency room and drove off in her car. She drove out to the main highway and deliberately drove her car, at a high rate of speed, into a bridge abutment. You may have seen a recent television commercial about the opioid epidemic where a young female unbuckles her seat belt and because of her need for drugs drives her car full speed into a trash bin. When the ambulance delivered Abbey back to the emergency room fairly well broken up, she told the ER doctor, "Told you I would be right back." I received information some years later that Abbey had passed away as a result of her chemical dependency. I was surprised that she lasted that long.

After one year, DC was allowed to obtain re-licensure with restrictions. During my tenure, DC never regained full unrestricted privileges. However, several years after my retirement I was informed that the board finally lifted all restrictions on his license. No problems were identified for DC during several follow-up profiles and no complaints were received by the medical board on him during the rest of my career.

I never told him I was his nephew and he never told me he was my uncle. I never found out if he knew or not. I suspect he did know, just did not want to get into "how is the family kind of conversation" and have to act as if he truly cared.

CHAPTER 17

THE RED BALL EXPRESS

Do as much as possible for the patient and as little as possible to the patient. – Bernard Lown, MD Cardiologist, inventor, author.

Occasionally a complaint is received by the medical licensure board that is difficult to put into just one of the "five D's" bad actor categories. The following is such a case and could really be put in a category by itself.

The original call came from a mother who related the following to me. She said her daughter had been treated or abused while a patient of a psychiatrist (I'll call him "Dr. Red"). Her daughter was currently under the care of a local psychiatrist who, after hearing what happened under Dr. Red's care, recommended she contact the medical board. The mother requested a meeting at the medical board to discuss her daughter's treatment/abuse by Dr. Red. She described her daughter as an adult (who I will call "Sara") and said she would be with her to provide information. The abuse had lasted for approximately two years and they wished to file a complaint with the board. A meeting was scheduled for the following week.

Whenever a female requests a meeting to discuss a possible complaint, every effort is made to have a female staff member of the investigative division present at the meeting. This provides a level of protection for MBML investigative staff from any type of untoward allegation against the investigative staff for improper behavior. It also provides a very important level of comfort to the women who are talking to complete male strangers about highly personal and intimate matters. Sometimes it can take a long time for some patients to achieve a comfort level to talk to anybody about these issues. Male investigators who are total strangers just add to their hesitancy.

The following week, Sara and her mother arrived at the set time of the meeting. They were taken into the board's conference room and were joined shortly by me and Investigator Neil Breeland. Unfortunately, a female staff member was not available as originally planned. Since the couple had traveled a long way for the meeting, we decided to give them the option of continuing the interview or postponing it. Fortunately, they decided to continue.

Sara and her mother had brought a box containing several items that they said might be useful as evidence. The box contained what they described as several pornographic tapes of Sara and the doctor having sex at various locations along with a red rubber ball approximately the size of a tennis ball. Sara commented how she kept the box of tapes and the ball because Dr. Red was married, and he did not want his wife or staff to come across the items accidentally. The tapes speak for themselves; more on the ball later!

Since Sara was an adult, I asked her to tell us the facts and circumstances of the doctor/patient relationship and details of the abuse. At the beginning of an interview of this type, it is helpful to explain to the patient/victim how important her role is in communicating the precise details of what she has been put through. The two were assured investigators understood how difficult this could be and encouraged Sara and her mother to pause and take a break if necessary. We were open to all options. It can be especially difficult for a daughter to discuss these matters with a parent present, even as an adult. I have found that some sexually abused patients struggle with feelings of guilt because they feel responsible for what happened. I assured Sara and her mother we would listen, ask questions when needed with no intention to embarrass or judge. I explained to them our goal was to help her in any way we could and, if possible, to conduct a successful investigation into her complaint.

The mother was supportive at this point by commenting about being familiar with the Mississippi medical board's reputation for dealing with physicians that had abused patients. She said the psychiatrist that had referred her to the board had assured her the board would take the matter seriously and could be trusted to do a proper investigation. The referring psychiatrist had been an expert witness on several previous cases before the board. I assured Sara and her mother that they were in good hands with Sara under his care. She and Sara had discussed at length how difficult this might be for both and were prepared to provide the details of what had taken place.

These comments seemed to instill confidence in Sara as she began to explain just what had happened. She started seeing Dr. Red several years earlier for various problems such as depression and feelings of insecurity. After a few months of treatment, Dr. Red began to move the sessions in the direction of a personal relationship. On occasion, Dr. Red would provide her with gifts and comment on how he was very attracted to her. Sara admitted to being equally attracted to Dr. Red even though he was married.

The treatment then changed and very quickly developed into a full sexual romance with her treatment consisting of her having sex with Dr. Red. During this time, Dr. Red continued to prescribe various anti-depressants for her to take orally. Sara said they had sex in his clinic office, car, residence, and in various motels in a small town approximately twenty-five miles from his office. Sara described Dr. Red as a little on the kinky side. The motel encounters consisted of them having sex with various acts of a sadomasochistic nature. Dr. Red liked having her tie him up then spank him very hard. Sara said she did not like to be tied up or spanked. However, Dr. Red would spank her anyway. She said she did this for his gratification. The tapes were made by Dr. Red for them to watch as they were having sex.

The tapes provided by Sara and her mother were reviewed several days after the interview. They were determined by Board Attorney Stan Ingram and me to be of such poor quality they could not be used as evidence.

Sara then discussed the red rubber ball that was in the box. We could tell this was difficult for her and offered her a break before starting. Sara declined and commented how she just needed to get through this. Sara said that on several occasions, about two or three times a year, Dr. Red would travel to various psychiatric training seminars or conferences at locations in Mississippi and across the country. Dr. Red rarely took his wife. When the wife did not attend, he took her as his administrative assistant. She was expected to join him at the conference tables and sit by him. Sara said she was instructed to always bring the red rubber ball with her to the conferences and have it with her at the table. Sara went on to describe in detail what Dr. Red liked for her to do at the table sitting beside him. Sara was to act like she was doing her duties as an administrative assistant. The arrangement of the tables would vary. Sometimes they were circular, sometimes they were set up in rows, one behind the other. Most of the time other attendees were sitting at the same table, but not every time. While Sara sat beside Dr. Red, he would reach under the table, and while hidden by the tablecloth, remove her panties. Dr. Red would then begin to massage her genitalia as if engaging in foreplay before sex. After several minutes, he would have her remove the red ball from her briefcase and give the ball to him. Dr. Red would then begin inserting the red ball into her vagina, retrieving it, then reinserting it over and over. All of this being done with other conference attendees sitting nearby, sometimes right next to them! This happened at all the conferences or seminars she attended.

Sara was not aware of any other patients being "treated" in such a manner and the relationship as described with Dr. Red lasted almost two years. She had just recently, with her mother's help and that of a different psychiatrist (the expert used by the medical board), begun to break away from Dr. Red. She finally realized he was just using her weakness and illness to prey on her and take advantage of her. Sara described her current relationship with Dr. Red as good and said they occasionally talked to each other on the phone, but said that she would not return to him for treatment. She told investigators she would be willing to testify, sign any releases for files, and cooperate fully. Since Dr. Red paid for the motel rooms, she did not have any motel receipts. He had probably destroyed all receipts because he was afraid his wife or staff might find them. Sara did not know if he used his real name or not when he rented the rooms. She provided a list of the pharmacies used to fill most of the prescriptions Dr. Red had written for her.

I explained to Sara and her mother the next steps in the process. First, all the information collected would be put in the form of a complaint and presented to the executive officer and board attorney for possible action. Then a decision would be made by the executive officer concerning whether and when to proceed. I explained that decisions were usually made quickly, and if the decision was to investigate, we would contact her. In the meantime, we requested Sara not initiate any contact with Dr. Red, but talk with him normally if he made any contact with her. She was to avoid any future direct contact with Dr. Red, if at all possible until she was under the supervision of medical board investigators.

A few days later I was given authority by the executive officer to pursue an investigation. I contacted Sara and her mother to tell them of the decision, and to gather any new information on the case. In anticipation of approval, I put together a tentative investigative plan to hopefully obtain a strong case. The plan also had to cross that all-important bridge of making the patient credible in her testimony before the full board.

Since Sara and the doctor seemed to be maintaining some semblance of their relationship, we seemed to have a real opportunity. Sara had indicated in her initial complaint that even-though she had stopped seeing him for "treatment," she and Dr. Red had maintained a good relationship by staying in telephone contact. I felt this was a situation in which we had an advantage. In the state of Mississippi and federally, one-party consent is all that is required to legally record telephone conversations. Such calls are fully admissible in any court or hearing if they are legible, clear, and follow proper rules of evidence. During a one-month period and at the direction of investigators, Sara made three phone calls to Dr. Red that were recorded. The calls originated from the offices of the MBML to Dr. Red at his clinic and residence. The recording equipment was set up and managed during the calls by Investigator Neil Breeland and Mickey Robbins. Sara had previously indicated that she and Dr. Red were still on good terms and the three calls clearly established that fact.

During the recorded calls, Sara and Dr. Red would discuss details of their personal and sexual relationship including the places where they had sex, the motels, his residence, clinic, and car. She would talk about how she did not really like the "rough sex." Dr.

Red expressed how he did, especially her spanking him and, of course, the red ball. During one recorded conversation investigators directed Sara to ask about the motel receipts. Dr. Red said he paid cash and always destroyed the receipts to make sure his wife and staff would not find them. He said he had to use his real name because they always wanted to see his driver's license. Dr. Red occasionally asked how she was feeling medically and if he needed to call in something for her. They also discussed Dr. Red's wife and if she had any idea about their relationship. They discussed how they felt about each other and the possibility of continuing the sexual relationship. From the tone, it was clear Dr. Red wanted to renew the sexual relationship.

After the board attorney, Stan Ingram, listened to the three tapes, he said three would be enough for a hearing. With the three phone calls recorded, we could now proceed with the more overt portion of the investigation. When investigators go into pharmacies when investigating a specific physician, somebody always lets the physician know what is going on, it never fails! This allows the physician an opportunity to destroy evidence, make up evidence, or just get their story straight. We visited the pharmacies where Sara told us that she had filled her prescriptions from Dr. Red. The prescriptions issued to her by Dr. Red were seized as evidence to establish the ongoing doctor/patient relationship during the time of the sexual encounters. One might ask, what Dr. Red will do when he is told we are picking up prescriptions on patient Sara? At this point there is very little he can do. If he destroys Sara's patient file and denies a doctor/patient relationship, how does he explain the prescriptions without a file? If he tampers with the patient file, how does he explain the sexual relationship, which is verified by the taped phone calls? Either way, Dr. Red has nowhere to hide.

Since sources, even those who are cooperating, do not always tell the truth, the whole truth, and nothing but the truth, we profiled many additional pharmacies in the area. We had to be certain Sara was not holding anything back. Investigators and prosecutors do not like to be ambushed on a case. Fortunately, nothing contradictory was discovered. We also visited the motel where Sara and Dr. Red had their rendezvous and located many of the original receipts. Sara could not remember how many there were after such a long period. As a business that caters to the public, motels must be very careful to protect their guests. The motels require a signed release from the payor, a search warrant, or a subpoena before releasing any receipts. The motel receipts that could be located were later seized pursuant to a subpoena from the board.

While we were doing the field portion of the investigation, I worked with the board's attorney, Stan Ingram, drawing up several legal documents. These items included an administrative inspection and search warrant to seize Sara's patient file. In addition, a suspension order, summons, and affidavit for a licensure revocation hearing were prepared. The suspension order suspends the license of the doctor immediately and until such time as a hearing is held on the evidence. The doctor cannot legally practice medicine once the suspension order is served. The summons requires the doctor to appear at the hearing at a specific date and time in the hearing room at the offices of the MBML. The affidavit to the summons details the specific charges against the doctor. In this case, the charges are unprofessional conduct likely to deceive, defraud, or harm the public. To say the least, it is generally understood that it is unprofessional conduct for any physician to engage in sexual contact with a patient.

Investigator Neil Breeland took the prepared inspection and search warrant to the senior circuit judge in that district. The judge provided Investigator Breeland a similar experience as I had in "The Pill Doctor" case but for totally different reasons. The judge said since he was not familiar with the Mississippi State Board of

Medical Licensure, he would call in his court reporter to record the entire question and answer session. Investigators were trained and prepared for such occurrences to educate the judges on the authority and functions of the MBML. Investigator Breeland provided the judge copies of state statutes establishing the authority of MBML to investigate doctors, serve warrants, and seize evidence including patient files. Unlike the judge I faced in "The Pill Doctor" case, this judge reviewed all of the appropriate statutes and then read the affidavit. He questioned Investigator Breeland about the patient's credibility. Obviously satisfied that the case and warrant had merit, he had Investigator Breeland sworn in, who was then asked to testify that the affidavit was true and correct. The judge then signed the warrant. He told Investigator Breeland to make the return to the Circuit Clerk's office and not to him personally. That is the usual procedure. After approval, Investigator Breeland served Dr. Red at his clinic. Without much fanfare or conversation, Dr. Red provided Sara's patient file.

Investigator Breeland returned to the offices of MBML with the file in hand. An analysis of the patient file established that a doctor/patient relationship existed during the entire time of the sexual encounters. The file contained an initial examination, detailed patient history, initial evaluation and diagnosis, treatment plans, and records of prescriptions issued to Sara. Everything in the file indicated Sara was a current patient and had not been discharged, fired, or referred to another doctor.

At the staff meeting the following Monday morning, we briefed Dr. Morgan, the executive officer, on the details contained in Sara's patient file. There was no denying that Dr. Red had crossed boundaries in his relationship with Sara. After the staff meeting, Dr. Morgan had me take all of the case evidence to the psychiatrist, frequently used by the board as an expert, for his review. I was to stay with him to answer any questions he might have had. After reviewing all of the evidence, it was his opinion that Dr. Red had violated the doctor/patient relationship and was guilty of unprofessional conduct that most likely had, in fact, already inflicted great harm on the patient. Even though the board could not use the expert in a hearing because he was now treating the patient, we could use his opinion as part of our management of the investigation.

Based on the expert's opinion, Dr. Morgan authorized a visit to Dr. Red to give him a chance to surrender his license and avoid a public hearing. Should he refuse, we were instructed to serve him with the suspension notice and the summons and affidavit to a full hearing.

After a couple of phone calls posing as future patients to Dr. Red's primary clinic, we learned that he was in a secondary clinic in another city. Investigator Charlie Moses and I traveled to that clinic to see Dr. Red. After a brief wait, we met with him in a treatment room. We identified ourselves to him and explained the reason for our visit. I detailed just the highlights of the case to him. I did not play our entire hand. I explained to him that the executive officer was offering him the opportunity to voluntarily surrender his medical license, thus avoiding a public revocation hearing. He refused to even consider a surrender of his medical license claiming he had done nothing wrong in treating patient Sara. I reminded Dr. Red that we could prove that he had numerous sexual encounters with a very disturbed, seriously ill patient while he was treating her, which constituted a clear violation of the medical practice act and clearly established boundaries in the doctor/patient relationship. I suggested he may want to reconsider his position. He chose poorly and refused to surrender his license.

We then served Dr. Red with the suspension order and summons and affidavit for a hearing. I again explained to Dr. Red some of the details of the case against him. The patient file, prescriptions, and recorded telephone conversations showed that

Sara was a patient under his care. I again offered Dr. Red the opportunity to voluntarily surrender his medical licensure and avoid a public revocation hearing. Dr. Red declined, denied any wrongdoing, and said he had nothing further to discuss with us. We reminded him of the suspension of his license and hearing date. If he or his attorney had any questions, they could contact the board's attorney. We then left the clinic and reported the results of the visit to the board's executive officer.

Dr. Red and his attorney, a well-respected former prosecutor, decided to proceed with a public hearing before the full board. Prior to the hearing, the defense requested through discovery to be able to listen to the recorded conversations between Dr. Red and Sara. Investigators Neil Breeland and Mickey Robbins set up the tapes for the defense. Dr. Red and his attorney came to the offices of the MBML for the listening. They both listened to the tapes, made a few notes, then departed without much fanfare. They did not even ask for copies to be provided.

A hearing before the full board follows almost the same procedures as a criminal trial. There is usually a litany of pre-hearing motions before the start of the hearing. Once these are handled, the case starts with opening statements and then proceeds to the presentation of evidence. Each witness that testifies is subject to cross-examination by opposing counsel. The board is also afforded the opportunity to ask questions in regulatory hearings. Once the prosecution rests, the defense presents its case with appropriate witnesses. Both sides are allowed closing statements before the board goes into executive session for deliberation.

During the hearing, all the evidence was presented to the board over several hours going late into the night. Sara testified how and why she originally went to Dr. Red for treatment and how her "treatment" evolved into an almost two-year sexual romance. She described in detail the sexual encounters and other activities including the red rubber ball and videotapes and how they were used. Curiously, the spouse of the doctor was present during the entire hearing. It was clear that she had a very difficult time throughout the process. Sara's patient file was introduced along with her prescriptions as well as the tapes of the three recorded telephone conversations. All established that Sara had been a patient during the sexual contact. The board's expert witness, a psychiatrist, testified on behalf of the board to the inappropriate treatment of patient Sara by Dr. Red. He described the sexual contact with a fragile, mentally ill, and vulnerable patient as a boundary that should never be crossed in any valid doctor/patient relationship. As expected, throughout the hearing, the defense objected to the admission of every piece of evidence. An attorney from the Mississippi Attorney General's office was always assigned to oversee board hearings as a neutral observer and to make legal rulings when points of contention arose. The AG assignee overruled almost every objection from the defense. Almost all the evidence was admitted for board consideration.

A slight digression is in order here. Investigators put a lot of pressure on Stan Ingram, the board's attorney and prosecutor, to set the tone of the hearing while he made his opening statement. We begged him to gently toss the infamous red rubber ball in the air from hand to hand while making his opening statement. The reaction of the doctor and his attorney would have been interesting. The ball was sealed in a clear evidence bag. Unfortunately, he refused! He would not even touch the ball. I really don't blame him!

After all evidence and testimony were presented, the board went into executive session. After several hours of deliberation, the board decided to revoke Dr. Red's medical license. As in all cases of revocation of a license in Mississippi, by statute, a licensee can seek reinstatement of that license after one year. However, the last I heard of "Dr. Red" before I retired was that he was running a motel. How appropriate! I understand that his spouse remained with him after the entire episode concluded.

CHAPTER 18

THE MOBILE CURE

The truth must be quite plain if one could just clear away the litter. – Agatha Christie.

After working with doctors, either as appointees to the Mississippi State Board of Medical Licensure or as expert witnesses on cases, certain things become abundantly clear. Most doctors seem to have a real disdain for attorneys, the media, and anything requiring transparency where a doctor is concerned. This lack of a free flow of public information fostered in and helped nurture what was and still is known as the concept of "the mobile cure". As a result, the mobile cure developed into a frequently practiced technique which allowed a doctor to hide their nefarious background by simply moving from one state to another. Unfortunately, in the past twenty or so years, transparency has been mostly a dirty word. Medical board reporting of actions to the public and the Federation of State Medical Boards data bank have seemingly declined somewhat because of the misdirected priority of protecting the doctor, thus enabling the mobile cure concept to continue to function.

The mobile cure concept illuminates the situation the medical board faced when a well-known thoracic surgeon (I'll call him "Dr. Mobile") from another state attempted to relocate his practice to a very small Mississippi hospital. He was trying to escape his past problems and hide his past treatments for chemical dependency. His drugs of choice included Demerol, a narcotic in Schedule IIN, and some non-controlled substances, Stadol and Nubain. Stadol and Nubain had significant abuse potential like Demerol and Dilaudid. Dr. Mobile had contacted a very small Mississippi hospital and had convinced the administration and the chief of staff (I'll call him "Dr. Lyre") to "front door" the licensure processes all the while "forgetting" to tell them of his past issues. The "too good to be true" axiom went out the window.

Experience and common sense in these issues is the best teacher. Why would a professor of thoracic surgery in his prime years practicing at a major teaching university outside of Mississippi want to relocate his practice to one of the smallest, if not *the* smallest, hospital in Mississippi? He was also giving up his teaching position and tenure? Why would any physician want to move from one of the largest and most successful medical referral centers in the country to a town in Mississippi with a population of fewer than 2,000 people? Well, the obvious answer, if you just got off the turnip truck, is he wanted to help cure all the sick people in Mississippi. What else, right? Wrong!

Believe it or not, during this era in medicine throughout the United States, the mobile cure was commonly practiced because many state boards did not report or cooperate with one another. Thankfully, the situation is somewhat improved currently, but there is still a long way to go in Mississippi and nationwide.

Fortunately, the Licensure Division of the Mississippi State Board of Medical Licensure (MBML) had seen this movie before. Although the original license application submitted by Dr. Mobile did not list any previous problems, the licensure vetting process of the board did uncover former disciplinary action. On his application, Dr. Mobile had gaps of unexplained time when he did not seem to have employment. These gaps turned out to be time spent in treatment programs as required by his original state of licensure but not reported to the federation data bank or any other state. The doctor did finally cooperate when confronted directly about the inconsistencies on his Mississippi application. At first, Dr. Mobile decided not to pursue a license in Mississippi because he had been outed. Later, he reversed directions and decided to pursue a Mississippi license. Because he had falsified his original application and, along with the pesky little problem of having "forgotten about" action taken against him in another state, Dr. Mobile was told he could not receive an unrestricted license. However, he could be licensed with numerous restrictions. This procedure was a common practice in Mississippi and most other states. Dr. Mobile only needed to enter into a consent order (a public record) with the board that specifically spelled out the conditions for licensure. However, I emphasize that the conditions are numerous. One restriction, among many others, was that he had to submit to random, unannounced, and witnessed urine and or blood samples at any time. By "any time," I mean any time or place a board investigator asks for a sample, including weekends, the doctor shall comply or face board action for violation of his conditions of licensure. The urine and blood samples are tested for all controlled substances, alcohol, Stadol, and Nubain. Also, the doctor pays for all testing costs. The cost of the tests for Stadol and Nubain, at that time, was quite high due to their being new and unfamiliar drugs. Dr. Mobile agreed to the consent order and was granted a Mississippi medical license with conditions. The urine and blood testing started right away. It was the MBML's position to try and collect at least three samples a month for the first year in the monitoring program. After that, at least two samples a month were collected until the monitoring period was complete. Most consent orders in Mississippi, at that time, had a minimum of five years of monitoring.

Approximately three months after licensing, several clean samples had been collected from Doctor Mobile and everything seemed to be going well for the surgeon. Then, early on a Monday morning, I arrived at the hospital to collect a sample. I really liked collecting a sample on Mondays, especially early. That sample would look back over the weekend in case a relapse had occurred. At the time of my arrival, Dr. Mobile was already performing a procedure in surgery. For obvious reasons, a surgical suite is one of the areas investigators cannot go unannounced to collect a sample, so I had to hurry up and wait. After about an hour, Dr. Mobile exited the surgery suite. I met him at the door to the surgical suite and told him I needed to collect a urine sample for testing. At first, he requested to be allowed to clean-up, write his surgical notes, and check on the status of the patient. I told him that would be fine. However, he would have to be escorted by me until the sample was collected. Investigators were not permitted by policy, which was learned the hard way, to leave the presence of the physician until the sample was collected. Previous cases in which physicians had altered samples, by having advance warning of a board visit, taught the board a lesson rather emphatically. Remember, these are smart and sometimes very devious people. With that information, Dr. Mobile agreed to produce the sample immediately rather than try to explain to staff why a stranger was following him around the hospital. We stepped into a room just off the surgical suite area where Dr. Mobile provided the witnessed sample. When a urine sample was collected, there were two containers involved. They were plastic evidence sample bottles with screw-on tops approximately 100 cc/ml (3-4 oz) per container. Each container had to be at least half full to be a proper sample for testing. If the donor could not produce the required minimum, the investigator had to wait until they are able to comply. Once the samples were collected, they were sealed and covered with tamper-proof evidence tape, then marked and dated with the investigator's and doctor's initials. Both containers were delivered to the university toxicology lab operated under the supervision of Arthur Hume, Ph.D. One container was for the UMMC toxicology lab for testing. In case of a positive result, the second container was frozen by the lab and maintained for possible independent testing by a defense team. The actual testing, reporting of results, and testifying, when necessary, was done by Chief Toxicologist Lee Spencer. Not only were the tests performed in a timely manner, but the results were always spot on. Not a single independent test performed by a defense team was found to be different, a false positive, or in any way contradict the UMMC lab results.

Dr. Mobile was asked if he had taken or been prescribed, administered, or dispensed any medication by anyone that might need to be explained. Dr. Mobile said there was not. I took the samples to the lab at UMMC and personally delivered them to the chief lab tech for testing. Strict chain-of-custody had to be maintained at all times. Dr. Mobile's samples were to be tested for all controlled substances, alcohol, Stadol, and Nubain. Stadol and Nubain required the samples to be sent to an off-site specialty lab and required several days extra time for testing.

After approximately three weeks, I was contacted by Lee Spencer and told that the sample from Dr. Mobile tested positive for Stadol and Nubain metabolites and that the results indicated large amounts or probable multiple injections of both drugs. Sophisticated testing labs do qualitative testing and quantitative testing when necessary to not only determine what drug(s) are present in the blood or urine but just how much is present. No other substances were detected. All the lab results were reported to the executive officer and board attorney. The board's attorney was authorized to draw up an order to suspend Dr. Mobile's license and summon him to a hearing for possible revocation of his license, based on violating his consent order with the MBML.

Approximately three days after the lab results were received by the board, the executive officer received a telephone call from a doctor on staff at the same hospital as Dr. Mobile. He stated he had recently been contacted by Dr. Mobile and requested to create a medical file for him indicating he had given Dr. Mobile an injection of Stadol on the day before the urine sample was collected. The doctor told the executive officer that Dr. Mobile said he needed the file to document and justify an injection of Stadol he had self-administered for a migraine. The doctor refused to prepare the file. The executive officer did not disclose the positive result for Nubain, nor the excessive amounts detected in the sample. He requested the doctor provide the board a written statement and be available to testify if necessary, and he agreed. The next day I met confidentially with him at the hospital and picked up his prepared statement. The doctor then told me he had recently learned of a second doctor at the hospital that had been requested by Dr. Mobile to prepare a medical file to reflect a Stadol injection. That doctor had also declined Doctor Mobile's request. The executive officer authorized me to contact the second doctor and request a written statement. Initially, he refused. After some thought and a brief discussion about the consequences of not cooperating, he reluctantly agreed to provide a statement.

Before the suspension order and the summons and affidavit were prepared and served on Dr. Mobile, the executive officer for the MBML was contacted by the hospital owner and chief of staff, Dr. Lyre. Dr. Lyre told the executive officer that Dr. Mobile had made him aware of the sample collected. Dr. Lyre said the sample was probably positive for Stadol because he had himself provided

Dr. Mobile an injection of Stadol the morning of the sample collection due to a migraine headache. He agreed to provide the board the medical file documenting the injection authorized by him. Again, no mention was made of the Nubain or the excessive quantity of each drug in the sample. I was immediately dispatched to Dr. Lyre's clinic to pick up the medical file on Dr. Mobile reflecting the injection. Dr. Lyre was not available at the clinic; however, he had made arrangements with his staff to provide me the original file and leave the clinic a copy. The file contained one solitary injection of Stadol and no mention of Nubain.

The file was delivered to the board attorney for consideration in the case. After the board's attorney reviewed all the evidence, I was directed to visit Dr. Lyre and advise him of the case to date, which included the results of the urine sample, the other doctors who were asked to falsify a medical file, his own medical file data on Dr. Mobile, and then to wait for his explanation.

When I met with Dr. Lyre, I detailed the entire case to him, especially the part about the Stadol and Nubain and the quantities identified in the sample. I told him I knew his file to be a false reflection of the facts and I wanted to get his response. After being presented with the details about the other two doctors being approached to prepare a medical file, Dr. Lyre, realizing he was in a corner, kind of laughed and then acknowledged that he created the file at the request of Dr. Mobile. He said he thought he was somehow helping the situation. I told Dr. Lyre that a more appropriate word might be "enabling" the situation rather than "helping." Dr. Lyre was told he may well face charges himself for his serious actions in this case. I suggested that it would be a show of good faith if he would provide a statement and agree to testify concerning his actions should Dr. Mobile decide to pursue a full hearing for violation of his consent order. Dr. Lyre reluctantly but eventually provided a statement and agreed to testify.

The following day a suspension order and summons and affidavit were served on Dr. Mobile. Once served the doctor cannot practice medicine in Mississippi until there is a resolution to the charges in the summons and affidavit. Dr. Mobile never sought to challenge the suspension of his license. He never responded to the summons and affidavit resulting in the board revoking his Mississippi medical license in his absence.

Dr. Lyre had his license placed on probation and, fortunately, never had to appear before the board again.

The mobile cure never cures!

CHAPTER 19

DR. HAMILTON

It's not appropriate for a doctor to sit behind the patient to examine the breasts. Ideally, in fact, doctors should be visible to the patient. – Erica Hinz, MD. "Doctors and Sex Abuse," Atlanta Journal Constitution, 2016.

A little-known fact about licensing doctors can cause confusion among patients and a lot of bad outcomes in patient care if one is not careful. Most medical boards, including Mississippi, do not license doctors based on a particular specialty. A doctor is licensed to practice medicine only when they complete training at a qualified medical school and pass the Federation Licensing Exam. If they choose a particular specialty, which most do, they are then certified in that particular specialty when they complete the residency course of training. They can then practice and obtain hospital privileges to treat inpatients in their specialty. A licensed pediatrician can apply to a hospital to perform neurosurgery if he or she has completed the appropriate training in neurosurgery. If not, the hospital will not grant that doctor privileges to perform in neurosurgery. That actually happened in one case. The pediatrician could not get hospital privileges in neurosurgery so he began to perform neurological procedures in his clinic. The trusting and misinformed public had numerous bad outcomes. Eventually, it did not end well for the doctor. He had a consistent record of bad decision making. Some not involving medicine but did involve female patients that eventually cost him his license. He considered himself untouchable, but that is another case for another time.

This case involves a retired doctor who chose to continue to practice medicine in retirement, but not in the specialty for which he was trained and in which he performed successfully for decades. After he retired, he was hired by a hospital to treat patients that, for one reason or another, had no place to care for them. They were unable to care for themselves for a variety of reasons. The government had to house, feed, clothe, and manage their medical problems. The medical problems are where Dr. Hamilton (not his real name) began to attract unwanted attention.

Most hospitals are always recruiting doctors for staff privileges. Some hospitals, depending on location, find it fairly easy to recruit and retain doctors while others find it difficult for various reasons. The usual cause of a doctor leaving a hospital is "greener pastures." They do not feel they are making the money they should or could elsewhere. Government-run facilities are continuously dealing with high doctor turnover mainly due to low salaries based on limited government funding. Dr. Hamilton was limited where he could find a job in retirement due to his former specialty. The hospital that did hire him desperately needed doctors and would allow him to practice what would be considered a general family practice. He would be responsible for the day-to-day medical complaints of the general population patients confined to the hospital. This involved several hundred patients that had no other place to go. In effect, they were a captive patient population. Many had physical challenges along with serious mental challenges.

The initial complaint originated from a doctor at the hospital. Remember the first rule of medical board complaints. If a doctor is complaining about another doctor, you need to pay attention! The doctor indicated that over the past several months, numerous complaints had been received from staff members concerning Dr. Hamilton's conduct with female patients. The staff members were complaining that Dr. Hamilton's examinations of female patients along with his comments were inappropriate, embarrassing, and abusive. Most of the patients were powerless to resist or defend themselves. Attempts to counsel him had resulted in brief periods of improvement with him only returning to the improper behavior. An equally troubling aspect was that the inappropriate exams and comments were in the presence of and witnessed by other health care professionals, most of them women. The complaining doctor indicated that the hospital, short of firing Dr. Hamilton, was at the end of its rope and was requesting help from the medical board to deal with him. Also, the doctor said it was almost impossible to fire a government employee. Firing him was not enough, they wanted something done to address his ability to treat patients in the future. The doctor offered any number of witnesses from the hospital to testify if and when necessary.

I briefed the executive officer on the complaint and was advised to make it a high priority case. We wanted to move as fast as possible to preserve as many witnesses as possible. Witnesses sometimes tended to quit or get cold feet when testifying was in their future. I contacted the original complainant and set an appointment for the following day.

At the meeting, I was provided a list of at least eight employees who had repeatedly witnessed the misconduct of Dr. Hamilton. Most were RNs, or LPNs, and two were psychologists. I did not recall a single case in which I had such a strong list of reliable, competent witnesses to testify. Usually, it was like pulling teeth to obtain full cooperation. These witnesses were mad as hell and could not wait to tell what had happened. Finally! Why could they not all have been like that?

The witnesses were summoned one at a time to the hospital conference room where they were interviewed individually by me. The statements obtained followed a similar pattern. At the hospital, medical rounds were made daily to each building housing patients. Some patients could be managed by the nursing staff, others would be referred to see the doctor at morning rounds. At each morning round, there were several staff members present in the room used to examine and evaluate each patient. It was common practice to have more than one person present during the examination to prevent just what Dr. Hamilton was doing. In addition, they recorded the doctor's orders for the treatment of the patient. The staff usually consisted of an RN, an LPN, a psychologist, sometimes an orderly (depending on the patient's stability), and Dr. Hamilton. Initially, the examinations were conducted appropriately and professionally. After several months Dr. Hamilton began to take liberties with certain female patients, especially if they were younger or had what he referred to as "a nice ass" or "nice tits." He would also make various inappropriate comments about their possible sexual history or activity, usually while he was examining the patients' genitals. He frequently would sit behind a female patient and reach his arms around under their arms, cup a bare breast in each hand, and juggle them up and down while making inappropriate comments or laughing. Each witness described the behavior as occurring several times a week over the last several months despite hospital efforts to curb the conduct.

All of the statements were reviewed by the executive officer and board attorney. They both suggested Dr. Hamilton be contacted and offered the opportunity to surrender his medical license or be charged and summoned to a full revocation hearing. When contacted, Dr. Hamilton refused to surrender his license. Stan Ingram prepared a summons and affidavit detailing the charges and requiring Dr. Hamilton to appear before the full board.

At the hearing, all of the witnesses that had provided statements testified to the actions of the doctor. None of the patients could be called due to their being incompetent to testify. The doctor who called in the original complaint testified concerning the hospital's repeated efforts to get control of the situation and Dr. Hamilton's repeated failure to cooperate in the effort.

During the hearing and after the prosecution rested, Dr. Hamilton, who was represented by counsel, took the stand in his own defense. His wife was also present for the full hearing that took several hours and ran late into the night. During the hearing, the doctor testified he meant no harm and denied that he harmed any of the patients. He offered no medical reason for his inappropriate actions and no defense for his comments. Stan Ingram pressed the doctor on the way he conducted the breast exam, especially the way he cupped the breast and performed a juggling motion. Stan demanded a medical reason for such exams. Dr. Hamilton could not provide one. Stan pressed him further on his experience in performing appropriate breast exams since his previous practice did not involve breast exams. The doctor said he felt he knew how to perform an appropriate breast exam. Stan excoriated the doctor on his lack of proper care for defenseless patients and told him it seemed doubtful that he did know how to perform a proper breast exam.

By this time, the exchanges had become heated. After Stan Ingram's last comment to the doctor, the doctor's wife had had enough. She stood up at the defense table and screamed at Stan, "What do you know about breast exams? Just how many breasts have you examined, Mr. Ingram?" The president of the board banged his gavel for order and called a short recess before continuing. During the recess, Stan walked over to me at the prosecutor's table and sat down. He leaned over to me and commented, "Can you believe that woman shouting that?" I leaned over to Stan and quietly commented how the question was very interesting and told him that he should take the stand and answer the question. "Just how many breasts have you examined Mr. Ingram?" He looked at me with a perplexed look on his face, then realized he had been had! I told him, "Well, we are waiting, how many?" He finally just exhaled, relaxed, shook his head, and started laughing.

The hearing reconvened. No expert witness was presented since it was not necessary. There are nine experts that sit on the board well-trained in proper breast examination. The defense only offered up a glowing history of Dr. Hamilton's past performances and assurances he meant no harm to the employees or the patients.

The board went into an executive session to consider the evidence. After about an hour they returned with a verdict of guilty of unprofessional conduct. They ordered his license to be revoked. As a condition of reinstatement, Dr. Hamilton had to be examined for mental competency and successfully complete a course on medical ethics. The board then adjourned.

To my knowledge, Dr. Hamilton never returned to the practice of medicine.

The question that Stan Ingram was asked by the doctor's wife was memorialized in a plaque that the medical board investigators provided to Stan as a Christmas present. The actual transcript was provided by the court reporter. There was a postscript added at the bottom of the transcription. Let the record reflect that Mr. Ingram refused to answer the doctor's wife's question. "Just how many breasts have you examined, Mr. Ingram?" To this date, and to his credit, he has never answered that question.

CHAPTER 20

DR. STAVROS and DR. AVILLA

Most people who become addicted [to opioids] like me, do so after a prescription for a painkiller following a medical procedure. Once the phenomenon of craving sets in, it is often too late. – Jamie Lee Curtis, movie star and recovering addict.

Most physicians do quite well financially and do not resort to "entrepreneurial" tactics for enrichment. Some doctors, however, are not interested in patient face-to-face contact or are uncomfortable managing sick patients due to a lack of skill. These individuals usually play with fire and sooner or later get burned. They set up some form of "make money fast and furious" scheme, regardless of the patient's well-being, until the hammer falls.

The investigation of Dr. Stavros (not his real name) started with one patient of interest and grew to eventually involve, and ultimately threaten, thousands of unsuspecting victims. The original patient was a very young man, single, with no living parents (I will call him "Jodie"). Jodie lived in a medium-sized Mississippi oil town and had inherited producing oil wells from his family. I was never informed exactly how Jodie came to inherit the wells, but he was doing quite well until an accident resulted in a long hospital stay. While in the hospital, Jodie had several surgeries and as a result was administered large amounts of Dilaudid, Demerol, and other drugs. After several weeks, he was discharged to the care of his primary surgeon. After approximately six weeks of convalescence, he was released by the surgeon to be cared for by his primary care physician of choice. Since Jodie did not really have a regular family physician, he was referred to Dr. Stavros, who continued to prescribe him large quantities of Dilaudid 4 mg on an outpatient basis. The prescribing to Jodie was eventually identified by the board's monitoring program and a visit to Dr. Stavros was approved by the executive officer. Dr. Stavros readily agreed to discontinue the prescribing and have the patient evaluated for chemical dependency. After a first-time visit to any doctor by MBML investigators, a follow-up warning letter was sent by the executive officer urging the doctor to appropriately manage patients and avoid just maintaining them on controlled substances and that a follow-up profile would likely take place in a year or so to evaluate the situation. The patient, Jodie, went in for an evaluation that resulted in a confirmed diagnosis of chemical dependency. He went in for treatment. However, the treatment was not successful, and Jodie returned to Dr. Stavros for drugs.

Dr. Stavros did not relish the attention from the medical board and did not want to continue the prescribing of Dilaudid. He changed the prescriptions for Jodie from Dilaudid to Stadol. Stadol was a new drug and had all of the properties of Demerol and Dilaudid, but was not yet a controlled substance. It also had the same potential for abuse and was frequently substituted for other, more commonly abused controlled substances. Dr. Stavros continued to prescribe the Stadol in an injectable form on an outpatient basis for Jodie. Since Stadol at the time was not controlled, it did not appear on anyone's radar.

Then it happened. Information was received by the medical board from an anonymous source who identified herself as a friend of Jodie's. She said that Jodie was continuing to receive injectable Stadol prescriptions from Dr. Stavros. He was completely addicted and unable to operate his business in his best interest. According to her, the prescriptions had been issued for the last two years whenever Jodie wanted the drug. She also said that there was a rumor going around in the oil business that Jodie had transferred over, not sold, a producing oil well to Dr. Stavros. The executive officer immediately approved a follow-up investigation into the complaint.

Oil and gas wells are bought and sold almost every day and it is perfectly legal. However, the source said it was transferred, not sold. Why would anyone just transfer a producing oil well to someone without something in return?

The next step was to conduct pharmacy profiles to identify just how much Stadol Dr. Stavros had been prescribing to Jodie. The profile took much longer than normal because Stadol was not yet a controlled substance, therefore the prescriptions were mixed in with all the regular non-controlled substance prescriptions. Fortunately, some of the pharmacies were just beginning to use computers which shortened the process somewhat. After several weeks of profiling, a clear pattern had developed indicating that Jodie had been receiving as many as ten to twenty 10 cc vials of Stadol weekly for almost twenty-four months. The normal decision at this time would be to visit Dr. Stavros and determine the medical justification for prescribing the Stadol over such a long period. However, this situation deviated somewhat from the norm. Most patients do not give their doctor oil wells! I suspected a quid pro quo. Everyone thought I was way out on a limb. The board attorney said he had seen people give away oil wells, but it usually involved family or corporate transactions. None of that applied here. It was hard to imagine a patient giving a doctor an oil well for prescriptions. It was even harder, at the time, to believe a legitimate doctor would stoop so low as to involve himself in such nefarious activity. However, my experience with some doctors had taught me to never say never.

I proposed to visit Jodie first, not the doctor. It took some doing, but I was finally able to talk the executive officer and board attorney into the patient visit first. Should I just walk in or call and make an appointment? Fifty/fifty either way. It is usually easier to say no over the phone than in a face-to-face meeting. On the other hand, in person, you can get a body language reading. However, an impromptu visit might have the effect of scaring him off. I decided to give him a courtesy call to try and set up a meeting.

On the phone, I introduced myself to Jodie and requested to meet with him to discuss some medical board related business. I asked him to please just hear me out before he hung up. I told him I wanted to talk to him about the prescriptions for Stadol he had been receiving from Dr. Stavros and particularly about some of his business dealings with the doctor. I said that I was the investigator responsible for having Dr. Stavros stop the Dilaudid prescriptions two years ago and referred him for treatment. I do not expect you to consider me a friend but the medical board is not knowingly going to allow a doctor to destroy a patient by overprescribing addictive substances. I also told him that I had heard of his transferring to Dr. Stavros a producing oil well for no obvious compensation, other than possibly drugs. I suspected a quid pro quo but I was not certain of that. I told Jodie to please feel free to stop me if I got too far out of line. He never told me to stop, so I continued. I assured him he was not in any type of trouble with the law as far as I knew, but I could not say the same for Dr. Stavros. I wanted very much to hear his side of the story in person. Now, I fully expected Jodie to tell me it was none of my business. To my surprise, he did not!

Jodie said he was not certain what he should say or if he should say anything at all. I repeated that the board was not investigating him, only Dr. Stavros. I suggested he consult with his attorney and offered to answer any questions I could to help convince him to talk with me. I told him I only ask for one thing, the entire truth. Jodie said he needed some time to talk with his attorney before saying anything to me. I asked him to give me a call as soon as he made a decision. I had taken my best shot, but I did not expect to hear from him ever again. If he did not call me back in a reasonable period of time, I would follow plan B, i.e., making the standard visit to Dr. Stavros to discuss the overly suspicious Stadol prescriptions to Jodie.

My second surprise came two weeks later when Jodie called me at the medical board and said he would talk to me. We agreed to meet in two days in my room at a local motel that I frequently used when I worked in that city. He arrived at the room at approximately 6:00 p.m. He came alone and was carrying a notebook with what looked like a legal document protruding from one end. Jodie had an extremely youthful appearance. If I did not know better, I would have guessed he was not a day over twenty-one. Actually, he was approaching thirty. He first wanted to know exactly what I planned to do with my investigation of Dr. Stavros. I explained how the MBML was an administrative agency, not a criminal one and told him I hoped to gather enough evidence with his help to address the doctor's practice of medicine in Mississippi. I told him that if what I suspected happened actually happened, with his cooperation and testimony, I could charge Dr. Stavros with enough violations of the medical practice act to bring him before the board in a revocation hearing. Jodie asked me what I thought had happened. I told him that I was operating on the theory that Dr. Stavros, either by design or happenstance, had prescribed Stadol in sufficient quantities over a long enough period to addict him. As a result, either he talked you into transferring an oil well to him in return for Stadol or you offered him the oil well. Either way, Dr. Stavros had gone way off the reservation by accepting the oil well as a quid pro quo and was clearly not acting in his patient's best medical interest. The board calls that unprofessional conduct likely to deceive, defraud, or harm the patient. It could cost him his medical license and make him subject to other restrictions deemed necessary by the board.

Jodie said he was addicted to the Stadol and probably still was but had stopped using thanks to a local physician that was instrumental in helping him to get off the drug. He admitted he had offered the oil well to Dr. Stavros in return for him providing the Stadol for the rest of his life. He admitted that at the time he was addicted and out of control. However, now he was very reluctant to get involved any further because of the embarrassment for himself and credibility in the community and the oil business. I told him I could not do it without him. He inquired if this would in any way help him recover the oil well. I told him that question was a legal issue that was way beyond my level of expertise. Seizing the opportunity, I asked Jodie to show me the contract papers transferring the well to Stavros and he did! The key components identified the oil well location and site for the property location. It was transferred to Dr. Stavros in return for compensation provided to Jodie as determined necessary and appropriate. Jodie made clear that the compensation was understood to be Stadol, whenever he wanted it. The other thing made clear was that Dr. Stavros would be the sole owner of the well. Done and done. Now, could I convince Jodie to hang with me and testify if necessary? Jodie expressed a real need to keep the case out of the public eye. I told him I could not make that promise. If the case went to a hearing, it would be open to the public. Eventually and with great reluctance he agreed to testify. A release was executed to obtain

Jodie's medical file from Dr. Stavros. To say the least, Dr. Stavros reluctantly provided Jodie's medical file to the board. The analysis of the file revealed little to no medical indications or justification for two years of Stadol prescriptions and virtually none of the prescriptions were documented in the file. Dr. Stavros refused to meet or talk with me concerning the patient file.

Before Dr. Stavros could be formally charged, he worked out an agreement through his attorneys with the executive officer and board attorney to surrender schedules II, IIN, III, and IIIN of his DEA certificate, and agreed to a ban on his administering, dispensing, or prescribing any form of Stadol or Nubain. The time period for the suspension was five years. Dr. Stavros could petition the board for the return of the DEA privileges at any time, but the board was not under any obligation to act. I was advised of the agreement by the executive officer. I strongly objected to the wording. The truth is that there was no requirement to seek my opinion on any case settlement and, in fact, it was never done. Still, I strongly urged that Dr. Stavros be required to surrender his medical license, not just his DEA certificate and that, as a condition of reinstatement, he be required to return the oil well obtained from Jodie under duress. My suggestion was completely ignored. It was worth a shot, I felt I owed Jodie that much and I told him so.

As a result of the loss of his DEA certificate, Dr. Stavros was limited in the type of practice he could operate. Also, with a restricted DEA certificate, at the time, he could not be granted hospital privileges. It was during this time Dr. Stavros began to practice in the area of bariatric medicine (weight loss). This required no hospital privileges. Since he had been allowed to retain Schedule IV of his DEA certificate, he was in business big time. Most controlled diet pills were, and still are, in Schedule IV. His bariatric business began slowly but in a relatively short time grew like gangbusters and as his practice grew, he began to explore ways to increase revenue. After only a few years he was considered to have one of the largest weight loss clinics operating in the southeast. He literally had busloads of patients coming to the clinic daily. At one time he started a valet parking service for patients. As frequently happens with large scale operations, people look for shortcuts or other ways to increase revenue and reduce costs of the operation. Bariatric or weight loss practices are quite common and patients frequently have success in their carefully managed weight loss efforts. There is nothing suspicious or nefarious about such clinics as long as the doctor and the clinics follow the rules and practice medicine appropriately. However, not everyone does.

Weight loss clinics did not garner a lot of attention from the medical board at the time and were generally considered fairly benign in their operation. However, that was about to change. Complaints began to come in from multiple sources concerning Dr. Stavros' weight-loss operation. Complaints from patients indicated they could not get prescriptions filled at their hometown pharmacy because the prescriptions were issued in some form of code that Dr. Stavros would not release. He would tell the patients to get them filled at one particular pharmacy that had the codes and the proper drugs he wanted to be used. It was later revealed he owned that pharmacy, imagine that! Medical board regulations require that the patient have freedom of choice on where to have their prescriptions filled. Patients complained about not ever being seen by a doctor or sometimes being seen by a "doctor" who they suspected was not a real doctor. Parents and spouses were alarmed that their loved ones were getting weight loss diet pills when they did not need to lose any weight. Patients complained about bad reactions requiring hospitalization and the treating physicians complained about not being able to get information on the drugs the patients were taking, placing them at great risk. The pharmacist filling the prescriptions was instructed to not reveal the drugs and Dr. Stavros would not do so.

I received information that Dr. Stavros was frequently traveling out of the country and taking large quantities of cash from the clinic operation with him without reporting it to United States Customs. I was also informed that he had foreign bank accounts with large balances of money from the clinic that he did not report on his income tax forms. I contacted a friend of mine with IRS criminal division and one with Customs and told them of the possible financial irregularities. They expressed real interest in following up on the information. Just from how the conversation flowed, call it investigator intuition, I suspected they were already on to Dr. Stavros's tax and money smuggling scheme, but I was never told for sure.

I also received information that during his foreign trips, Dr. Stavros had Arnufalo Avilla, MD (not his real name) practicing in the clinic. According to my source, Dr. Avilla was licensed in a nearby state, but not Mississippi. I checked our licensure division on Dr. Avilla and they confirmed that fact. Finally, the same source told me that whenever Dr. Stavros was out of the clinic, he provided his staff pads of pre-signed prescriptions for Dr. Avilla to use when prescribing to the patients. The only thing the staff or Dr. Avilla had to add to the prescription was the patient's name, address, and date. Of course, they also collected the money for the visit. The vast majority of payments were made in cash. Very few insurance companies covered medical weight loss programs and Dr. Stavros did not accept any insurance.

Most diet clinic prescription regimens followed a similar pattern. They generally consisted of five to seven basic drugs. A Schedule IV diet pill, vitamin pills (B12, B6, etc.), a thyroid pill, a fiber pill, a stool softener, and a diuretic. Dr. Stavros had a letter code system for each drug prescribed that worked fairly simply. On the prescription, the patient would see their name, address, and date. Below that, where the drug(s) were supposed to be listed were a series of letters such as A, C, O, T, Q, etc. in column format with directions on how to take them by each letter. The actual drug name was not identified even on the pill bottle itself, after being filled! Sometimes the prescription had just one coded drug on it. Others had two or more and some even had five or seven coded drugs, depending on what was prescribed.

Just when the executive officer had given the go-ahead for a full investigation on Dr. Stavros, I got a call from my IRS and Customs contacts who said that they had opened a joint criminal investigation. I told them that I had just been authorized to begin an administrative investigation. They requested that we delay our investigation or at least any overt actions and allow the criminal case to go first. Really, I did not have much choice. If I did not delay my investigation or if I in any way interfered with their case, I could be accused of obstruction. Also, I needed them more than they needed me. They did not want to spook Dr. Stavros into changing his habits, nor did I. I was told they had located foreign bank accounts containing very large amounts of money that Dr. Stavros had failed to acknowledge and pay taxes on. A review of the transactions by IRS verified that every few months, deposits from $20,000 to $80,000 were made into the accounts. Customs did not have any reports of transfers of cash out of the country. Federal law at that time required that any transfer of cash out of the country in amounts of $10,000 or more must be reported to U.S. Customs. Dr. Stavros had not made any reports.

I took the news of the criminal case to the executive officer and told him they had requested we do nothing at the time. No one realized how long the criminal case would take. After almost two years of seemingly no action, I complained to my contacts at Customs and IRS about the long delay and how we at the medical board were being inundated with complaints and criticism for a lack of action on Dr. Stavros. Federal agencies do not have to explain or report anything to state agencies, not even cooperating ones that help them initiate a case. However, most of the time they communicate fairly well. In this case, I was afforded some explanation to provide my executive officer who was getting a lot of irate calls from other doctors and the State Medical Association, believe it or not, on Dr. Stavros! The IRS explanation made perfectly good investigative sense but did not help our situation. To establish criminal intent for the tax not paid on the foreign bank accounts and the failure to acknowledge the existence of the accounts, there is a substantial waiting period that must pass. Once a taxpayer files a tax return and omits, for whatever reason, that he has foreign bank accounts thus avoiding any tax, the IRS must wait until the time period for filing an amended return has passed so the taxpayer cannot successfully claim it was just an oversight. For each tax year, there was considerable wait time to pass that threshold.

Also complaining loudly and frequently to me about the operation of Stavros' diet clinic was my old boss at the Mississippi Bureau of Narcotics. He had retired from state employment and was now working for the city as the chief of police. He kept calling me about the complaints that he and the mayor of the city were getting and wanting me to do something immediately to stop Dr. Stavros' practice and all the diet pills that were flooding the town. I tried to explain to him the complication I faced with trying to cooperate with IRS and Customs on the case. He was not sympathetic. He kept right on calling and complaining to me about how I needed to cut through the federal red tape, do my job, and shut this doctor down – and fast! Finally, I responded to him, "Talk about me not doing my job!" I then reminded him of an internal affairs case at the MBN that he had assigned to me, exclusively, with no help, over my strong objections and that of my terminally ill supervisor who was near death from cancer. The case involved two agents, who while intoxicated, arrested, kidnapped, and assaulted two heroin case defendants, husband and wife, and beat them mercilessly while they were handcuffed to a tree in the woods. Even though the evidence was overwhelming against the two agents, I reminded him, "You did basically nothing to them but a suspension. I strongly recommended termination and prosecution, but you said you just could not bring yourself to do that." I also reminded him how, a few months later, one of those same agents attempted to have me approve his offer to toss a different well-known heroin smuggler under a running soybean combine to kill him. He told me all I had to do was say the word and walk away, and it would be done. I reminded the agent that we wore the white hats. We did not operate that way and that he had not learned anything from his last experience. That agent had a reputation for covertly recording everything and everybody, but did not know I was recording him. I gave the recording to my boss. I am confident the agent was recording me and planning to do the same, had I authorized him to kill the smuggler. When it became clear the agent was going to walk again, I gave my thirty-day notice and resigned from the MBN.

I also reminded my old boss of a rather well-known, long time operation in his city of a "ladies of the night" red light establishment that catered to local, state, and Washington politicians along with wealthy suitors from all over the country. Even several Secret Service agents were said to have partaken of the "goods" when a certain President of the United States paid the town a visit. I advised him of my investigation of another local doctor in his town who was supplying the madame and her girls with controlled substances in return for trips to the doctor's clinic by his choice of the week from among the working girls. Three of those girls had been talking to me for some time concerning the day-to-day, tit for tat (no pun intended) operation. Two of them were a mother/daughter team (how sick is that?). The mother was concerned because the daughter had become dependent on the controlled drugs and wanted help getting it stopped. The third girl was just sick and tired of having to give "freebies" to the doctor.

Eventually, the board did take away that doctor's DEA certificate. However, the real solution to that problem occurred when the doctor came in second in a knife fight (literally) in New Orleans. It left him, more or less, in a vegetative state. That did much more for the community than anything we could do. I then told my former boss to stop calling me about Dr. Stavros until he did something about those two criminals posing as MBN agents and the world-famous whorehouse operating right under his nose. He said there was nothing he could do now about the two agents and that he would have a better chance of shutting down the First Baptist Church than that whorehouse! After that conversation, he called me about many things, but never again about Dr. Stavros. Many years later, at one of his grandson's baseball games we attended together at North West Rankin High School, he did finally admit, in a rare moment of regret, that he should have fired the two agents and referred the case for prosecution.

During the long delay waiting for IRS and Customs to act, we continued our investigation covertly into the diet pill operation. Investigators from the medical board made undercover visits to the clinics to assess the entire practice objectively and document the treatment regimen. Prior to the visits, one investigator was given a thyroid pill by our consulting expert to increase his thyroid level to see what the doctor would prescribe to him. During the UC visits, both investigators were examined by the unlicensed Dr. Avilla, had a blood screen run, were weighed, were required to see a film on weight loss and breast self-examination (which even male patients were required to view), and then met again with Dr. Avilla. He then provided them prescriptions for the diet regimen including controlled diet pills. The prescriptions had all been pre-signed by Dr. Stavros, a really big "oops" in our favor! The investigator with the elevated thyroid level was still prescribed more thyroid to take. (This was later determined when we found the drug code decrypt sheet.) In a real case scenario, our expert said that any patient that took the extra thyroid could have been put into heart failure with fatal results. All the prescriptions issued were in the code used by the clinic and Dr. Avilla did not identify the drugs prescribed. They were referred to the specific pharmacy to have the prescriptions filled. They paid the fee and departed the clinic. A similar operation took place two weeks later at a remote clinic operated by Dr. Stavros in another part of the state with similar results. The female undercover investigator loaned to us by MBN was not a weight loss candidate. Regardless, she was still prescribed the entire weight loss regime. The prescriptions had Dr. Stavros' signature on them, but she was seen by Dr. Avilla. Based on the undercover visits, investigators began to prepare an inspection and search warrant to serve on the clinics.

Just as the warrants and affidavits were being prepared, I received a call from a deputy sheriff in the city who had been helping us unofficially on the investigation. He indicated Dr. Stavros had recently left the city on a trip overseas. He had Dr. Avilla working in the clinic and had provided him and the staff with a large box containing pre-signed prescription pads to use in his absence. Here was the opportunity we had been waiting for. We had reliable advance notice that Dr. Stavros was not only out of the clinic but out of the country. While I knew it might upset the IRS and Customs by doing something this overt, I felt we could not wait any longer or for a better opportunity. Here was the chance to go into the clinic at a time when patients were being seen and provided prescriptions bearing Dr. Stavros' name and we could prove that he was not even in the country. I briefed the executive officer and board attorney on the status. They both thought the time was ripe to go in. We had waited more than long enough for the Feds to act.

It was about this time I received updated information from my friend, MBN Agent Steve Campbell, that he and other MBN agents, DEA agents, and FBI agents had also been conducting a parallel investigation including undercover visits on Dr. Stavros. During their undercover visits, they were seen by Dr. Stavros, not the unlicensed practitioner, Dr. Avilla. They were all prescribed the standard weight loss regimen "in code." Agent Campbell at the time was a long-distance runner and in impeccable shape but was diagnosed by Dr. Stavros as morbidly obese. A female MBN agent that was borderline anorexic had also been diagnosed as obese. The FBI agent and DEA agent were in top physical shape but had also received the same diagnosis of obesity. The exam, which was done by Dr. Stavros, included listening to their heart with the stethoscope five inches away from the chest. All were described as having normal heart rhythms. Dr. Stavros was examining as many as six to eight patients at a time in this manner. When Agent Campbell and the others were with Dr. Stavros, all he wanted to talk about was Texaco Oil. Probably because he was in the oil business thanks to Jodie giving him the oil well for the Stadol prescriptions.

After the visit, Steve Campbell took his prescription from the UC visit to a regular pharmacy in the town to fill. He was told by the pharmacist that he could not fill the prescription because he had no idea what was prescribed. Agent Campbell was referred to the pharmacy owned by Dr. Stavros. At that pharmacy, the coded prescriptions from all of the UC visits were filled for phentermine (a Schedule IV diet pill), vitamins, and several other non-controlled substances. The drugs were identified by the Mississippi State Crime lab, not the pharmacist. The main difference between the MBML UC visits and the MBN UC visits was that one group had been treated by Dr. Stavros and the other by Dr. Avilla. The case was rapidly becoming what was known as "an airtight case."

The MBML warrants and affidavits for the clinic and pharmacy were prepared, reviewed, and approved by Board Attorney Stan Ingram. Investigators Charlie Moses, Neil Breeland, Mickey Robbins, and I convoyed to the clinic site to set up surveillance with the warrants and affidavits in hand. While the clinic was being surveilled, Investigator Moses and I located the senior circuit judge and presented the affidavits and warrants for the clinic and pharmacy. The judge carefully reviewed the affidavit data and after approximately an hour of legal research and questions, approved the search warrants. We went by the police department and picked up a detective that had also helped us on the case. I told him we had a warrant to serve and wanted him with us but did not tell him who it was on until he was in the car – no leaks allowed, even if by accident. I also contacted the deputy sheriff who had called me about Dr. Stavros being out of the country to see if he wanted to meet us and go in on the warrant, but he declined. He said his boss was elected and it might cost him votes and/or his job since Dr. Stavros was so popular in the community. I knew he would not say anything or alert anybody because he had some skin in the game through his status as a source on the case.

It was late in the afternoon when Investigator Moses, the detective, and I finally arrived at the clinic with the signed warrant. The parking lot, normally full of cars, was almost vacant. The investigators doing the surveillance told me that Dr. Avilla was still in the clinic but there were few if any, patients. In we went, with Investigator Moses, Investigator Breeland and I through the front door and Investigator Robbins through the back door to prevent anyone from leaving. We announced ourselves to the nurse who greeted us and who we asked to speak with the doctor on the premises. She said that would be Dr. Avilla and left to go get him. She came back after three or four minutes and said he was driving away, out of the parking lot. Through the side windows, we saw him driving out of the parking lot at a high rate of speed. The nurse said she did not get to talk to him, he was already leaving when she got back to his office. He must have heard us when we entered. I began to worry about where Investigator Robbins was. Had he been attacked or hurt or worse by the fleeing doctor? I ran to the back door and out into the back parking lot. I did not see Investigator Robbins anywhere, so I shouted his name loudly several times. I finally heard a response from an area where kudzu vines were growing all over tall pine trees on the edge of a bluff over-looking a section of the city. I could see Investigator Robbins using the kudzu vines to pull himself up and over the edge. Once on top, he walked over to me and said he had an emergency call of nature and had to take care of some very important business. Relieved, I told him, "You scared the hell out of me. I thought the doctor driving away might have run you down or something."

There were at least two "moons" over the entire city that evening and one of them belonged to Investigator Robbins. I sincerely hoped no one saw that one! We never let him live that down. Fortunately, Investigator Robbins was fine, but the unlicensed doctor got away. Except for that, we had a good laugh and still do, to this day. Now everybody knows!

We still had a warrant to serve. According to the remaining clinic staff, Dr. Stavros had been out of the clinic for at least the last five working days. Several hundred patients had been treated during that time period by Dr. Avilla using prescriptions pre-signed by Dr. Stavros. I asked one of the nurses if she could explain why Dr. Avilla used prescriptions signed by Dr. Stavros? She said that she did not know and only did what Dr. Stavros told her to do – the standard, over-used defense when nothing else is available. Next, I asked what appeared to be the head nurse in the clinic the same question. She was more perceptive and said she suspected Dr. Avilla was not a real doctor but did not know for sure. Dr. Stavros had taught them to do what they were instructed to do and not ask any questions. I told her, "You get the prize! You are mostly correct in that Dr. Avilla is apparently a doctor, just not licensed to practice in Mississippi." She began to have a sinking spell and sat down hard. I then said, "Your actions may expose you to a lot of liability and legal action. I strongly suggest you and the rest of the staff have a come to Jesus meeting and cooperate fully. You might come out of this with your nursing license intact and be able to work somewhere else." They all said they would cooperate, and they did.

I told the police detective with us that I had hoped he would have been able to arrest Dr. Avilla on charges for the unlicensed practice of medicine. I was planning on personally filing the charges for the arrest. Since he had absconded, I asked the detective to fill out the warrants and I would prepare the affidavits the next day. He used his portable radio handset to call a marked police car to pick him up. I told him to tell his boss, my old boss at MBN, that we had served a warrant on his favorite doctor and had all the evidence we would need! As the detective departed the clinic, he assured me he would prepare all of the warrants and affidavits to be signed later. The documents would be on file in case Dr. Avilla shows back up or he is found in the city at which time he could be arrested on the outstanding warrants. We later learned that Dr. Avilla immediately left town that night and went back to his own clinic/home in a state that adjoins Mississippi. Since the unlicensed practice of medicine is just a misdemeanor criminal charge in Mississippi, the city prosecutor would not extradite. It is just too expensive to go to that much trouble for a misdemeanor.

The clinic staff provided all of the files of patients treated by Dr. Avilla over the last five days when Dr. Stavros was out of the country and the files from the previous undercover visits. We also obtained the files of cooperating patients who had complained about their care and/or complications.

Investigators Breeland and Robbins were very good sleuths – they could dig up and find almost anything. They found box after box of pre-signed and pre-written prescriptions (in code) including controlled substance diet pills. All the prescriptions needed were patient names, addresses, and dates. Anyone with access to the pre-signed and pre-written prescriptions could give them out to anyone and apparently, that happened frequently. Once the boxes of the above mentioned prescriptions were found, the clinic staff became much more cooperative. The nurses in the clinic eventually confessed to giving out prescriptions even when neither doctor was on the premises. They also found one of the prescription drug code reference sheets that decrypted the drug codes used on the prescriptions. Just because one letter such as an "A" is written on the prescription, the decrypted codes revealed it could stand for as many as four different brands of the same drug. Finally, we obtained written statements from each employee. We also seized all of the boxes containing thousands of pre-signed and/or pre-written prescriptions signed by Dr. Stavros. We technically had no authority to "close" the clinic, however, I cautioned the nursing staff they did not want to get caught treating patients again without a doctor present. We prepared a detailed return listing the items taken based on the authority of the warrant, left a copy with the head nurse, and departed. I left the decision to close the clinic with the clinic staff.

The next warrant to be served was on the pharmacy. By the time we had finished at the clinic, it was getting late and the pharmacy down the street had closed. The escaping Doctor Avilla may have alerted them but even if he did, it could not hurt our investigation. The evidence from the clinic establishing the case was securely in our hands. We would serve the pharmacy the following morning.

Upon entering the pharmacy, it was easy to see it was a different pharmacy operation. There was no front-end merchandise and no other drugs in the pharmacy area except for the drugs used in the clinic operation. The service of the pharmacy warrant was an arduous operation. Once served with the warrant, the pharmacist mostly disappeared but did provide us access to all of the store's prescriptions. The prescriptions we wanted to seize would have to be found without any help from management. We targeted mostly those patients treated in the last five days while

Dr. Stavros was out of the country. There were several hundred prescriptions that matched the patient file names and dates, seized from the clinic, the previous day. I recommended to the pharmacist that he might consider not filling any more prescriptions from the Stavros clinic bearing his name until he was certain that Dr. Stavros himself was back in the clinic. I told him that every prescription he had filled over the last five days that had the name of Dr. Stavros on them was illegal. Dr. Stavros had been out of the country and an unlicensed doctor was in the clinic issuing pre-signed prescriptions. The pharmacist said he had no way to know that. I replied, "Forgive me, but this is a small town, everybody knows everybody, and everybody knows Dr. Stavros owns this pharmacy. Therefore, I really do not believe you." I told him all of this would be reported to the Board of Pharmacy for any action they deemed necessary.

Strangely enough, I heard nothing from the IRS or Customs investigators about our actions with the warrants we served. We for the most part had a complete case. It would be several more months before Dr. Stavros was indicted by a federal grand jury on drug charges, tax charges, and money transfer violations and months longer until the case came to trial. Unfortunately, the United States attorney handling the case refused to include any of the drug charges in the final criminal settlement. The AUSA handling the case told me personally and rudely to my face that he had no interest in pursuing any drug charges in the case against Dr. Stavros. Not the attitude you expect from a supposedly responsible federal prosecutor when the evidence clearly showed hundreds of thousands, possibly millions, of controlled substance diet pills were illegally diverted into the cities and towns in Mississippi and other states.

In the meantime, an order of suspension was prepared and served on Dr. Stavros by MBML after he returned from his trip, prohibiting him from practicing medicine until such time as the criminal and administrative cases could be heard. Dr. Stavros eventually pled guilty to just one count of criminal tax evasion and was sentenced to pay the back taxes, a penalty, fined, and required to serve twelve months in federal prison. He completely got away with all of the drug diversion because the AUSA would not pursue the charges.

In addition to the federal conviction, Dr. Stavros faced thirty-three counts before the Mississippi medical board including: violating board regulations by issuing pre-signed prescriptions including controlled substances, unprofessional conduct (e.g., lack of freedom of choice, use of codes), aiding and abetting in the unlicensed practice of medicine, prescribing controlled substances outside the course of a legitimate professional practice, and being convicted of a crime involving moral turpitude. His attorney, John Colette, was successful in obtaining three continuances but the fourth continuance request was denied. Dr. Stavros did not bother to show for the hearing and since his client did not appear for the hearing, his attorney refused to participate in the hearing and left the building. Dr. Stavros was tried in absentia and found guilty on all counts. His license to practice medicine was revoked. To my knowledge, he never again practiced medicine. When he was released from federal custody, I heard he left the country. I also heard he returned after several years and was now living in the same city.

Several months after Dr. Stavros' license was revoked, on a trip to another state to collect a urine sample from a doctor in the board's urine monitoring program, Investigator Charlie Moses and I dropped by the clinic operated by Dr. Avilla. Surprisingly, he met with us. Just in case he did not know, I told him of Dr. Stavros going to prison and of his license being revoked. I told Dr. Avilla that I had signed affidavits and had two warrants issued for his arrest for the unlicensed practice of medicine in the State of Mississippi. They were based on his treating the two MBML undercover investigators at a time he did not possess a license to practice in Mississippi. I told him the charges are misdemeanors in the state, so no one was going to arrest him for extradition. However, if he ever was caught in Mississippi for any reason by a law enforcement agency or pulled over for a traffic violation and they checked for outstanding warrants, he would be detained and the MBML would follow through on the charges. I told him if he ever thinks about applying for a medical license in Mississippi, he might want to keep that in mind. “In all fairness,” I said, “we just wanted you to know.” He just said thank you for the information. We then departed the clinic. Dr. Avilla was never heard from again, at least while I was working for the board.

What happened with the oil well? I hate to say this, but to the best of my knowledge, Dr. Stavros got to keep the well. I do not know if Jodie took any legal action but if he did, I was not called as a witness. During the remainder of my career, Jodie never appeared on any prescription profile that the MBML was involved with.

All of our information was provided to the Mississippi State Board of Pharmacy concerning the pharmacy owned by Dr. Stavros. To my knowledge, no action was taken against the pharmacists who filled the illegally coded prescriptions.

CHAPTER 21

DR. VERN and PATIENT GROSS

This has been a problem in the making for a decade. The main driver is that we have prescribed too many prescriptions [for] opioids for too long. – Benedikt Fischer, Ph.D. Criminologist, scientist, academic researcher.

On occasion, the medical board had to deal with patients that at first glance made the doctor look like a bad actor when in reality, he was not. As I stated in my introduction, and now is a good time for a reminder, the majority of physicians are well-trained, caring professionals who strive to do the right things for their patients. Most emergency room (ER) physicians and staff are included in that good category but are plagued with "frequent fliers," "doctor shoppers," or "professional patients," who are just seeking drugs in the ER for personal addiction or fun and profit. These criminals

(I refuse to dignify them by calling them "patients") create real problems for ER doctors and staff.

During a personal visit to an emergency room in 2019, I had the opportunity to discuss the current Mississippi medical board with the ER doctor who took care of me. He had asked about my work history and the topic of my tenure with the medical board came up. I told him I had retired in 1998 long before the pendulum swung in a "different direction," away from protecting the public to protecting the physician. I was curious to see how he would respond to my comment. The doctor sat down in the treatment room with my wife and I and just began talking. I thought I was going to get a lecture on how important it is to have more doctors practicing, not less or something like that, but he surprised me. With somewhat of a quizzical look on his face he said, "I think I know what you mean. I had never thought about it that way, meaning the pendulum thing." He then commented how many of his ER colleagues at that hospital and others had expressed concern over a lack of serious action that should have been taken by the board in past cases, especially over the previous several years. At one time the board was taken seriously, but in the last few years, not much seemed to be happening. A recent case of an Ob-Gyn doctor may signal a change and the board may be getting back on the right track.

He then talked generally about frequent fliers in the ERs that made the job very difficult and cost the hospital time and vast amounts of money to deal with. They are never sick, really, and never pay or have insurance, but they cannot be denied care. Once they are outed, they become angry and threatening because they do not get their drug of choice and complain about not getting proper care. Hospital management does not like to send anyone away "unhappy." He said he did not want to lose his job or license because he refused to prescribe their drug of choice that they had been prescribed previously by unscrupulous physicians. On top of that, the medical board did basically nothing to deter the physicians who caused the problems. I could tell he was fairly upset. He vented further. Even when professional patients are tossed out of the ER, they are smart enough to find some other doctor that will sell them a prescription. Why doesn't the board deal with those bad actors? They need to be out of business! I told him that I completely agreed, but that we appeared to be in the minority.

I then told him about a case I had worked on involving a professional patient that frequented ERs including the one I was currently in. I told him I was curious to see if he possibly had the displeasure of treating her. This criminal (I'll call her "Patient Gross" or "PG" for short) was good at what she did and even suffered from a form of Munchausen syndrome. I was aware of some patients who would swallow forks or open pocket-knives and even smash their car into bridge abutments just so they could get Dilaudid, Vicodin, or some other drug of choice. Sometimes surgery would be required to retrieve the objects. The more cutting required, the better.

PG was unique in that she would inject fecal matter into her breasts to generate an abscess and infection, then present for help at an ER or doctor's office. These people were desperate and often well-organized. It was common for many years for doctors to leave blank prescription pads in exam rooms or clinics for ease of access. PG never missed an opportunity to steal as many as she could get her hands on so she could forge prescriptions and sell blanks to other forgers. All she needed was a template to go by. Any doctor's handwriting would do. When the ER or other doctor wrote her a prescription for anything just to get her out the door, she was in business. She could duplicate the handwriting perfectly and write the script for what she wanted on the stolen pads. She and her cohorts had a reservoir of DEA numbers and knew how to match the correct letter of the doctor's name to the DEA number to get it by the pharmacist.

During one of my pharmacy profiling efforts looking for suspicious prescriptions, I identified several prescriptions for large amounts of Dilaudid 4 mg to PG who was using several of her known alias names. The real tip-off of a problem was the so-called authorizing physician. The prescriber was a well-known pathologist, Dr. Vern (not his real name), who I knew personally. He did not deal with live patients per se, just parts or samples of patients. I also knew he had never written a Dilaudid prescription in his entire career. Yet, there they were, and lots of them. I seized approximately forty of the prescriptions to take to Dr. Vern for his review.

As was standard operating procedure, I briefed the executive officer on the prescriptions and was authorized to contact Dr. Vern to advise him of the situation. The executive officer and I felt we knew the situation, but had to cut the cards. As expected, when I met with Dr. Vern, he got a good laugh, but also a little upset that his name had been used. The handwriting and signature on the prescriptions were very close to his. He offered to fully cooperate and testify against the patient if a good case could be developed by the MBN. Since the MBML did not work criminal forgery cases, I passed on the information to a friend of mine at MBN. Had I not personally known Dr. Vern, the situation would have looked bad for him, at least on the surface and at least at first glance. Dr. Vern was so upset his name had been used that he sent his DEA number back and requested to surrender schedules II, IIN, III, IIIN, and IV. He retained his number with only Schedule V. He did not want this to happen again.

I told the ER doctor about another female professional patient that I knew who had been in every ER in Mississippi and several other states. She also hit doctor's clinics as a way of life. She was a drop-dead gorgeous strawberry blonde female, and the best drug con I had ever seen. I had documented at least ten to fifteen aliases she operated under throughout the southeast. She was so good-looking when sober that she could talk almost any doctor out of one hundred Dilaudid 4 mg in a heartbeat. I never heard of her doing the drugs for sex thing, but she did not have to, she was just a silver-tongued she-devil. Whenever I was able to cut her off from her latest doctor conquest, she would invariably call me at the medical board and cuss me out. We had many interesting one-sided conversations. I always tried to talk her into going into treatment, but she gave me the same line, "How would I make a living?" and discussed her knowledge of my mother in ways I won't mention here.

The ER doctor said he had not seen a patient that had injected fecal matter in her breasts yet, but he probably would sooner or later. He said the description of the strawberry blonde rang a bell, but he never wrote prescriptions for Dilaudid, so if he saw her, she went away a little disappointed.

The doctor emphasized the board truly needed to crack down on the over-prescribers and not just play nice. He continued to say that over-prescribers do not practice the same type of patient care that most doctors do and legitimate doctors do not like to be put in the same category as them. These prescribers frequently hide behind being themselves impaired, but still, they create and perpetuate the problem with opiates. I told him, "I think you and I are the only ones who realize that. Everybody wants to blame the drug companies. They are putting the blame in the wrong place." I then told him that I just need about 100 to 150 Oxycontin, and I should be just fine! The ER doctor said with a laugh, "Oh, that's good, that's very good!" I am glad to say that he took really good care of me that night – no Oxycontin!!

The last I heard of PG before I retired in 1998, she was still hitting up doctors and emergency rooms all over the state. To my knowledge, she was never arrested.

I know for a fact that the strawberry blonde was going strong when I retired. I had a personal project to get her prosecuted for obtaining controlled substances by use of fraud or subterfuge. However, not a single district attorney would prosecute her for any of the hundreds, if not thousands, of prescriptions she obtained using fake names and identification. She did not have to forge a doctors' signature on a prescription. She was convincing enough to get the doctor to write it themselves. She just posed as a patient using fake names daily, across Mississippi and the southern United States. At times I had prescriptions that clearly documented her getting Dilaudid or Percodan prescriptions from as many as eight to ten doctors in one day! All were issued under different names. Because she was so attractive, the pharmacists easily identified her from photo lineups as the person filling the prescriptions. The monitoring programs will not ID this major source of diversion because of so many different names. Investigators have to grind out the data in the field. Then the doctors have to be educated to not prescribe the drug.

Most of the doctors that are taken in by professional patients such as PG and the strawberry blonde are not necessarily the unscrupulous repeat offending doctor that causes most of the illegitimate diversion of controlled substances. These doctors are duped or easily conned and need to be addressed by training and education, at least at first. This requires constant vigilance and visits by the medical boards to investigate the prescriptions, see the patient file for documentation, and emphasize to the doctor to not give the patient what the patient says seems to work for them. Red flags are just that, red flags!

CHAPTER 22

X-RAYS and DIVERSION

Life is barely long enough to get good at one thing; so be careful what you get good at. – Matthew McConoughey, movie star and actor.

This case, the last in the series, identifies, explains, and reinforces why I identify the prescriber/doctor as the most significant contributor to the opioid epidemic in this country. It is yet another classic example of trust and intellect tossed out in order to gain fun and profit through controlled substances. It also graphically illustrates the power of controlled substances to rule a person's life, even that of a well-trained doctor, not to mention the depths they sink to, to try and maintain access to the drugs. It all happened in just a period of a few weeks.

This case was initiated by a call from a pharmacist that had worked well with medical board investigators in previous cases. He stated a Dr. Phillips (not his real name) had been coming into his pharmacy recently and writing hydrocodone prescriptions to himself and other patients and picking up the filled prescriptions. Sometimes the patients would accompany him into the pharmacy when the prescriptions were picked up. Dr. Phillips usually paid for the prescriptions, but not every time. The pharmacist described the doctor as a large muscular man who, although young, was completely bald. Since the bald look had not caught on, I asked if the doctor could have alopecia. The pharmacist said he did not think so because he had dark but shaved eyebrows.

A check with the licensure division indicated that Dr. Phillips was currently licensed to practice in Mississippi and was in a residency training program at UMC in radiology. He had a current and unrestricted DEA certificate. What was immediately interesting was that the registered location on the DEA certificate was an apartment in a small town nearby. Most doctor's DEA certificates bear the address of the location where they see patients or, in a case like this, where they are in a training program.

A profile at the pharmacy where the prescriptions had been filled documented several hydrocodone prescriptions to Dr. Phillips and two other people, a man and woman with different last names. The couple had on occasion come into the pharmacy together, with the doctor. The pharmacist did not know anything about the other two patients. An expanded pharmacy profile in other pharmacies in the area revealed a few additional prescriptions for hydrocodone to the doctor and the other two patients.

The MBML was still receiving fairly consistent access to ARCOS reports from the DEA indicating what controlled substances were being ordered under what DEA number in Mississippi. By "regular access," I mean at least once or twice a year. Since Dr. Phillips had only had a DEA certificate for approximately one year, the orders credited to his DEA number were small according to the last ARCOS printout MBML had received. I decided to cut the cards and requested an update for current purchases or orders under his DEA number. This period would cover the past four to six months. The amounts ordered were startling. Just during the previous six months, he had purchased several thousand Percodan tablets, Valium 5 and 10 mg tablets, Xanax 1 mg tablets, and hydrocodone tablets. The orders were sent by multiple vendors to his apartment address, not a medical facility.

The executive officer was briefed at the next staff meeting on the developing situation. He suggested that we were probably dealing with an impaired doctor and recommended that we immediately proceed with an inspection and search warrant and conduct an audit to account for the drugs. Impaired physicians were still considered the highest priority for the board since they are deemed to pose the greatest threat to the healthcare-consuming public. The EO said that if Dr. Phillips could not account for the drugs, to offer him the opportunity to surrender his DEA certificate and immediately enter an approved treatment program. If he refused, we were to serve him with a suspension of his license. The suspension, as a tool, was being used more and more by the board's executive officer because it accomplished almost the exact same thing as a revocation without the time and expense of a full revocation hearing.

I contacted Board Attorney Stan Ingram and briefed him on the details of the case developed thus far and the executive officer's instructions. He said he would start immediately on the inspection and search warrant and a suspension order. He requested the exact name and address of the apartment and a detailed description of the apartment complex. He emphasized that we were to make absolutely certain of the apartment number and a description of the actual door to the apartment. Since this was not a medical facility, traditionally easy to identify, he wanted to be sure to describe the correct location in the warrant and affidavit to avoid any possibility of a mistaken address.

Investigator Charlie Moses and I traveled to the apartment complex location and took pictures. There is nothing better to ensure an accurate description than current photos. We photographed the complex, the apartment location from several angles, and especially the correct apartment number and door. The apartment was located on the bottom floor of the two-story complex with Dr. Phillips' door facing one of the parking lots. The color photographs were provided to the board attorney to ensure an enhanced, detailed description of the apartment location in the warrant.

A brief period of surveillance on the apartment over the next several days documented that a large muscular white male apparently resided alone in the apartment. By large, I mean *really* large. At least 6'5" or 6'6" tall and clearly a gym rat. We observed him coming and going from the apartment many times. He did not appear to be attending any regular residency training program or classes and always wore only muscle shirts, tight shorts, athletic shoes, and a baseball type cap, on a bald head. We were hoping to observe him going to a pharmacy to obtain prescriptions but we were not that lucky. He mainly went to a local gym, grocery store, or video store.

We updated the drug purchases and prescriptions we could locate in order to have the latest information for the affidavit for the warrant. It appeared Dr. Phillips had to account for at least 10,000 Percodan, 10,000 10 mg Valium, 5,000 5 mg Valium, 5000 1 mg Xanax, and 5,000 various forms of hydrocodone products purchased over the last few months. This was a huge number of controlled substances ordered for any doctor much less someone in a radiology residency, not even a regular practice. It also explained why he was not going to any pharmacies. He seemingly had all he needed, or so we thought.

Once the warrant and order of suspension were completed, Investigator Moses and I met with a circuit judge to obtain the signed warrant. Once approved, we traveled to the apartment complex. We observed the doctor's car in the usual parking spot. I told Investigator Moses, "Go knock on the door to see if the good Dr. Schwarzenegger was in. If there is any trouble, I will go for help. Somebody has to live to tell the story." Investigator Moses made some kind of off-beat comment like, "I think the chief investigator should take the lead into combat." Both of us started laughing. I told him this was not the *old* army; this is the *new* army. The leader has to lead from behind to direct the attack. As we got out of the car still laughing and thinking we were probably going to die, all I heard from Investigator Moses was, "Not so, Chief Investigator, not so."

I knocked on the door and prepared to present my identification. The human being that answered almost filled up the entire door frame. I told him in the strongest, nicest voice that I could muster that we were from the Mississippi medical board and were trying to find Dr. Phillips. He responded that he was Dr. Phillips. I told him we needed to speak with him and he invited us in. We presented identification and told him we had been documenting some large quantities of controlled substances he had been purchasing. I then presented the inspection and search warrant and explained how it allowed us to search the premises and audit the controlled substances delivered to this apartment address. He took the warrant and began to read it. After just a few minutes, he asked permission to call his attorney. Since we had the area secure, I told him he could make the call. It appeared he was a gentle giant and not steroid enraged, thank goodness for us!

After Dr. Phillips spoke with his attorney, he handed the phone to me. He said his attorney wanted to speak to me. After introductions, the attorney asked if we would wait to serve the warrant because he would like to have an opportunity to see the document for himself. He said he could be there in less than thirty minutes. I told him we would wait, but that he should not make us wait too long. The lawyer said he was on his way and hung up. We sat down in the apartment to wait. The doctor, dressed in his usual muscle shirt and shorts, was cordial but not conversational. Investigator Moses and I knew that we did not have to wait for the attorney to arrive, but it is important to at least try to make these legal processes as cordial as possible. I asked Dr. Phillips how his residency training was progressing? He only said he had dropped out for the year. While waiting for the attorney, I was able to get a close up look at Dr. Phillips. He was bald and no visible hair was on his arms, legs, or eyebrows. His skin was red and raw-looking like he had shaved himself too close, and had a razor burn all over. After an extended wait, the attorney finally arrived and immediately began to review the warrant and affidavit. When he finished his reading he asked, just to be sure he understood clearly, that we needed to account for the purchased drugs by an accountability audit. I told him that was basically correct. We needed to see the inventory, count the doses in the inventory, then account for all doses not found in the inventory by reviewing the required ledgers and patient files reflecting the use of the medication. He asked for permission to talk to his client in private. I told him to proceed as long as it was outside the apartment where he could not touch anything inside or in his car until we finished. They went outside into the parking lot for approximately ten minutes, then came back into the apartment. The attorney said we could initiate the search warrant, but his client was not in a position to answer any questions right now. I asked if he would show us where he kept the drugs he had ordered. The attorney said, "We will not answer any questions." He said all that I can say is that Dr. Phillips was not currently in his residency training program due to being treated by a psychiatrist for OCD (obsessive-compulsive disorder). The symptoms manifested themselves in an obsession to shave off all the hair on his body. At times he would shave himself so much that he would literally begin to skin himself alive. It was thought by medical professionals that the stress of the training program may have been the catalyst for the obsessive activity, which is why he was currently taking a break from the training.

I invited the attorney to accompany us on the search if he wished. He declined. I then asked him if his client understood the purpose of the warrant and what we needed to do? He said he did. Charlie and I searched the entire two-bedroom apartment: all rooms, closets, drawers, shelves, appliances, cabinets, bathrooms, boxes, suitcases, and containers. Any item or location we could possibly conclude that drugs could be stored or hidden was searched. Even ceiling tiles that could be lifted or loosened were checked. His car was also included in the search since it was considered under his control and access. We found nothing, no drugs, no patient files, and no records. The only thing found were unused DEA order forms. I told the attorney since the drugs could not be accounted for; we were seizing the order forms pursuant to the warrant until it could be determined what Dr. Phillips had done with the drugs. I told the attorney in the presence of Dr. Phillips that failure to account for the drugs was a violation of federal and state regulations. I reminded them that under the regulations, every single dose, tab, and pill had to be counted. I also told them that since Dr. Phillips' DEA certificate had his apartment as the registered location, the only place the drugs could be legally stored was right there in the apartment. I asked them about the possibility of a substance abuse problem and explained how the board had a program for treatment and recovery for doctors but we needed to talk right then to begin that process. The attorney again stated that his client was not able to talk with us. I then told them that the consequences of not accounting for the drugs would be a suspension of Dr. Phillips' license until he complied with the board's requirements. The attorney again indicated his client could not make any comment at that time. I told him I had no choice other than to serve Dr. Phillips with the order of suspension until such time as he could account for the drugs and comply with the board's requirements. I reminded them that the suspension of the license also negated his DEA number and that DEA would be formally notified by the board. A doctor cannot have a valid DEA number without a current medical license. That means Dr. Phillips could not write any more prescriptions or order any drugs until the board reinstated his license. I gave Dr. Phillips' attorney the telephone number and name of the board's attorney in case they had any questions. I also gave them a copy of the prepared return listing the order forms taken. Investigator Moses and I then departed.

After we returned to the MBML offices, I briefed the executive officer on the negative results of the search warrant. I told him about the doctor following his counsel's advice and refusing to offer any explanation of what happened with the drugs or even to acknowledge that he had ordered them.

Approximately six months after the doctor's license was suspended, the male patient to whom Dr. Phillips was writing controlled substance prescriptions was arrested by a sheriff's department, with MBN assistance, in possession of approximately 5,000 Xanax tablets. He refused to implicate any other person. By connecting the dots, one might conclude that Dr. Phillips was the major supplier and using runners for deliveries.

While I was still employed with the medical board, Dr. Phillips never attempted to have his license reinstated. To my knowledge, he never returned to the practice of medicine.

However, it is possible he got a license in another state. Some states issue unrestricted licenses despite actions in another state. Remember the mobile cure, where a doctor seeks to hide their past and a state just ignores the evidence from other states or does not request it in the first place, perpetuating the problem.

EPILOGUE

The first duty of the physician is to educate the masses not to take medicine. – Anonymous.

After reading this in its entirety, I want to make sure the reader keeps the proper perspective of medicine in general by repeating my opening comment from the preface. *The good news is that the majority of physicians are well trained, perform as expected, and genuinely want to help their patients be free of suffering from any disease*. So, I pose the following question. Who or what is responsible for the opioid epidemic of the 1980s through the present day and beyond? The diplomatic political response from weak leadership says it is a multifaceted, complex, cultural phenomenon based on economic deprivation caused by excessive jailing of criminals, education shortcomings, white supremacists, and, of course, corporate greed by manufacturers. Heavy emphasis on corporate greed because that is where the real money is. That is the bull version. Decorum prevents me from a more graphic word use. The basic reason is much simpler and much closer to the truth and home. If the prescriber (physician, dentist, etc.) does not write or authorize the prescription or divert by other means, the controlled substances are not going out the door into the community. If the real drug dealers are left in jail as they should be, they aren't on the streets smuggling and dealing. Leading politicians from both major political parties have created a resurgence in dealers by supporting the release of thousands of criminal drug dealers out of jail early with more on the way. Just in time for the regeneration of the marijuana and opioid epidemic 3.0. Those people never work, never have what would qualify as genuine employment, but they always have a job and gobs of tax-free cash. Legalizing marijuana is only going to make it worse. Are we not as a nation putting enough poison in our bodies already? Many feel that marijuana is the gateway drug directly to pharmaceutical and street drug paradise. I personally saw that result too many times. Several were described in this publication. I might add, as a result, the funeral home directors do quite well.

Read the following words very carefully. *The opioid problem lies at the feet of the prescribers and nowhere else!* Shut down the unscrupulous prescribing or diversion by providers and you shut down the pharmaceutical opioid sources. If this is not done, after the lawsuits against manufacturers are settled and drug prices are raised to pay for the settlements, it will leave a problem in place to continue. A drug-abusing patient cannot get a single prescription from a manufacturer. It simply cannot be done. Only a doctor can issue the prescription. A manufacturer cannot fill a prescription. It can only be filled by a pharmacist. A patient cannot order any controlled substance from a manufacturer, supplier, or even Amazon. It can only be done with the authority of a DEA number that can only be held by providers. The prescribers know full well the dangerous and addictive qualities of opiate drugs. Regardless of the sales pitch from manufacturers and distributors, the prescribers know that opiates are addictive and dangerous and should not be used except for terminal or short-term major trauma or illness. They also know there is a large amount of money to be made by selling the prescriptions. It also makes their lives easier. They don't have to take the time to actually practice medicine and deal with difficult pain management, non-compliant patients who need real management. They just prescribe what patients say they want; not what patients necessarily need. Doctors also take incentive money from the manufacturers, but if anyone questions their selling prescriptions or over-prescribing, they turn around and blame the manufacturers. Unfortunately, too many medical boards let the prescribers skirt away with a slap on the knuckles.

Lawsuits may put a lot of money in the pockets of trial lawyers and families of deceased drug abusers, but the opioid problem will persist until the medical boards step up and deal with bad actors who inappropriately prescribe or divert controlled substances. The only reason the trial lawyers go after the manufacturers and distributors is that the financial return is larger.

Pharmaceutical opioids are a market-driven commodity just like corn, gold, or oil. The price on the street is determined by supply and demand. In 1981 the average street price of a Dilaudid 4 mg tablet in Mississippi was in the $50 range because the supply was plentiful. By 1983/84 the price had risen to the $150 – $200 range. The MBN and DEA had dried up major heroin sources out of Mexico. Dilaudid, used as a heroin substitute, had become scarce in part due to similar MBN and DEA efforts along with the area development project by the Mississippi medical board investigating *every single prescription* for Dilaudid that was written. If a board investigator found a prescription for Dilaudid, the prescriber was paid a visit and required to produce thorough documentation justifying the prescription. Getting the largest known prescriber (see the "Pill Doctor" case in Chapter 1) shut down with federal prosecution also sent a huge message. If you want to be next, just keep up with your excessive, not medically indicated prescribing. The same can be done with Oxycontin and other controlled pharmaceuticals if the will is there to do it. These programs had nothing to do with the manufacturers of the drugs, only the prescribers.

With all the pressure on Dilaudid, what happened next? I was not a student of physics, but it seems like I recall Mr. Boyd, my high school physics teacher, telling my class that Newton's third law states that for every action, there is an equal and opposite reaction. That law applies in several ways.

With the focus on Dilaudid seemly working to reduce availability, as indicated by rising street prices, and heroin being scarce, along comes "Ts and Blues," the next heroin or Dilaudid substitute. The T in Ts and Blues was Talwin (pentazocine), a Schedule IV controlled substance. The Talwin, by itself, had a high risk for dependence and addiction. The Blues was Pyribenzamine. Pyribenzamine is nothing more than a prescription antihistamine. However, when combined with Talwin and injected, voila, you produce heroin-like effects and big-time abuse problems as a substitute for heroin or Dilaudid. Another rabbit trail to follow. The same focus was done with Talwin as Dilaudid and amazingly the latest drug fad faded away. Also, the Mississippi legislature listened early about the Ts and Blues problem. Through efforts by MBN and MBML, Talwin injectable was moved from Schedule IV into Schedule II in Mississippi, which dramatically helped reduce the prescribing of injectable Talwin. When the effort to move Pentazocine to Schedule II in Mississippi started, the manufacturer organized a massive lobby campaign by the big lobbyist guns in Mississippi and nationally to shut down the bill. Why? The issue of money is the only honest reason. They wanted doctors to be able to prescribe it and have refills available that were not available on Schedule II products. If not for the Director of MBN making a passionate appeal for the bill in committee, it may have not seen the light of day. Still, even with all of the pressure and incentives from manufacturers, doctors know the dangers to the patients of over-prescribing Talwin, Dilaudid, Oxycontin, and other controlled substances.

Perhaps you are beginning to see a pattern here. Next came Stadol and Nubain problems. In the mid-1980s Mississippi had one of the early problems with abuse of Stadol and Nubain, especially by doctors. Of interest, one county in Mississippi was considered the Stadol and Nubain capital of the world. Several of the cases in this publication describe the problems with these drugs not only in the general population but among doctors in particular. Stadol or Nubain in combination with promethazine became a highly abused heroin substitute on the street. Pressure on those two drugs by MBML and the State Board of Pharmacy brought in the hydrocodone epidemic, with abuse of such products containing hydrocodone like Vicodin, Lorcet, Lorcet Plus, Endal HD, Tussionex, etc. This led us to the Oxycontin problem. If the effort is put forth on an Oxycontin project like it was Dilaudid and Talwin, Oxycontin prescriptions would become as rare as hens' teeth, at least in Mississippi. Such projects do not prevent a doctor from writing the prescriptions when medically indicated. It just makes sure the documentation, medical indications, and real medical management (not just maintenance), really exist and provides severe consequences when they do not. In other words, the doctor really has to earn his or her pay. The medical boards must cut the cards to be certain the prescription is for a valid justified medical need. Oxycontin at any dosage is not valid for chronic pain, migraine headaches, or toothaches. That is like using a nuclear bomb when a firecracker would do.

However, if the doctors do not fear repercussions or no entity is holding them accountable, the prescriptions will flow. It was not that long ago when Mississippi went from first in medical board disciplinary actions to dead last in the United States in a very short period. Does that indicate a willingness to protect the public? The precipitous drop in board actions clearly reflected that a different purpose and mission had been adopted by the Mississippi board. The responsibility to curb the flow of inappropriate prescriptions rests with the medical boards. One cannot just wait for the phone to ring, an email, or a review of an MPMR (Mississippi Physician Monitoring Program) report in order to act. Developing the right confidential sources, using the right databases, and extensive face-to-face field projects will identify a target-rich environment to be investigated. Once the targets are identified and investigated, the boards themselves must have the courage and political will to take serious and final disciplinary actions and to keep the public informed on every action, not just provide lip service. I do not claim to have all the answers, I just know that over the last twenty years, we have shown that inaction simply does not work! The best approach is to attack the source, the over-prescribers, and to deal with them with finality. Otherwise, people will most likely continue to die.

ACKNOWLEDGEMENTS

To paraphrase Winston Churchill, a half-American (his mother was American) whom I consider more American than most Americans, "Never has one individual owed so much to so many." I am referring to the development, writing, and editing of this book. The list of individuals that were consulted and who contributed is long, but each deserves my heartfelt appreciation and gratitude. I especially thank my wife, Jane, who had to repeatedly reassure me that I could complete the project, despite my doubts and a complete lack of any significant writing ability or experience and my *woeful* computer skills. Jane has such a novel way with words and phrases to fit the situations and provided perfect descriptions. She also found out how Mrs. Lois Gulley, my seventh and eighth grade English teacher (one of the finest people I have ever had the privilege to know), even with her best effort, was unable to teach me a proper grasp of English and written communication skills. It was not her fault; she did not have much of a student to work with.

I also owe much to Gary Theis, a retired US Navy Commander. Gary is an almost lifelong friend, with whom I hunted and fished together while growing up around Grenada and Grassy Lakes in Mississippi, and is my current golfing partner. He endured the early drafts and performed the first edits, which helped me escape most of my law enforcement, ROI writing style. I owe a debt of gratitude to my brother and sister-in-law, Paul Beddingfield and Beth Kennedy, for their early support, encouragement, suggestions, and their extraordinary editing skills. I thank my good friends and former neighbors, Debra and David McIntosh, for their support and for connecting me with a professional editor and publishing opportunities. Finally, for Vince Evans from Phoenix, AZ, whom I have never met, and may never meet, but endured my emails and still took on the project for editing. I would be remiss if I did not mention the presence, for almost every word typed, of my canine assistants Mr. Stuckey, Ms. Lucy, and Ms. Vivi (an occasional, visiting, in-lap consultant), as well as my feline assistant, Johnnie.

I must add my heartfelt appreciation to the people at Foundations Book Publishing. Steve Soderquist, chief editor and director, and Laura Ranger, owner/editor/CFO, have been a Godsend to me. They have provided so much in the way of explanations, answering questions, and most importantly, patience! They actually do not laugh at my questions...at least not yet! Their editing has been phenomenal. They helm an extraordinary company for a first-time author to work with, and I sincerely thank them and their whole team.

As I discovered during the writing process, sometimes the hard way, the passage of time can blur, change, blend, and fade case facts and circumstances, and names can disappear or become distorted. All of the individuals listed below had a key role in most of the investigations, prosecutions, or hearing security, and played important roles in putting pieces of this publication in the proper place. They include, in no particular order, Charlie Moses, deputy sheriff and MBML investigator; Neil Breeland, USM campus police, MBML investigator, and cattle farmer; Mickey Robbins, US Marine, MBN and MBML investigator, and MS National Guard; Steve Campbell, US Marine aviator, MBN, police department executive, and sheriff's deputy; Randy Corban, MBN, and USA liaison officer; William Chadwick "Chad" Lamar, attorney, assistant United States attorney, and appointed United States attorney; Jim French, assistant chief, Jackson Police Department and bank security; Ken Fairly III, attorney and county judge; Gordon Kennedy, MBI investigator, and secretary of state investigator; Sammy Webb, district attorney investigator and youth court executive; Sam Aldridge, MBI/DEA task force agent, and DOJ investigator; and

Jerry Nickels, deputy sheriff, director of training, Federal Express, and corporate security consultant.

Last and definitely not least, I thank my good friend, Larry Burris, (now deceased) former Chief of Operations when I worked at the Mississippi Bureau of Narcotics, for the time he took to read and offer suggestions and in-sight to the manuscript.

There are several other attorneys and individuals who were of tremendous assistance that shall, at their request, remain unnamed, because of factors that might negatively affect their immediate situation.

I am not fully able to express appropriately how sincerely I appreciate everyone's contribution. THANK YOU SO VERY MUCH!

Just Call Dr. P.D.

P.D. treats them all
From minor aches to major falls
He'll prescribe you Demerol
All you have to do is call.

If you feel that you are ill
Or even if you think you did,
He will give you Dilaudid.
All you have to do is call.

When a sickness is at hand
Dr. P.D is your man.
He will give you Percodan.
All you have to do is call.

He can lance any pus pocket
If, your home, you will hock it.
He will then give you rectal rockets.
All you have to do is call.

From Septicemia to Amnesia
He knows your problem before he sees ya,
Don't expect Milk of Magnesia.
All you have to do is call.

Dr. P.D. is really a nice man.
Ask any drug addict, if you can.
They will tell you of his plan.
All you have to do is call.

Dr. P.D. knows the facts.
He knows a needle never leaves tracks.
It's just a simple anxiety attack.
All you have to do is call.

Let P.D.'s office set a date.
If you can stand or sit and wait,
He'll reward you with Morphine Sulfate.
All you have to do is call.

From Corinth to Bude,
Whether rude or nude,
He'll prescribe you Quaalude.
All you have to do is call.

No matter how often the patients came
The medical complaint was always the same,
"I'm suffering from Severe Pain."
All you have to do is call.

Even if the patient was "clean",
Or a patient he had never seen,
He would give them Amphetamine.
All you have to do is call.

When patients called "Need a Prescription Refill",
Dr. P.D. would give them a thrill.
He knew all along they were "really ill".
All they had to do is call.

Then one day the law showed up.
At P.D.'s clinic the "long arm" struck.
P.D. said he would not obstruct.
All you had to do is call.

The trial began, it was a gem!
Television cameras – they did film.
The prosecution summoned Steve,
Richard, Dr. Morgan, and Tim.
All they had to do is call.

The Federal Judge on the bench did sit.
The defense constantly throwing a fit,
As the addicts described how they obtained their hits.
All they had to do was call.

The Judgement was finally waning near.
Final arguments, the jury would hear.
P.D. slowly to the bench would stroll.
Upon the stand, his story he told
Of how he treated the young and old.
All they had to do was call.

The jury listened with eyelids down.
The Judge at times was not around.
Only the court reporter recorded the sound.
All we had to do was call.

And ready to pounce were Henry and Tucker.
On each file, the facts they would muster.
They knew P. D. was a no-good sucker.
"Guilty" was their favorite call.

Many experts took the oath
Upon the stand by the black cloak.
They told their story quote for quote.
All the lawyers did was call.

The defense gang, the trial had stifled.
The Judge shouted, "You shall not trifle!"
The Defense then sat meekly idle.
The Court had made its call.

Government, and Defense, the 12
would steer.
And hoped they had heard their call.

In Mississippi, the M.D.'s sat in shock.
The Pharmacists reduced their controlled
substance stock.
There's one less M.D. on the local mailbox.
The Jury has answered the call.

Written by Richard Allison during the course of the trial in 1984. Note, I took out the real doctor's name for obvious reasons.

Read by Richard Allison at the conviction celebration party held at a local restaurant. The stress had been tremendous, everybody needed a laugh.

P.S. The more people drank at the party, the more they liked the poem!

GLOSSARY

acetaminophen – An over-the-counter pain medication; primary ingredient in Tylenol.

AD – See "area development profiling."

affidavit – Legal document listing the probable cause to justify issuing a search warrant or for listing evidence for formal charges in a summons to a hearing.

AMA – 1. American Medical Association. 2. "Against medical advice."

ARCOS – Automated Report and Consolidated Order System, used by DEA to record purchases of controlled substances by individual DEA numbers.

area development profiling – A process used by Mississippi Board of Medical Licensure investigators to identify suspicious prescriptions in pharmacies.

Assistant Attorney General – Assigned by the Attorney General to a state agency to provide legal advice.

Attorney General – Chief law enforcement officer of the state and one who advises state agencies on legal matters.

AUSA – Assistant United States attorney.

B and E – Slang for "breaking and entering."

bad actor(s) – Physicians not conforming to acceptable standards of practice.

benzodiazepine – A class of drugs used for treating anxiety.

Blue Cross and Blue Shield of Mississippi – Mississippi's largest health care insurer.

Blue Rooster – A restaurant in Flora, MS.

Blue and White – A restaurant in Tunica, MS.

Blues - Street term for Valium 10 mg.

board attorney – The attorney contracted to prosecute the board's administrative cases and advise the staff.
Board of Nursing – State agency responsible for licensing and regulating the practice of nursing and nurse practitioners.
Broadwater Beach Hotel – A former four-star hotel that was located on the beach in Biloxi, MS. Destroyed by Hurricane Katrina in 2005.
Bureau of Drug Enforcement – Created by the Mississippi legislature in 1971 as a division of the MS State Board of Health and the forerunner to the Mississippi Bureau of Narcotics.
chancellor – The institutional head of the University of Mississippi Medical Center.
chief investigator – Person responsible for the supervision of the MBML investigative division.
code 10 device – Term used to describe a covert transmitter and microphone worn by undercover agents to record surreptitious conversations.
consent order – Order of the board entered with a licensee to avoid a full hearing. Usually contains various restrictions based on the type of charges.
constructive possession – Legal term whereby a suspect takes possession of evidence in such a manner that he cannot reasonably deny ownership.
contract pharmacist – Pharmacist that fills in for pharmacists at various locations.
Customs – Former agency responsible for monitoring United States borders or ports to identify illegal smuggling, including money, in and out of the country.
Dalgan – A non-controlled opioid analgesic with the chemical name dezocine.
DEA – United States Drug Enforcement Administration.
DEA certificate – Authority by which doctors can handle controlled substances.

DEA number – A unique number provided to a practitioner or provider who handles controlled substances.
DEA Diversion – Division of DEA responsible for monitoring pharmaceutical drugs in the United States.
Delta State University – University in Cleveland, MS.
Demerol – Schedule IIN narcotic used for treatment of severe pain.
Department of Public Safety – Umbrella name for the agency comprised of the
Mississippi Highway Patrol, Mississippi Bureau of Investigation, Mississippi Bureau of Narcotics, crime lab, intelligence and data center.
DNA – Refers to a testing procedure of material used to identify a specific suspect based on their genetic make-up.
DOJ – Department of Justice.
dextroamphetamine – Schedule II stimulant.
Dilaudid – Schedule IIN narcotic analgesic.
Disabled Doctor's Program – Precursor to Recovering Physicians Program.
disabled physician – Any physician deemed to be suffering from chemical dependency including alcoholism or mental or physical impairment affecting their ability to practice medicine with reasonable skill and safety.
district attorney – Chief prosecutor of the district in which a county is a part.
diuretics – Drugs prescribed to assist patients who are retaining fluids to void excess fluids.
doctor shopper – Individual who travels from one doctor to another seeking controlled substances.
DOJ – United States Department of Justice.
ED – Erectile Dysfunction. A condition whereby a male is unable to achieve a functional penile erection.
EO – Executive officer, MBML.

ER – Emergency Room.
executive committee – President, Vice President, and Secretary elected by the full medical board to work with the executive officer on day-to-day decisions as necessary.
executive session – A closed door session of the full medical board to consider hearing decisions or other matters requiring confidential deliberations.
Federation of State Medical Boards – Private nationwide organization funded by state medical boards for communication and coordination of efforts in legislation and operations.
FLEX exam – Federation Licensing Exam administered to medical students to assess their knowledge and training in medicine.
FISA – Foreign Intelligence Surveillance Court, used by federal agencies to obtain authorization to surveil suspected foreign agents.
frequent fliers – Drug(s) abusers who frequent ERs seeking controlled substances
grand jury – A jury of eighteen people assembled by prosecutors to consider charges/indictments against suspects.
general surgery – Practice of surgery in a non-specialty type.
grossly obese – A diagnosis of patients who are generally at least thirty or more pounds over their ideal body weight.
Hinds General Hospital – Former name of the hospital located on Chadwick Dr. Jackson, MS.
hydrocodone- Schedule II Narcotic for treatment of pain.
hydromorphone HCL – Chemical name for Dilaudid a Schedule IIN narcotic for treatment of severe pain.
impaired physician – See Disabled Physician.
inspection warrant – Document authorized by a judge that allows the MBML to inspect and seize items in a doctor's clinic.
IRS – Internal Revenue Service of the United States.
late bloomer – Refers to a student who enters medical school in their late twenties or early thirties.

MBML – Mississippi State Board of Medical Licensure.
MBN – Mississippi Bureau of Narcotics.
Mepergan Fortis – Schedule IIN controlled substance chemically/ known as meperidine and promethazine. It is an opioid used for the treatment of severe pain.
Mississippi Bureau of Narcotics – Division of the Mississippi Department of Public Safety responsible for enforcing the state-controlled substances laws.
Mississippi Medical Board Licensure Division – Division of the MBML responsible for issuing licenses to physicians and other practitioners practicing in Mississippi.
Mississippi Medical Practice Act – Statutes in Mississippi code that spell out the laws governing the practice of medicine.
Mississippi State Board of Pharmacy – State Agency responsible for licensing and regulating pharmacists.
Mississippi State Crime Lab – Division of the Department of Public Safety responsible for processing evidence for state agencies, local police, or sheriff departments.
Mississippi State Department of Health – Mississippi Public Health governmental body responsible for public health in Mississippi.
mobile cure – Moving around from state to state to avoid or hide from previous bad conduct or disciplinary action.
MSMA – Mississippi State Medical Association, state medical association.
Munchausen syndrome – Condition whereby a patient will harm themselves in order to obtain controlled substances or for other reasons.
nalbuphine – A synthetic, non-controlled opioid used for pain. Chemical name for Nubain.
Nembutal – Schedule II barbiturate for sleep induction, anxiety etc. Chemically known as pentobarbital.
Nubain – See nalbuphine.

Numorphan suppository – Rectal suppository containing oxymorphone for pain management.
Ob-Gyn – Doctor who specializes in obstetrics and gynecology.
OCD – Obsessive compulsive disorder.
order of suspension – See suspension order.
Oxycontin – Schedule IIN narcotic for treatment of severe pain.
oxymorphone – Schedule IIN narcotic used for treatment of pain and extreme anxiety.
papaverine – Prescription vasodilator.
pathologist – Physician specialty for tissue examination and diagnosis.
PEER - Performance Evaluation and Expenditure Review Committee of the Mississippi Legislature.
pentazocine – Chemical name for Talwin, a Schedule IV controlled substance used for treatment of pain.
Percodan – Schedule IIN narcotic analgesic. Chemically known as oxycodone. Also contains 325 mg aspirin. Used for treatment of pain.
Physician's Desk Reference – Publication by drug manufacturers that contain information on the drugs that they manufacture. Commonly referred to as a PDR.
Preludin – Phenmetrazine, a Schedule I stimulant, no longer legal in the USA.
president – Physician elected by other medical board members to preside over meetings and/or hearings.
professional patients – Drug abusers who travel from town to town and doctor to doctor seeking controlled substances.
Propoxyphene – An opioid analgesic previously in schedule IV used for relief of mild to moderate pain. No longer available in the United States.
psychiatrist – A doctor trained to diagnose and treat mental disorders.

psychologist – Therapist trained to counsel mental and emotional disorders.
Pyribenzamine – A prescription antihistamine.
Quaalude – Methaqualone, a Schedule I sedative hypnotic, no longer legal in the USA.
radiologist – Physician trained to read X-rays, MRIs, and other radiological tests.
radiology – Physician specialty for interpreting X-rays, CAT scans, and magnetic resonance imaging.
Recovering Physicians Program – Organization to assist impaired physicians in recovery.
Ritalin – Schedule II stimulant used in the treatment of attention deficit disorder and narcolepsy.
Roe v. Wade – United States Supreme Court decision legalizing abortions in 1973.
ROI – Report of investigation; documents details in a case.
Schedule for controlled substances – Federal and state law lists controlled substances in the following manner: Schedule I, II, IIN, III, IIIN IV, and V.
Schedule I – Drugs that have no legitimate medical use in the United States. Heroin (diacetylmorphine), LSD (lysergic acid diethylamide), Quaalude (methaqualone), Preludin, marijuana, etc.
Schedule II, IIN – Drugs that have legitimate medical use in the United States but a high potential for abuse or addiction. Oxycontin, morphine, methadone, Percodan, Percocet, Demerol, hydrocodone, Dilaudid, fentanyl. Schedule II (non-narcotic) include: Ritalin, Adderall, cocaine, amphetamine, methamphetamine, dextroamphetamine, Seconal (barbiturate).
Schedule III, IIIN – Drugs that have legitimate medical use in the United States but supposedly have less potential for abuse or addiction. Anabolic steroids, codeine with Tylenol combinations, low dose barbiturates.

Schedule IV – Drugs that have legitimate medical use in the United States but supposedly have an even less potential for abuse or addiction. Valium, Xanax, Ambien, certain diet pill medications.
Schedule V – Drugs that have legitimate medical use in the United States but supposedly low potential for abuse or addiction. Low dose opioid cough syrups, low dose codeine cough syrups.
Schedule IV diet pills – Medication prescribed that may suppress the appetite of obese patients and help in weight loss. Used for very short-term only.
Seconal – Schedule II barbiturate for sleep induction and seizures.
secretary – Physician elected by the full board to theoretically document all actions by the full board.
Secret Service – Agency of the United States government primarily responsible for protecting the president of the United States.
Stadol – Butorphanol Tartrate – Partial synthetic opioid in Schedule IV used for pain management.
summons – Legal document of the MBML requiring a physician to appear before the full board in a hearing.
suspension order – Order entered by the MBML suspending the license of a physician. The length of suspension may vary.
Talwin – Pentazocine injectable is a Schedule II controlled substance in Mississippi. The tablet form is in Schedule III in Mississippi. Used to treat pain.
The Bureau – Mississippi Bureau of Narcotics.
thyroid pills – Refers to medication sometimes prescribed as part of a diet plan to speed up metabolism rates.
traveling pharmacist – Pharmacist who fills in for various pharmacist at various locations as indicated.
UMC – University Medical Center.
UMMC – University of Mississippi Medical Center.

United States attorney general – Chief law enforcement officer in the United states and head of the United States Department of Justice.
United States Marshals – Federal agency responsible for federal courtroom security, fugitive recovery, and service of federal court orders.
UPS – United Parcel Service.
US attorney – Prosecutors for the United States government assigned by districts in each state.
USA – United States Attorney.
Valium – Schedule IV sedative. Chemically known as diazepam.
vice president – Physician elected by the full board to serve in the absence of the president of the board.
Vicodin- Schedule II narcotic for treatment of pain. Primary active ingredient is hydrocodone.
Xanax – Schedule IV controlled substance for anxiety.

About the Author

Richard P. Allison was the Chief Investigator for the MS State Board of Medical Licensure for approximately nineteen years. During that time, he was recognized by DEA for significant contributions in the field of controlled substance pharmaceutical diversion investigations. He received the 1993 United States Department of Health and Human Services Inspector General's Integrity Award for contributions to HHS to improve the quality of medicine practiced in Mississippi.

More from Foundations Book Publishing

How do past U.S. presidents avoid global panic?

Create a secret agreement with visiting extraterrestrials.

This well-researched, nonfiction book will give you a detailed, logical look at the most exciting presidential saga ever. Follow along with researcher/author Paul Blake Smith as he pieces together an explosive puzzle which reveals that President Eisenhower met with friendly aliens and that other American presidents likely renewed Ike's secret agreement with the visitors, to remain aloof to this day, to avoid triggering social chaos.

You won't see the UFO/ET topic the same way after this read.

Where is Gabriel Clay?

The search is on for missing twelve-year-old, Gabriel Clay. Few know Gabriel has a secret. Dangers are built-in with his secret. Seasoned detectives, Ben Schwartz and Al Di Natale have joined the rest of Boston in what many call a fool's errand.

Empty Doorways has many secrets. Gabriel Clay has his, City Councilor Marty Doyle has his own.

Foundations Book Publishing
Copyright 2016© Foundations Book Publications Licensing
Brandon, Mississippi 39047

10-9-8-7-6-5-4-3-2-1

Healers or Dealers?
Richard P. Allison

ISBN: 978-1-64583-048-1

CPSIA information can be obtained
at www.ICGtesting.com
Printed in the USA
BVHW062122271221
625028BV00002B/122